THE LONG ROAD HOME

The Long Road Home

THE AUTOBIOGRAPHY
OF A MAVERICK

James P. Warburg

GARDEN CITY, NEW YORK

Doubleday & Company, Inc.

1964

187979

Library of Congress Catalog Card Number 64-14277
Copyright © 1964 by James P. Warburg
All Rights Reserved. Printed in the United States of America
First Edition

CONTENTS

ILLUSTRATIONS

Acknowledgments

I owe the original impetus toward writing this book to my wife, Joan, and the temerity to attempt it to the encouragement and helpful advice of my good friend, Joseph Barnes. He and another superb editor, Anne Freedgood, have given me invaluable assistance in organizing and reducing to what I hope are readable proportions the mass of material accumulated in the course of a long and active life. My sister, Bettina, and my daughters Andrea and Kay filled in a few gaps in my recollections. My secretary, Ruth G. van den Bogaert, besides patiently typing and retyping the manuscript, has contributed a number of useful suggestions. Louis A. Siegel has helped me to read proof. To all of them, my thanks and appreciation.

The author wishes to express his appreciation for permission to include personal correspondence from James M. Cox, former President Dwight D. Eisenhower, the late President John F. Kennedy, and the late President Franklin Delano Roosevelt, and Adlai Stevenson.

PREFACE

LAST SUMMER, at the age of sixty-seven, I took my twelve-year-old son on his first trip to Europe to show him something of the Old World, where fourteen generations of his forebears had lived before his grandparents emigrated to the United States. I particularly wanted to take him to the little medieval town in Westphalia from which he derives his name.

Our ship passed through the Azores, skirted Cape Trafalgar and stopped briefly at Gibraltar. The first time Jimmy set foot on European soil was at Genoa, where we visited the house of Christopher Columbus. From there, we went to Naples and thence to Rome. The Eternal City seemed a good place at which to begin an introduction to European culture, although, had time permitted, I would have begun our journey at Athens. However, I wanted to spend a few days in Rome with my oldest daughter, whose two teen-age children I had not seen in some years.

From Rome, we went by train to Milan, past the Italian lakes and through the Alps to Zurich, where I showed my son the offices of the Swiss banks upon which, long before he was born, I used to call in my annual trips to Europe as a banker. The hall porter at the Dolder Grand Hotel told Jimmy that he had known members of our family for over forty years.

From Zurich, we flew to Frankfurt, where my cousin Eric and his fourteen-year-old son met us, and we all four motored north some 150 miles to the town of Warburg. Oddly enough, I had never before visited the town, but, years ago, I had looked up all the old family records and had acquired copies of the early town register.

Warburg, originally Warburgum, was founded by Charle-

magne in A.D. 777. At first incorporated into the medieval bish-
opric of Paderborn, it later joined the North German Hanseatic
League.

In the year 1559 there came to Warburg a Sephardic Jew
known as Simon von Cassel, presumably because he had come
from the nearby Hessian city of Kassel. (In those days, Jews
were not permitted to have family names.) It was said that
Simon's forebears had for many generations lived in Spain or
Portugal until driven out by the Inquisition. Since that time,
rumor had it that they had lived in Italy, but there are no
written records prior to Simon's appearance in Westphalia.

According to the Warburg town register, Simon von Cassel
was a "money changer, pawnbroker and lender of funds against
grain"—a business that was continued by his son and succeeding
generations. It is further recorded that Simon came to the town
of Warburg under a *Schutzvertrag* (protective agreement)
signed by the Prince-Bishop of Paderborn, which guaranteed
"safe residence for ten years" to Simon, his family and his
Hausgesinde—a term that probably meant servants or assistants,
or possibly distant relatives and friends whom Simon was supporting. In either case, it suggests that Simon was a man of
some means, and also that the Prince-Bishop must have considered this particular member of a generally looked-down-upon
minority worthy of his protection. Later pages of the town
register, in fact, state that Simon, his son, and his grandson
became highly respected leaders of the Jewish community in
the whole principality of Paderborn and record that the town
synagogue was located in the Von Cassel home.

Thus, the pattern of banking, originally of a primitive money-
lending and money-changing variety, as well as the pattern of
concern for and leadership in the Jewish community was set for
the Warburg family by its earliest known ancestor.

The twofold pattern was transferred in 1668 from Westphalia
to the north, when Simon's great-grandson, Juspa Joseph, moved
the family business from Warburg to Hamburg-Altona. At about
the same time, another branch of the family established a similar
business in Sweden, while still another moved to England. All
three changed their name from Von Cassel to Von Warburg, the
"von" being, as before, not a title of nobility but merely a designation of geographical origin. Shortly after Juspa Joseph moved

to Hamburg, the "von" was dropped, and the family name became Warburg.

We four latter-day Warburgs were enthusiastically welcomed
by the *Bürgermeister* (mayor), whom my cousin had advised
of our intended visit. He told us that the town had some ten
thousand inhabitants of whom about one half, including himself,
were refugees from the lost East German provinces. Over coffee
and cake in his farmhouse—he raised grain and cattle—His Honor
told us with pride that the field just outside of the town had been
the scene of a battle in 1730, at which the Duke of Marlborough
had defeated the French and thereby caused Canada to be
transferred from French to British sovereignty. What he did not
know was that, in 1945, the town had come into brief world-
wide prominence when the two wings of General Dwight D.
Eisenhower's armies joined forces there, completing the encircle-
ment of the Ruhr and sealing the fate of Hitler's Third Reich.
At the time, he had been fleeing from the Russians.

My cousin and I were able to show our sons the twelfth-cen-
tury walls, with a round stone watchtower at each of their four
corners, which still enclose the *Burg* up on the hill and the narrow streets lined with medieval houses that wind down to the
valley of the Diemel River. There are now no Jews living in
Warburg. The Nazis took care of that. But we saw the ancient
Jewish cemetery where our earliest ancestors lie buried and
the Judengasse where they probably lived.

The Jewish burial ground is a long, narrow strip lying between the walls of the Altstadt (Old Town) and those of the
Neustadt (New Town) because Jews were not allowed to be
buried within the town limits. Actually, the so-called New Town
was no longer very new when Simon von Cassel settled in Warburg. Some years prior to 1559, the two towns had merged, and
the cemetery thus fell within the city limits.

The mayor was more anxious to show us the few industries
and the modern school building outside of the old town than he
was in visiting the antiquities that most interested us. After joining him in a glass of excellent Warburger *Bier* at a modern
tavern, we thanked him and continued our journey northward
to Hamburg.

Here, my son could see the house on the Mittelweg where his
great-grandparents had lived; my parents' house on Gross Fon-

tenay, where I was born and lived until I was almost five years old; and the family banking house which, for almost a century and a half, had housed the firm of M. M. Warburg & Co., until it was "Aryanized" and taken over by the Nazis.

Fifteen miles north of Hamburg, I showed him the Kösterberg, his great-grandparents' country estate, where we stayed with Eric and his family in the original seventeenth-century farmhouse. Two other houses, built by my grandfather and by Eric's father, are now convalescent homes. My parents' house, where they lived during the European summers of my early childhood, had been sold and was about to be demolished. I was lucky to be able to show it to Jimmy and to take some last pictures of it before the demolition began.

Under the Hitler regime, M. M. Warburg & Co.'s name was changed to Brinckmann Wirtz & Co. After the restitution, my cousin Eric went back into the firm and hopes to restore it to its original name. Jimmy saw all the old portraits of the long line of Warburg partners and the rooms in which they worked. He was, I think, equally interested in the garage, recently built into the basement of the building, and the way in which trucks loaded with money and securities drove in and out of it.

From Hamburg, we flew first to Copenhagen and then to Amsterdam, where I took my son to the Rijksmuseum, as my father had taken me at about the same age, to see the Rembrandts, Vermeers, and other sixteenth-century Dutch masters.

During an all too short stay in London, Jimmy saw almost everything from Buckingham Palace, Westminster Abbey, the Houses of Parliament, Trafalgar Square, and Piccadilly Circus to Hampton Court and Windsor Castle. I would have liked to take him to Oxford and to the places where I had worked at many different times and in many different capacities in peace and war. But our time was up, and, frankly, I was tired.

Since we have been home, Jimmy has been arranging and rearranging his collection of postcards, slides and the many photographs we took on our travels. The other day, he said: "You know, Dad, it's like living it all over again."

That brings me to the reason for writing this autobiography.

All my life, particularly after my father's death, I have regretted that neither he nor any of his brothers left any record of their lives or any history of their family. I do not want my chil-

dren and their children to have any such regret. In the pages
that follow I have set down what I have been able to learn of
our family's history, partly out of old letters and papers, but
chiefly dredging up the memory of anecdotes that I was told as a
child. When it comes to my own story, I have told it as simply
and as honestly as I can, up to the time when my life became a
matter of public record. So far as the past twenty-five years are
concerned, there is little that I can add to my published works,
except to sketch in the context of world events in the kaleido-
scopically changing times during which I have been privileged
to come into close contact with many of the persons who have
left their indelible imprints upon the pages of history.

Perhaps the most significant change that has occurred during my lifetime is that men no longer mature in the age in
which they were born, or grow old in the age in which they
reached their maturity. More than half of man's store of knowledge has been acquired since I went to school. This explosion
of change, discovery, and invention has created a hitherto un-
heard-of demand for accommodation to altered circumstance.

Unlike many of my contemporaries, I have found the times in
which I have lived challenging and exciting, full of great danger
but also replete with great opportunity. During much of the
postwar period, I have been out of step with public policy and
majority opinion. At times, I have felt like the drunken Irishman in the St. Patrick's Day parade who cried out: "Musha-
God-love-me! They're all out of step but me!" To what extent
I have been right or wrong in my dissent remains for others to
judge.

Since 1961 I have been happy to find myself once more in
broad agreement with our nation's leadership. As I write this, I
view the future with greater confidence than I have felt at any
time since the first atomic bomb exploded over Hiroshima.

Greenwich, Connecticut,
November, 1963

Part One

CHAPTER I

Money-Changers of Modest Means

AT THE TIME when the Warburgs moved to Hamburg-Altona, Germany was recovering from the fearful ravages of the Thirty Years' War which had reduced its population from about thirty million to a mere twenty million souls. Actually, there was then no German nation but only hundreds of feudal kingdoms, dukedoms, and principalities, plus the free Hanseatic cities, all owing a loose allegiance to the Holy Roman (Austrian) Empire. Hamburg was the most important of the Hanseatic cities. Neighboring Altona, later to become a part of Hamburg, was Danish in 1668 when some of the Warburgs settled there; later it became Prussian and so remained until Prussia ceased to exist after Hitler's defeat.

Much of the relative prosperity and tranquillity the early Warburgs seem to have enjoyed was undoubtedly due to the fact that the Hanseatic cities were able to remain comparatively aloof from the wars that wracked Germany in the sixteenth, seventeenth, and eighteenth centuries. In any case, during the four centuries in which it dwelt in Germany, the Warburg family moved along from generation to generation without spectacular ups and downs, in consistently comfortable though never luxurious circumstances. This was in sharp contrast to many Jewish and other families whose fortunes seemed to rise and fall in accordance with the adage "three generations from shirtsleeves to shirtsleeves." The consistent characteristic that seemed to link the Warburg generations was that at least one member of each possessed a talent for making money without considering the accumulation of wealth as important as the use of it for constructive purposes. Sometimes the money-earner would support members of the family engaged in non-lucrative pursuits—an occasional artist, rabbi, historian, or scientist. Mostly the money-maker's benefactions concerned the general welfare of the Jewish community.

Unlike the later-blooming Frankfurt Rothschilds, the Warburgs developed no attachments to feudal rulers, pulled off no spectacular financial coups, built no castles, sought no titles, and cherished no dreams of empire. Their patriotism remained local —Hanseatic rather than German—and even in their local habitat, they were for centuries content with being not the wealthiest but merely among the most respected of the Hanseatic merchants and merchant bankers.

In 1798—the same year in which Alexander Hamilton obtained the first private bank charter in the United States—Moses Marcus Warburg and his brother, Gerson, consolidated the family enterprises in a firm henceforth to be known as M. M. Warburg & Company.

The brothers were not congenial. According to a story often related by Sara Warburg, the daughter-in-law of Moses Marcus, they refused to speak to each other during a year-long quarrel. Their seats on the stock exchange were back to back, and a certain broker made a handsome living throughout the year, buying sterling exchange from one brother and selling it to the other.

From all accounts, Sara, who married Aby, the rather indolent son of Moses Marcus, dominated the firm not only during her husband's life but for many years after his death.

Sara was greatly respected and admired. Among her friends were the poet Heinrich Heine, who dedicated a poem to her, and Prince Otto von Bismarck, who corresponded with her and received from her each year a package of Jewish Passover cookies. One year, however, Sara became outraged at the anti-Semitic preachments of the imperial court chaplain and quite unjustly held her friend Bismarck responsible. When no cookies arrived that Easter, Bismarck inquired through an intermediary why he had not received them. Sara replied, "If he doesn't know, tell him to ask me himself. But he won't ask. He knows quite well." Poor Bismarck never got his cookies again.

In the century following the Napoleonic Wars, the Free Port of Hamburg became a major shipping center and the most important point of trans-shipment in northern Europe. Hamburg bankers did a flourishing business in foreign exchange, in discounting drafts upon foreign bankers, and in financing imports and exports, and M. M. Warburg & Company acquired a leading share of this business, partly because the firm was one of the first among the merchant bankers to establish intimate relations with a considerable number of private banks and bankers in other countries. Among them were Hope & Company, Amsterdam; R. Henriques, Copenhagen; and the three Rothschild banks in London, Paris, and Vienna.

Sara outlived her husband by twenty-seven years. Until her death in 1884, her two sons—Moritz, who became my grandfather, and Siegmund—regularly reported on the day's business at her house on their way home from the bank to their families; and Moritz' strict adherence to Orthodox Jewish customs was inspired by his love for and fear of his mother. He was deeply troubled by the gradual apostasy of his sons, who maintained Kosher households only out of respect for him. As long as he lived, he gathered his children and later his grandchildren about him on Friday evenings to celebrate the Sabbath. The Sabbath ended at sundown on Saturday, and I can remember how he would sit at a window facing the West with an unlighted cigar in his hand—he was a passionate cigar smoker—waiting for the sun to sink below the horizon.

I can also remember the shock with which I discovered that Grandfather Warburg wore a wig. (As a matter of fact, he had three wigs: one to make him look as if he needed a haircut, a second to represent having just had a haircut, and a third for the intermediate period.) I must have been about five years old when my mother sent me upstairs to Grandfather's bedroom to pay him a visit because he was not feeling well. To my horror, I found him sitting up in bed completely bald. Thinking that he must be frightfully ill to have lost all his hair, I asked him what had happened. He roared with laughter, reached for the wig that hung at his bedside on a contraption something like a modern lady's hatstand, and put it on, saying, "Now, do you like that better?" For some time thereafter, I looked carefully at the back of men's necks to see if they, too, wore toupees or if their hair was their own.

By German standards, the Hamburg of Moritz Warburg's day was relatively liberal. He was the first of the many generations of Warburgs who had lived in Hamburg to be granted citizenship, and one of his sons, Paul, who became my father, was the first Jew to be elected to the *Bürgerschaft* (Lower House) in the Hamburg government.

Citizenship, Moritz Warburg discovered, entailed the duty of serving in the Hamburg militia. Being a peaceable and also a somewhat lazy man, he decided to become a trumpeter, since it was easier to carry a trumpet than a gun.

Moritz was not an outstanding businessman. He loved people, enjoyed music, and, like most of his forebears, felt a responsibility for the Jewish community. He founded both a Jewish orphanage and a hospital and contributed time and money to a number of other charitable institutions. At that time the leading Jewish family still fulfilled to some extent the role later assumed by organized charities. According to Jewish tradition 10 per cent of one's income must be given to the poor, and it is only when a Jew gives in excess of that amount that charity may be said to begin. Moritz's wife had a whole list of people who called at Mittelweg 17 regularly once a week to receive a small stipend.

The Moritz Warburgs had seven children—five sons and two daughters. In the roomy but modest house where they grew up there was almost always music of one sort or another and, in later years, usually a family play in preparation or rehearsal. My father, Paul Warburg, who had inherited a talent for writing from his mother, a frequent contributor of feature stories to the Frankfurt newspapers, supplied most of the inspiration for these performances.

By the time M. M. Warburg & Company celebrated its hundredth anniversary in 1898, the firm and its foreign connections had developed the custom of exchanging future partners for training as unpaid apprentices.

Moritz' oldest son, Aby, was entitled by family tradition to be trained as the future senior partner of the firm. He, however, renounced his rights in favor of the next oldest son, Max, in order to devote himself to the study of symbolism and iconography in the history of art. "You can have the oldest son's place in the firm," he said to Max, "I don't want it, provided that you will always buy me the books I need." Little did Max realize what this would involve.

Aby was a tiny man with bristling black hair and mustache, twinkling brown eyes, an incredible capacity for indignation, and an irrepressible sense of humor. He could tell hilariously funny stories in any number of dialects. A distinguished Renaissance scholar, he eventually wrote a number of significant books about the history and meaning of art and assembled a unique library which he gave to Hamburg University when he was appointed to a professorship at that institution. (Later, Eric Warburg transferred the library to London in the nick of time to save it from Nazi destruction, and it ultimately became established as the Warburg Institute of London University. A wholly new system of cataloguing has made the institute unique and a model for students in the field of history of art.)

The money for the library came in annual donations, sometimes accompanied by audible groans, from his brothers in the banking business. Aby had no compunctions about assessing them for what he considered the only worthwhile product of their mundane endeavors.

Max Warburg was the inevitable businessman of a Warburg generation. He and his younger brother, Paul, who would have preferred to become a civil engineer, were destined for partnership in the family concern. Because of the tradition that a senior partner could introduce no more than two sons into the firm, the two younger brothers had other careers planned for them. Felix was expected to become a diamond merchant in Frankfurt under the tutelage of his mother's gifted brother, Paul Oppenheim. Fritz, the youngest, was to be a lawyer.

Before being apprenticed to one of the bank's London connections and later to another in St. Petersburg, Paul was sent on a trip around the world. He journeyed by train to Genoa, thence by ancient sail-bearing steamer to Suez and Aden, where he transferred to the comparatively luxurious British liner *Oriental* which took him to India, where he visited Delhi and Calcutta. He went on to Ceylon, Singapore, Saigon, Hong Kong, Macao, and Shanghai. After a visit to Japan, he crossed the Pacific to Vancouver and traveled by train to Seattle, Portland, San Fran-

cisco, Chicago, Niagara Falls, and New York City before returning to Bremen.

A partial and almost illegible carbon copy of his diary contains some interesting and prescient observations. Unfortunately,
the original was sent home in letters to his parents and has been
lost.

One passage about Egypt expresses surprise and resentment
that a people of ancient civilization and culture should have
sunk into such squalor and apathy. Another sharply criticizes
the British Raj in India and foresees that country's emancipa-
tion. "The gloomy Middle Kingdom" (China) did not appeal to
him, but he was enthusiastic about the beauty and the cleanliness of Japan. In one letter, he figured out in detail that Portugal could save $286,000 a year by relinquishing its colony at
Macao, which he described as "a remnant of imperialistic vanity." There are no comments about the United States, probably
because he expected to get home faster than any letters written
on the last leg of his journey.

Paul was not the first Warburg to visit the United States. His
brother Aby had spent some time studying the Pueblo Indians
in Arizona and New Mexico. But it remained for Felix, who
was not even being trained as a banker, to establish the connection in New York that was to mark the beginning of a new era
for the Warburg family.

CHAPTER II

From Modest Means to Great Wealth

Up to this point, money had played a relatively unimportant part in the family. Warburg family life had been rich in music, in variegated interests, and, above all, in humor. There was a strong recurring streak of laziness which probably acted as a healthy brake upon excessive ambition. But there was also a pronounced sense of duty to work at something worthwhile. Manners were important, especially punctuality. A person who enjoyed the advantages of a comfortable home and a good education owed it to others to set an example in consideration. *Hubris* was one of the cardinal sins; modesty one of the cardinal virtues.

The turn of the century introduced new elements into this long settled background, when both a family and a business connection were established in New York.

After the abortive revolution of 1848, Solomon Loeb, one of the thirteen children of an impoverished wine dealer in Worms, Germany, had emigrated to America. For a time, he lived in New York, in a garret on Canal Street, then traveled to Cincinnati by Erie Canal boat to join a distant relative, Abraham Kuhn, in managing Kuhn, Netter & Company, a dry-goods and clothing concern. The business prospered, especially during the Civil War, when it had government contracts to make uniforms and blankets for the Union Army. By 1867, Solomon Loeb had amassed a fortune estimated at $500,000. He had also learned that Kuhn, Netter's New York bank made more money at less risk than was to be made in the dry-goods and clothing business in Cincinnati. Accordingly, he proceeded to found the New York banking house of Kuhn, Loeb & Company.

On the day the new firm opened its doors, the president of the National Bank of Commerce, with whom Solomon Loeb had long done business, came to pay his respects and announced that he was sure the new firm would be a success. When Loeb asked him why, Mr. Coe replied: "Because you know how to say 'No.'" Years later, Loeb advised his son, James: "Learn how to say 'No.' You can always change your mind and say 'Yes,' but once you have said 'Yes,' you are committed."

This became a family joke. Whenever Loeb's wife—a warm-hearted lady of generous instincts—wanted to help some needy person or to make a gift to some charity, she would say to her husband: "Now, Solomon, first of all say 'No.' Then let me tell you my story."

Betty Gallenberg Loeb was an accomplished pianist, and, although her husband was tone-deaf, all of the children were musical. At an early age they played string quartets. Nina Loeb, who became my mother, played the violin. Her favorite brother, James, for whom I was named, was an excellent amateur cellist who founded the Institute of Musical Art, later to be merged with the Juilliard School of Music.

Neither of the Loebs made much of their Jewishness. Solomon was an avowed agnostic; his wife was religious in her own strictly personal way but felt drawn toward good works rather than toward membership in a congregation.

Their sons were not attracted by the banking business. Both graduated from Harvard University. Morris, the elder, became a distinguished chemist and a professor at New York University. James, after a brief, filial attempt to become a banker, devoted himself to music, archaeology, and the publication of the Loeb Classical Library.

Having no sons to succeed him, Solomon Loeb took in a number of outside partners. By far the ablest of these was Jacob H. Schiff, who later married Loeb's oldest daughter. Aggressively ambitious, adventurous, opinionated, and strong-willed, Schiff raised Kuhn, Loeb & Company to a pre-eminence among American private banks, second only to J. P. Morgan & Company. By the time of Solomon Loeb's retirement, Schiff had not only assumed command of the firm but had established himself as the self-elected devoutly Jewish patriarch of the family. The religion he practiced and preached was a strange mixture of orthodoxy and ritualistic liberalism he had concocted for himself and which the Loeb family found difficult to accept. Yet he was extremely generous, founding and making large contributions to any number of charities.

In 1893, Schiff took his wife and two children on a visit to his native Frankfurt, during which his daughter Frieda met and fell in love with young Felix Warburg. A year later, they were married in New York, and Felix entered Kuhn, Loeb & Company as a junior partner. At the wedding, Paul Warburg met Loeb's youngest daughter, Nina, whom he married a year later and took back to Hamburg.

Thus began a period in which the hitherto frugal Warburgs began to tap the sources of great wealth, thereby materially altering the background against which the next generation was to grow up.

Another new factor entered the picture at about the same time. The Warburgs had always been strictly city people. However, Moritz had for a long time had his eye on a country estate high over the eastern bank of the Elbe River, about fifteen miles northeast of Hamburg, but the price was prohibitive. Suddenly, in 1896, the owner asked him to bid on it. Moritz offered one quarter of the price previously asked and was promptly accepted. (Later, he learned that the former owner was anxious to get rid of the property at any price because his wife had betrayed him there.) So Moritz came into possession of a fine old estate, its wooded acres stretching from the hills to the bank of the Elbe, with a seventeenth-century farmhouse, a coach house and stable, gardens, and broad, well-kept meadows. The family's head was now a country squire. Simultaneously, two of his sons began to acquire the kind of wealth the family had never known.

The old days were over. A new era had begun.

CHAPTER III

Bilingual Boyhood

THE NEWLYWED Paul Warburgs lived on Gross Fontenay, within a five-minute walk of Moritz Warburg's house and less than a mile from the family bank on the other side of the Alster Lake. Paul was the first Warburg to acquire a horse and carriage. He did so because his American bride was lame as the result of a childhood accident. Even so, the family frowned upon the luxury of a private equipage. The Warburgs had been bankers for twelve generations, but Grandmother Warburg still did not like to hear her husband say that he was a banker, because this seemed to her immodest; she preferred to have him describe himself as *"ein einfacher Kaufmann"*—an ordinary merchant or businessman. She considered her son's acquisition of a horse and carriage *"protzig"* (showing off). As a mother-in-law, she must have been a bit difficult for a somewhat pampered American girl to take.

On August 18, 1896 I was born and was immersed from the very beginning of my life in the traditions of two dissimilar families and the vastly different cultures of two continents.

When my mother was unable to nurse me, the German family doctor suggested a wet nurse—the usual procedure in those days. My father, Paul Warburg, was a shy and exceedingly modest man, and I have often thought what an ordeal it must have been for him to go to the broker's office in which a number of unmarried mothers waited on a long bench, prepared to exhibit their bosoms. The nurse he chose turned out to be not only good at her job but a highly amusing if somewhat bawdy character, named Anna Lanz. In later years, when I exhibited the usual signs of teen-age vulgarity, I can remember my father saying, "I don't know where you got such ideas or such language. It must have been through Anna Lanz's milk."

When I was eleven months old, I was taken to the United States to be shown to my American grandparents. Much to my mother's annoyance, since she was a wretched sailor, I learned to walk in mid-ocean and had to be kept in a laundry basket until the ship docked. This was the first trip of a childhood and young manhood that was to be punctuated by well over fifty ocean voyages and almost equally divided between Europe and the United States.

The Hamburg I remember as a child was in some respects very much as it is today. At the turn of the century, Hamburg was crisscrossed, as it still is, by many canals, with its heart built around the shores of a shining lake. Tiny passenger steamers scurried to and fro across the Alster, as they do today. There were no tall buildings. A multitude of churches pointed their sharp needles into the sky; they still dominate the city's silhouette. The beautiful medieval Rathaus (City Hall) was and still is its architectural gem.

But the streets of the Hamburg I remember were paved with rough cobblestones over which horse-drawn vehicles rumbled with a pleasing roar. Horse-drawn funeral cortéges were followed by professional mourners on foot, wearing medieval costumes of black plumed hats, white neck ruffles, black cloaks, and black knee breeches. Policemen carried swords and wore spiked helmets. Peasants in colorful native garb came from nearby Schleswig-Holstein bringing their produce to market. The lamplighter came at sundown. Black-faced little boys in top hats functioned as chimney sweeps. German soldiers wore colorful uniforms by which I learned to distinguish their regiments.

During the first four years of my life, three major events transpired on the international scene. Britain became involved in war with the Boers in South Africa. The United States fought a war with Spain. And the Boxer Rebellion broke out in China and was suppressed by the foreign powers. I learned about the second and third of these wars only when I later studied history. But the South African war provided me with a direct experience which impressed itself on my memory. The episode occurred in March 1900, when I was three and a half.

I was having afternoon tea with my English nanny when the

postman rang the bell, and I ran to the door. The postman was an old friend. On this occasion, he had brought a letter for Nanny which he gave me to take to her. I thanked him in German and then ran back to Nanny shouting in English: "Nanny! Nannee! It's for you."

Nanny opened the letter and began to read. Almost at once her wrinkled face screwed itself up into an unfamiliar shape, and great tears began to course down her cheeks. I had never before seen a grownup weep, and I was terrified. When Nanny was able to speak, she told me that she was weeping for joy—which puzzled me still more. Nanny explained that her brother was an English soldier; that England was fighting some "quite nasty people, called Boers," in a faraway place called South Africa; that her brother had been all but given up as lost because his regiment had been trapped in a town called Ladysmith; and that the letter now told her her brother's regiment had been relieved so that he would soon be back home in England.

Soldiers were a familiar sight in Hamburg, but I had not known that they ever shot at people in some sort of mass quarrel called "war." Nor had I known that there were "good" soldiers and "bad" soldiers. I now gathered that "war" was "good soldiers" shooting at or being shot at by "bad soldiers" who were "quite nasty people." The discovery seemed both horrible and exciting.

The next step in learning about international affairs came shortly thereafter, when the Kaiser (William II) came to visit his friend, Albert Ballin, founder of the Hamburg-American Line, whose house on the Badestrasse stood back to back with our house on Gross Fontenay. Between the two houses there were the usual two small back gardens, separated only by a hedge.

Nanny, greatly excited by the royal visit, called out: "Jimmy! Jimmy! Come quickly! The Keezer's in the Baddystrassy!"

I cannot remember whether I actually saw "the Keezer" on this occasion, only that there were a lot of German soldiers standing about in the neighbors' garden and I wanted very much to know whether German soldiers were "good" soldiers, like Nanny's brother, or "quite nasty people," like the Boers.

The unanswered question remained in my mind until two or three years later, after Nanny had departed and a German Fräulein had taken her place. My parents had built themselves a house on Grandfather Warburg's Kösterberg estate. One autumn, the German army maneuvers were held on the big heath near Kösterberg, and two Uhlan officers were quartered in the house while their batmen and horses were lodged in Grandfather Warburg's stable. Since I liked the two officers, particularly the red-faced one with the blond mustache, I came to the conclusion that German soldiers must be "good"—a belief that was not to be dispelled for some time to come.

Meanwhile, several important things had happened in my life. My sister, Bettina, had been born in 1900, after a mysterious period during which my mother remained in bed with the shades drawn and everyone tiptoed around the house. I had been promised "a great surprise" as a reward for being quiet and good during this time and was thoroughly disgusted when the surprise turned out to be not the hobbyhorse for which I had hoped but a squalling baby who pre-empted everyone's attention.

Grandmother Loeb had died, and my mother, although I did not know it at the time, had been urging my father to move to New York, where a partnership in Kuhn, Loeb & Company had been offered to him. In 1901, he somewhat reluctantly agreed, with the understanding that he would retain his partnership in the Hamburg firm and a promise to his parents that he would bring his family to live at Kösterberg every summer.

I knew nothing of the conflict of filial and marital love this decision involved for my parents, especially my father. By this time I had begun to feel a certain pride in all things German and a sense of belonging to Germany. Moving to America was exciting, but even at age five it was sad to leave the house on Gross Fontenay for good. Happily my beloved Fräulein came with me to America.

From 1901 until 1914, we spent the winters in New York and the summers, from May until September, in Europe. (Today, the accouterments of this annual hegira seem altogether incredible. We traveled with a valet-butler and lady's maid, as well as a nurse or governess. Wilhelm Toerber, the valet-butler, took charge of the baggage, which consisted of a number of large trunks for the ship's hold, hatboxes, blanket-rolls, "steamer trunks," and innumerable suitcases and valises to be stowed in the cabins. The cook and one or two maids traveled on a separate ship. Upon arrival, poor Wilhelm had to attend to the customs, while my father left the dock for the office and the rest of us were taken home by a waiting conveyance.)

In New York, I had private lessons for a year and then attended Miss Bovee's elementary school, which I hated. We lived in a house at 3 East 82nd Street that neither of my parents liked very much; but I did, because it had an electric elevator.

Another attraction was the fact that my father acquired an electric hansom cab, instead of a horse and carriage. This progenitor of a long line of family automobiles skidded prodigiously on wet pavement and had to have its battery recharged every night. Its professional driver sat on a high seat behind and above the passenger compartment.

Most of the summers were spent at Kösterberg, while my father and Uncle Max commuted to the family bank in Hamburg. But almost every year the whole family was taken along on business trips to various European cities and, occasionally, to a Swiss or Austrian health resort. "Taking the cure" was a regular feature of middle-class European life.

Throughout the early part of this transatlantic period I was unable to identify myself clearly as either an American or a German. Europe seemed as much "home" as America, perhaps because the summers in Europe were more exciting than going to school and being taken for walks with my sister in Central Park. The fact that English and German were spoken interchangeably at home increased the feeling of not belonging definitely to either country. Very likely, there was also a strong unconscious desire on my part not to face the necessity of identifying wholly with either an American mother or a German father.

In an odd way, I used to feel most like an American when I was in Germany, and vice versa. At Kösterberg, my family was referred to by its German relatives as "the Americans"; while at Bovee elementary school and later at Columbia Grammar School in New York, a boy who was not only bilingual in German but was also Jewish was made to feel something of an outsider.

On the whole, until I was about ten or eleven, I felt more European, though not necessarily more German, than American. America meant merely New York City; the family had not as yet begun to travel in the United States nor did we yet have a country home there. Europe, on the other hand, included, besides Hamburg and Kösterberg, such fascinating cities as Paris,

Amsterdam, Zurich, and, above all, London. What was more, life in Hamburg and Kösterberg had certain interesting cosmopolitan aspects.

From our house, high on the hills overlooking the Elbe, I could watch an endless procession of ships of many nations going to or coming from almost every part of the world. By the time I was eight or nine, I knew most of the flags and could tell to what nation and which shipping company a vessel belonged, where it was going, or in what country it had last called. At the approach of the big Hamburg-American liners I would run up to the attic to dip the American flag, hoping for and sometimes getting a whistle-blast salute in reply from one of the captains who knew the family as frequent passengers. Once, in 1903 or 1904, there was great excitement at Kösterberg when the Russian cruiser *Askold*, shortly to be sunk by the Japanese at the battle of Tsushima Strait, sailed up the river vigorously blowing an unfamiliar siren.

Diplomats, bankers, and businessmen from other countries visited M. M. Warburg & Company and not infrequently came to Kösterberg. One night, when the Russian consul general was having dinner with my parents and several other guests on the veranda I was asked to fetch his hat from the coatroom because a chill wind was blowing. When I returned with the right hat, my proud father asked me how I had been able to identify it. To his horror, I replied: "By the funny smell!" (Exit in disgrace.)

At about age eight, I became an ardent stamp collector—a hobby greatly facilitated by the fact that M. M. Warburg & Company carried on correspondence with almost every country in the world. When I was occasionally allowed to visit my father's office—which I was not permitted to do in New York until much later—Johann Ax, the kindly chief of the firm's mail department would give me a whole new packet of stamps or stamped envelopes from foreign lands. In this way, I learned a lot of geography and, because of the portraits on many of the stamps, gained a certain amount of familiarity with contemporary and past kings, queens, and presidents.

All these various opportunities to learn about the world centered in my European summers; little such stimulus derived from my winters in New York. The one compensation was that I saw more of my father. In Hamburg, his time was taken up with business, even on weekends; in New York he often took long weekend strolls with his children and, on week days, almost always walked me across the park to school. On rainy Saturdays or Sundays, I could sometimes persuade him to play upstairs with toy trains or tin soldiers. Playing with soldiers was stimulated by the Russo-Japanese war of 1904–5. Both my father and I wanted the Japanese to win—my father because he had fallen in love with Japan on his trip around the world and because he hated the Russians for their anti-Jewish pogroms; I because the Japanese were, in fact, winning and because I had read Ralph Henry Barbour's *Under Togo for Japan.* Being a kindly parent, my father usually consented to be General Kuropatkin while I was Marshal Oyama. (I did not know then that my father's firm had been responsible for floating a large Japanese war loan in the United States.)

When I was ten, my mother engaged Howard Berry, a young student at Columbia University, to teach me carpentry, help me with my homework (I had trouble with arithmetic), and make up for the lack of training in games and sports caused by our never being in the United States during the summer. Howard Berry supplied the most Americanizing influence to which I was exposed until I went away to boarding school. On expeditions to nearby New Jersey or Van Cortlandt Park, he taught me to throw and catch a baseball, skip stones across the water, and fish. Occasionally, he would take me to a professional baseball game at the Polo Grounds, where I became an ardent Giant fan— my first solid American allegiance—to New York City rather than to the United States.

It was not until my father became an American citizen in 1911 and I was sent to a New England school that I acquired a firm sense of anchorage on this side of the Atlantic.

CHAPTER IV

What Is a Jew? Why Is He "Different?"

UNTIL I reached the age of four or five, I took it for granted that all people were Jews. I was shocked and grieved to discover that my beloved Fräulein was something called a Gentile. I was equally surprised to learn that the Kaiser was not a Jew! As I grew older, I was puzzled as to what constituted the difference between Jews and Christians—a difference that, for some reason, appeared to be quite important to older people.

My father seemed to have rejected the traditional Warburg orthodoxy. My mother had had little if any religious training. When they moved to New York, both had, as a matter of fact become "twice-a-year Jews," attending the synagogue only on the Jewish New Year's Day and the Day of Atonement. My mother, who liked to read aloud to us, did read us psalms and stories out of the Old Testament. I liked the music of the psalms, but was interested in the Bible chiefly—as I later became interested in Webster's Unabridged Dictionary—because I hoped to learn something about the carefully guarded mysteries of sex and pro-creation. (My father was unapproachable on such subjects and my mother brushed off questions either by citing the well-known case of the bees and the flowers or else by telling me that these were very sacred matters into which I was not old enough to inquire.)

I felt warmly about Grandfather Warburg's Friday evenings and loved the sound of Hebrew. On the other hand, I was re-pelled by the proselytizing religiosity of my New York uncle, Jacob Schiff.

At school in New York, I soon discovered and was hurt by the fact that to be a Jew evidently meant being considered "different" and an outsider. A slightly older boy whom I rather liked used to insert an E between the letters J W with which I initialed my school papers until I put a stop to it by signing myself JPW. Apparently, the word "Jew" could be a term of opprobrium; and apparently there were some, or perhaps even many people who disliked Jews and looked down upon them. My mother confirmed that such was indeed the case. She said that because of this, a Jewish boy should always be very careful not to push himself forward. This puzzled me. It seemed like accepting some sort of second-class status.

I gathered the impression from both of my parents that, no matter what other people might feel, to be a Jew was something of which to be proud. Why this should be so remained unclear. Evidently, my parents wanted their son to feel that he had fallen heir to a precious heritage, but neither of them could or would explain just what remained of this heritage if the Jewish religion were shucked off. It seemed to me that nothing more remained than a *dis*belief in the divinity of Jesus Christ.

At age ten, I decided for myself that, if I was going to be a Jew and suffer whatever social or other disadvantages this might entail, I would be "a real Jew," like Grandfather Warburg. I even thought of becoming a rabbi. My parents were rather surprised— whether pleased or displeased, I could not tell—when I asked to be allowed to study Hebrew, to learn all about the Jewish religion and to be *bar mitzvah* in the traditional manner.

Fortunately, Judah L. Magnes, the rabbi to whom I was sent for training, was a rare and wonderful human being, deeply religious, yet tolerant and endowed with a rich sense of humor. I was fascinated by the Hebrew language, which I learned easily (and, alas, later forgot with equal ease), and by the history of the Jewish people; but I found it difficult to accept the Mosaic mythology and increasingly impossible to discover any relevance to modern times in most of the ancient Jewish laws.

Like all the old rituals, the *bar mitzvah* ceremony is beautiful and moving. I recall the feeling of reverence and pride with which I read my excerpt from the Torah and carried the sacred scrolls back to the Ark of the Covenant. But, by this time, I knew that I did not want to be a rabbi and was not at all sure that being a good Jew held any essentially different meaning from being a good Christian.

The next year I was sent to Middlesex School in Concord, Massachusetts. The headmaster, Robert Winsor, was a liberal-minded Unitarian whose ethical philosophy seemed to differ but little from that of my parents or Rabbi Magnes.

For a teen-age boy uncertain as to where he belonged in terms of both national and religious allegiance, Middlesex School was very nearly the ideal prescription. I owed my being sent there more to my uncle Felix than to my parents.

Felix Warburg was an outgoing, optimistic man who taught his children to ride horseback and play tennis and who fitted easily into an American environment and the possession of great wealth. He and my father were fond of each other, but their relationship was not nearly so close as that between my father and his older brother Max. This was intensified by the fact that my mother and my Aunt Frieda Schiff Warburg, besides being sisters-in-law, were aunt and niece; and the Loeb and Schiff inheritances were in many respects incompatible, so that Mother and Aunt Frieda alternated between excessive intimacy and mutual criticism of each other's children and ways of life. But the children of the two families were frequently thrown together and, on the whole, liked each other.

In the autumn of 1910, Frederick, my uncle's oldest son, was sent to Middlesex. Uncle Felix believed that boys should be sent away from home at the appropriate time. My parents were less committed to the boarding-school idea, but, when Fred was obviously happy at his new school, they decided to give me an opportunity to go there too. I liked the idea. I was not at all reluctant to leave Columbia Grammar School or concerned about leaving home. I was a little scared without knowing why, but I left my father on the Grand Central Station platform with less sadness than a feeling of embarking upon an exciting adventure.

Almost the first thing that struck me upon my arrival at Middlesex was the atmosphere of friendliness that seemed to say: "We don't care *who* you are; it's *what* you are that matters." The boys came from many backgrounds and many parts of the country. Most of them were from New England, New York, and Philadelphia, but among my classmates was one boy from Texas, another from Denver, and still another from Lake Tahoe.

I was never aware of the slightest trace of anti-Semitism among the teachers or the boys. One or two classmates, never having known a Jew, showed a friendly interest in finding out where the Jewish religion differed from Christianity, just as I was now interested in becoming familiar with the New Testament. Sunday chapel was compulsory and conducted by various visiting ministers of different Christian denominations. Out of this experience grew a feeling of skepticism with regard to Christian fundamentalism very similar to my rejection of Mosaic mythology and Jewish orthodoxy. On the other hand, I liked the hymns much as I had enjoyed the chanting of the Hebrew cantor.

By the time I graduated from Middlesex in 1913, I had formed an attitude toward religion that was to remain essentially unchanged throughout my life. Perhaps it could be most simply described as Jeffersonian deism—a belief in some sort of divine purpose, or Providence which required no formal affirmation, church affiliation, or ritualistic observance. Without such a belief, it seemed to me that the Declaration of Independence and the principles which it embodied would make no sense. The Darwinian theory of evolution seemed more credible to me than the Biblical story of the creation, but Darwin, too, left much unexplained—among other things, the evolution of man's reason and sense of justice.

From a theological point of view, I might at this point have chosen Unitarianism as easily as Judaism, if I had felt the need for any church affiliation. From a secular standpoint, however, I had strong pro-Jewish feelings. If the Jewish people had constituted the majority group in the American society, I would have seen little reason to stand up and be counted as a Jew. But so long as the Jews constituted an underdog minority, it seemed to me that to desert them would be contemptible. If, in the existing circumstances, I were to reject my heritage I would be nothing more than a renegade seeking social advantage, unless my renunciation of Judaism were motivated—as it would not be—by sincere conversion to and affirmative belief in Christianity.

As I look back, I am astonished that, as a boy, I apparently thought of Jews as being united only by a religion and by minority status, so that, if the religion were rejected, only the minority status would remain as a bond. Had I understood that the Jewish cultural heritage is perhaps more of a bond than Judaism, I would have better understood my half-conscious, quasi-tribal feelings of loyalty.

CHAPTER V

New England Makes an American

MIDDLESEX SCHOOL is situated only a few miles from the scene of the first battle of the American Revolution. Emerson's and Hawthorne's houses stand on Concord's elm-shaded main thoroughfare. Walden Pond lies within easy bicycle range. Louisa May Alcott's house and the historic Wright Tavern are other landmarks.

Frederick Winsor, affectionately but respectfully known as "the Boss," founded the school in 1901. He and his wife, a Boston Paine, were typical New Englanders—upright, frugal, friendly but taciturn.

The Boss was a chunky man of medium height, with slightly graying and thinning auburn hair, an English guardsman's bristling mustache, and bespectacled, steely blue eyes which, even in moments of austere severity, seemed always on the verge of a humorous twinkle. He walked with quick, short steps and always with a slight forward tilt, much as a sailor walks along an unsteady deck. He understood and loved boys but did not suffer parents gladly.

Mrs. Winsor was a small, delicate lady whose shyness made her almost inarticulate. Rarely seen on the campus, she was nevertheless utterly devoted to the school. It was her money, together with that of a small group of aristocratic Bostonians, that had enabled her husband to start it. The earliest school buildings bore the names: Bryant-Paine, Lee Higginson, Hallo-well, and Peabody.

The houses were typical red-brick-with-white-trim New England school buildings, separated by wide lawns and a circular road. "Doing rounds" on this road was the standard punishment for lateness at class or meals, unmade beds, or other peccadilloes. The number of rounds to be run or walked depended upon the offense.

The encounter with friendly taciturnity was a new experience for a boy who came of a family of enthusiastic conversationalists, but I quickly learned to appreciate the beauty of lean language and of occasional total silence. I also learned to appreciate dry humor, chiefly through the satirical dialogues of Finley Peter Dunne's Mr. Dooley and his saloonkeeper friend, Mr. Hennessey—relished and frequently quoted by the headmaster to illustrate whatever point he was making.

I had my first experiences in public speaking when I was elected to the debating team and through this activity learned to look up material in the Concord Town Library. In the annual debate against Groton, we successfully upheld the affirmative on the question: "Should the United States complete the Panama Canal?" My opponent was an eloquent boy from Virginia, Westmore Willcox, of whom I was to see more in later life.

Though not an outstanding athlete, I enjoyed and participated in various sports enough so that, in spite of my high marks, other boys did not consider me a "greasy grind." I dropped piano and learned to play the guitar with the Mandolin Club—a decision I later regretted. In one of the school's annual dramatic productions, I played Lady Macbeth. (My roommate's mother afterward told me that I looked more like Pocahontas than like a Scottish noblewoman.) As editor of *The Anvil*, I gained my first experience in journalism.

I do not remember what outside reading I did while at Middlesex. Either there or earlier, I know that I devoured the works of Robert Louis Stevenson and read most of the novels of Sir Walter Scott. I also read much of Charles Dickens, and Thackeray's *Vanity Fair*. The latter was, I think, prescribed reading. Robert Browning and Charles Algernon Swinburne were my favorite English poets, but I doubt whether I read much of their work until I went to college.

My favorite subjects were Latin and Greek. Latin was compulsory, but Greek had recently become an elective subject. As the only boy who chose to take Greek, I had an excellent teacher all to myself. Winfred ("Pud") Brown's love of Greek literature was contagious. In three years, he guided me through Xenophon's *Anabasis*, Plato's *Republic* and well into the plays of Aeschylus Sophocles, and Euripides.

Physics, a subject that did not greatly interest me, was taught by Chick Raymond, the baseball coach. I liked him better on the diamond than in the classroom. (Later I learned that Chick had had to learn physics himself while teaching it. By this time he had become a first-rate teacher.)

When it came to baseball, Chick Raymond knew his business. The Boss fancied himself as a pitcher and would occasionally pitch for the faculty team against the boys. He had excellent control, a dinky curve of which he was inordinately proud, but, as Chick irreverently put it, "no mustard on his fast ball."

One day, when he was sending me up to bat with a man on first base, Chick said: "Okay, kid. Go on up there and get hit."

"*Get* hit?"

"That's what I said. I don't want you hitting into a double play. Just stick your tail out a little. That nuthin' ball of the Boss's won't hurt, but it'll make him mad. Then maybe we'll get some runs."

It worked. The Boss, slightly distracted by knowing perfectly well the trick that had been played on him, walked the next batter after nicking me and allowed our cleanup hitter to drive in two runs. When I came back to the bench, Raymond said: "I may not know much about pacific (*sic*) gravity, but I know how to rattle a pitcher, even if he's the guy that pays my salary."

Dr. Reginald Heber Howe—known as "Doc" or "Heber"—was my housemaster. His wife, the sister of my classmate, Bill Barker, besides being the mother of two children, was half mother and half older sister to all the boys in Hallowell House. She was the perfect feminine antidote for homesickness. Doc Howe introduced me to botany, forestry, and natural history. Under his guidance, Charles Winsor, the Boss's son, and I wrote a paper on the Usneaceae of North America (lichens) which Doc had printed and distributed to the members of the Massachusetts Botanical Society. Doc was also the rowing coach and managed for years to train future Harvard varsity oarsmen on the school's half-mile pond. Later he founded and became the first headmaster of the Belmont Hill School.

Nowadays, Middlesex sends her sons to many universities and colleges. In my day, it was taken for granted that, if you went to Middlesex, you hoped to get into Harvard. As I remember, all but one of my classmates—who failed the entrance examinations—went to Cambridge. My own decision to try for Harvard antedated my going to boarding school and was conditioned by the fact that my uncles Morris and James Loeb had distinguished themselves as Harvard scholars and graduates, just as my love for the Latin and Greek classics derived at least in part from the fact that my Uncle Jim, a great classics scholar, had been held up to me throughout my childhood as an example to be followed. During my college days, he corresponded with me in Latin and occasionally in Greek.

I thoroughly enjoyed my three years at Middlesex. In later life, I could see only one shortcoming in the education we received there: a too puritanical indoctrination in matters of sex. This, however, was a common failing of most New England secondary schools in the last years of the Edwardian age. Though more explicit in its prohibitions, the Boss's Puritanism was essentially no different from the less articulate prudery of my parents.

Years later, after I had graduated from college and come out of the World War I Naval Flying Corps, I told the Boss that I thought this part of our education had not been helpful. Frederick Winsor turned his blue eyes upon me in horror and said: "Jimmy, don't tell me that you have acquired French morals!"

A prewar Middlesex education tended to create or reinforce Puritan priggishness, but this did not in any way alter the fact that when I received my diploma, I had, thanks largely to Middlesex, become an American.

CHAPTER VI

A Father Wins Fame and Faces a Dilemma

MY CLOSEST friends at Middlesex were Alan Clark, Eric Douglas, John Morgan, and Bill Barker. We decided to room together at college. There were then no freshman dormitories and no house system. Freshmen lived wherever they could find rooms, and none of my four friends had well-to-do parents. When my father generously offered to give me whatever allowance I wanted, I told him that I would like a hundred dollars a month, which was what my friends would have to cover tuition, books and living expenses. My father thought this "quixotic" but my mother supported me.

The five of us found a tumble-down little frame house on the wrong side of Mount Auburn Street, opposite the luxurious Claverly Hall—one of a group of such houses known as Tenement Row. I was seventeen at the time and have often thought later it might have been better if I had been older. Nevertheless all five of us spent a happy and somewhat hilarious freshmen year. Douglas and Morgan made the freshman football team. I competed unsuccessfully for football manager. Clark and Barker concentrated on their studies. After the football season was over, we went into Boston and got ourselves rather magnificently drunk, riding home in an old-fashioned, horse-drawn cab whose driver, an Irishman named Cusick, specialized in what he called "bringin' home the young gintlemen."

We went in white ties and tails to the sub-debutante dances given by Boston dowagers for their daughters. At one of these Johnnie Morgan met the girl he was eventually to marry. Eric Douglas had a steady girl in Buffalo, his home town. Clark and Barker did not like "getting into monkey suits." I thoroughly enjoyed these parties as well as the more informal Cambridge dances at Brattle Hall, patronized by the academic community.

At one of the latter, I met and fell for the daughter of my French professor. The second or third time I saw her, she expressed a longing for a parrot. A week or so later, I happened to see in the Boston Common a sailor sitting on a park bench with a big green parrot on his shoulder. The sailor said that he had bought the bird in Brazil and that it could talk, but only in Portuguese. A foreign-language-speaking parrot! What gift could be more appropriate for the beautiful daughter of a professor of Romance languages?

I bought the bird for two dollars.

For three days I kept the parrot in my room, during which time it never said a word. On the following Sunday, I had been invited to lunch at the professor's house. My inamorata was enchanted with the bird. The professor addressed it in Portuguese. The bird remained obstinately silent. At lunch, the parrot perched on the high back of the dining-room chair upon which I was seated next to my love. About halfway through the meal, the professor launched into one of his interminable anecdotes. Suddenly, the wretched bird spoke. "Aw, shut up you old fool!" it said. And then, as if that had not been enough, it added: "You stupid bastard."

End of romance.

While I was a freshman at Harvard, my father was appointed by President Wilson to the first Federal Reserve Board.

Even before he had taken out his first papers to become an American citizen, my father had begun to work for the much needed reform of the American banking and currency system. Beginning in 1907, he had published numerous pamphlets advocating the establishment of a central note-issuing bank and the creation of a discount market. The central bank would acquire the sole right to issue currency, in place of the then existing motley array of treasury certificates, greenbacks, and national bank notes. The new currency would be safeguarded by a fixed reserve of gold bars or gold coin. In addition, the central bank would be empowered to rediscount commercial paper for the private banks, provided that they endorsed it, thus providing a liquid reserve more reliable than stock-exchange loans or single-name commercial paper.

During the Taft administration, my father worked with the Monetary Commission headed by Senator Nelson W. Aldrich, (R) of Rhode Island. In 1911, Aldrich took a small group of men, including H. P. Davison (a Morgan partner), Frank A. Vanderlip (president of the National City Bank of New York), and my father to Jekyll Island, off the Georgia coast. To forestall any publicity, Aldrich let it be known that the group was going to shoot duck. My father, who did not know one end of a shotgun from the other, had to borrow a lethal weapon to camouflage himself as a duck hunter. There the group worked out the so-called Aldrich Plan for the establishment of a central note-issuing bank.

When Woodrow Wilson was elected a year later, my father shifted his efforts to win the support of the Democratic administration. Working chiefly through Colonel E. M. House, Wilson's closest adviser, and through the congressional committees headed by Senator Robert L. Owen and Representative Carter Glass, my father contributed to the drafting of the Federal Reserve Act (the Owen-Glass Bill). In 1914, he became vice chairman of the newly created Federal Reserve Board.

The most important difference between the Federal Reserve System as set up under the new legislation and the Aldrich Plan was that it provided for the creation of twelve regional Federal Reserve Banks with a Federal Reserve Board sitting in Washington, in place of the single central note-issuing bank contemplated in the earlier proposal.

Paul Warburg was generally considered to have been the father of the Federal Reserve System, but, when asked if this was actually the case, he once replied with characteristic modesty and humor: "I really don't know who was the baby's father, but, judging from the number of men who claim the honor, all I can say is that its mother must have been a most immoral woman."

Since his English, though excellent, was somewhat Teutonic in style, my father often asked me to make suggestions for stylistic revision in his reports. Thus, I was privileged to see much of the inside workings of the slow and painful process of political creation that culminated in the passage of the Federal Reserve Act.

My father's appointment necessitated giving up his lucrative partnerships in Kuhn, Loeb & Company and M. M. Warburg

& Company, as well as his withdrawal from numerous director-ships. He was highly amused when I wrote him from Cambridge that the Irish maid who cleaned our rooms had congratulated me upon my father's "getting such a foine job wid such a grand salary." The appointment also made it necessary for my parents to move to Washington. Before returning to Cambridge for my sophomore year at Harvard, I helped to settle my father in a temporary apartment in Washington, pending the redecoration of the house he and my mother had rented.

The German-Austrian declaration of war in August 1914 came like a bombshell. Few people in America had foreseen it. There had been a number of crises over the Balkan situation and over Morocco, but each crisis had passed. In 1913–14, Americans were more concerned over their relations with Mexico than over the affairs of Europe.

When Germany launched its attack, my father was deeply shocked and grieved. Whatever his feelings as to the compli-cated causes of the war may have been, his loyalty to the land of his birth and his dismay at its ruthless violation of Belgian neutrality created a painful ambivalence. Added to this was a deep concern for his family. His feelings must have been rather similar to those that Elmer Davis, also of German ancestry, ex-pressed a year later in an article published by the magazine *Forum.*

I am neutral with the bitter, soul-searing neutrality of the man whose reason tells him one thing while his emotions cry out the other. Through the tangle of plots and counterplots, conflicting national aspirations and interests, I think I can see a heavy majority of arguments in favor of the Allies; and yet I feel no joy over their successes . . . When von Kluck swept on from Ons to Lille, and then on to St. Quentin, Compiegne and Senlis, my blood boiled up and sang. Tannenberg[1] and Coronel[2] were to me personal triumphs, though I knew all the time that my enthusiasm must be repented in the chill, gray logical dawn of the morning after . . .

During the first months of the war, my poor father was tor-tured by much the same "soul-searing neutrality." Until the un-

[1] Hindenburg's first great victory over the Russians.
[2] A naval battle off the coast of Chile in which a British squadron was sunk by the German fleet.

restricted German U-boat campaign forced the United States into the war, he ardently supported Wilson's policy of keeping out of the conflict and of trying to mediate a "peace without victory."

Although my German blood, too, at first "boiled up and sang" over the initial German victories, I did not for long share my father's admiration for Wilson's policy. Sentiment at Harvard was predominantly pro-Ally. In my newly acquired feeling of Americanism, I could no longer root for the German Army about which, as a child, I had felt much as I felt about the New York Giants. I admired Theodore Roosevelt, and T.R. was now an outspoken critic of Wilson's cautious neutrality. The event that thoroughly crystallized my interventionist, pro-Ally sentiment was the thrilling experience of being invited by my classmate, Archie Roosevelt, to have breakfast with his illustrious father.

Hearing T.R. excoriate the "skulking cowardice" of Wilson's neutrality, the "evil wickedness" of the Kaiser (whom he himself in some respects resembled), while he expounded upon the "righteousness" of the Allied cause, made a deep and lasting impression. The resulting hero worship on my part became a sore subject with my father, who had little use for the swashbuckling former President.

At the time, I knew little or nothing of the wholly admirable domestic reforms initiated by Roosevelt during his presidency. What attracted me were his less admirable qualities—his pugnacity, his certainty of where "righteousness" and "evil" were to be found and his love of physical adventure. These seemed to me manly and authentically American qualities.

Fortunately for the relationship of father and son, I spent the following summer away from home on a geological survey expedition in the San Juan Mountains of Colorado, conducted by Professor Atwood of Harvard.

At the beginning of my junior year, my friend Graham ("Fuzzy") Blaine and I were elected editors of the Harvard *Crimson*. As such, we launched a successful campaign for "preparedness," involving the creation of a Harvard University training regiment. This was the first such military establishment in the history of the university and the forerunner of the Plattsburg camps and the Reserve Officers Training Corps.

Before the house system was established at Harvard, all freshmen and the bulk of the sophomores, juniors, and seniors ate their meals in the huge, hideous dining room at Memorial Hall or else in the various small commercial lunchrooms on Harvard Square. For the privileged few in the three upper classes, there were eating (and drinking) clubs. These were not fraternities. They provided no living quarters. But they were the focus of social status. A sophomore, if he came from the right prep school or from an established Harvard family, or if he was an outstanding athlete, was eligible for election to the Institute of 1770, known as Dickey (originally DKE) and to one of half a dozen so-called "waiting clubs." The latter were societies whose members hopefully expected to be taken into one of the "final clubs" in their junior year. The half-dozen final clubs, each with about twenty to thirty members of the junior and senior classes, constituted the apex of the social pyramid. Membership in one of the elite final clubs was considered extremely important not only by undergraduates but by many of their parents. To belong to the Porcellian, the A.D., the Gas House, the Fly or the Sbee constituted an open sesame to "society" and to later member-ship in exclusive men's clubs, as well as to ready employment in the Boston, New York, and Philadelphia banking and business world. The sophomore waiting clubs occasionally took in a Jew or a Catholic, but the final clubs maintained a rigid tradition of Protestant exclusivity.

In my sophomore year, I was elected to the Institute of 1770 and to the Phoenix, one of the choice waiting clubs, as well as to the Signet Society, a literary rather than a social organiza-tion. Aware of the anti-Semitic prejudice in the final clubs, I philosophically although regretfully accepted the fact that, in my junior year, I would be to some extent separated from most of the boys with whom I had come from Middlesex and from some of the other friends I had made at Cambridge. It was, therefore, an agreeable surprise when two upperclassmen came as a delegation from one of the choice final clubs to notify me of my election.

I said that I would be delighted to join the club if my election signified that the club had abandoned its religious discrimina-tion, but that I would be unwilling to be singled out as an ex-ception to a continuing anti-Semitic policy. The two friendly upperclassmen said that I was wanted as a member precisely because, they said, "You aren't like other Jews."

I asked: "How many other Jews do you know?"

They had known scarcely any. It was clear that what they meant was that I was not like the stereotype caricature of the Jew that had been handed down to them by their families. They were not saying: "We realize that there are pleasant Jews as well as unpleasant ones." They were saying: "We like you because you're not really a Jew."

Regretfully, I said that I would have to decline the invitation. Having done so, I could not help wondering whether it might not have been more constructive to join and break down the prejudice, thus opening the way for other members of excluded minorities. But whether I was right or wrong, this is the course I have pursued throughout my life. I have refused either to be made an exception to a prejudice or to retreat in the face of it into the sort of defensive ghetto symbolized by Jewish country clubs and a general aping of the Christian community.

At Harvard, in my favorite studies of the classics, the superb teaching of E. K. Rand in Latin and Chandler Post in Greek enabled me to take second-year and final honors. Oddly enough, considering my later career, the study of government and economics played only a minor role in my college education, the high points of which, besides Latin and Greek, were Bliss Perry's courses in English literature, John Livingston Lowe's lectures on English poetry and M. T. Copeland's evening reading sessions. The books which I best remember are: Plato's *Republic;* Walter Pater's *Marius the Epicurean;* Aristotle's *Ethics;* Thucydides' *History of the Peloponnesian War;* John Jeffery Farnol's *The Broad Highway,* a second-rate novel (read aloud by Copeland); the plays of John Galsworthy; *Fortitude* by Hugh Walpole; and the poetry of Browning, Swinburne, François Villon, and Baudelaire. In German, I remember Schiller's *Wallenstein's Camp* and Lessing's *Nathan the Wise.*

I received my only "C" in Professor Haskins' freshman history course, not because I did not like history but because I was bored by Professor Haskins. I was only mildly interested by F. W. Taussig's course in pre-Keynesian economics and later found that I had to unlearn much that he had taught me. (My father considered Taussig a great man.)

I deeply loved Bliss Perry. This great teacher became a cherished friend and a kindly critic of my later writings until he died in 1954 at the ripe age of ninety-three.

I was too light for college football (there were no JV teams then) and not good enough at baseball to make a team. At tennis, I was just barely good enough to be used, along with four or five others, as an occasional practice opponent for the varsity. My only athletic talent was as a natural quarter-miler, but here I had the bad luck to be running at a time when Harvard had three quarter-milers who could consistently break fifty seconds—a feat I accomplished only once and then with a strong wind behind me. Nevertheless, I enjoyed my unsuccessful efforts to win a varsity letter and eventually became manager of the cross-country team.

After three years, I completed the requirements for a B.A. degree but deferred taking it so as to be able to graduate with my class in 1917. Little did I realize that my class would have no commencement exercises because, by that time, the United States would be at war.

Having finished college at nineteen, I planned to go to work for a year and then to go either to Oxford or the Harvard Law School. Being the oldest male member of the thirteenth generation of a banking family, I felt that I should probably follow in the ancestral footsteps and eventually join my father in Kuhn, Loeb & Company, even though, from a personal point of view, I would have preferred to work under my Uncle Max in Hamburg rather than under Jacob Schiff in New York.

Kuhn, Loeb & Company's major business had long consisted of financing and occasionally reorganizing railroads; yet none of the partners, including my father, was closely familiar with the operating problems of the companies they financed. It seemed to me a sensible idea to learn more about them. Accordingly, I asked my father whether he thought it would be possible for me to be apprenticed for a year to a railroad where I could learn at first hand something about what, besides money, made railroads run. My father promptly arranged with his friend, Daniel Willard, president of the Baltimore & Ohio Railroad, to give me precisely this sort of opportunity.

When I presented myself in Baltimore, Mr. Willard told me that he had never heard of a railroad financier who had begun

his career by working on a railroad, and that he had often wished
that bankers had more direct knowledge of operating problems.
He suggested that I work first as a passenger agent, then as a
freight solicitor, then on a track gang, then in the freight yards,
then in the office of a divisional superintendent, and finally,
for a few weeks, in the executive offices. As it turned out, this
interesting schedule could be only partially completed before I
decided to volunteer for training in the United States Naval Air
Corps. Nevertheless, I learned much during the following six
months.

No one who has not sat in a switch tower or a train dis-
patcher's office can appreciate the continuous nervous tension
involved in regulating traffic so as to keep everything moving
at maximum speed while at the same time guarding against
accidents. One has to work all day on a track-repair gang, or in a
freight yard, loading bales of cotton into box cars to acquire any
comprehension of the backbreaking labor involved. Even selling
passenger tickets is a rewarding experience, for here one learns
how truly inconsiderate most people in a hurry can be. It was
fascinating for me to observe how one's point of view changes,
depending upon whether one is standing before or behind a
ticket window.

One day, when I was working in the Camden station, a train
pulled in with Mr. Willard's private car attached to the rear.
Out of the car came Mr. Willard, followed by a tall and very
handsome young man, not very much older than I, who said that
our fathers were great friends, that he had heard what I was
doing and that, as a director of the railroad, he was glad to
have me working for it. This was the first time I met Averell
Harriman, whom I was to know well and increasingly to admire
throughout the rest of my life.

Working in the freight yards with tough but on the whole
likeable men, I had to establish myself as not being a tenderfoot
or, worse, a company spy. I learned to chew and spit tobacco
as if I enjoyed it. The crucial test came in a fistic encounter with
a barrel-chested Irishman named John O'Toole. Acting that day
as temporary foreman of a freight-yard gang noted for laziness
and slack discipline, I foolishly delivered the kind of pep talk
I had heard Percy Haughton give Harvard football teams between the halves of a game. To this ill-advised inspirational

effort, O'Toole, the ringleader of the gang, reacted with a stream of obscene epithets that could be answered in only one way. Without much enthusiasm or confidence, I aimed a punch at O'Toole's jaw and came to about five minutes later to find him sitting on a barrel laughing at me. Again, there was only one thing to do. I did it, with the same result . . . When next I recovered consciousness, I had sense enough to realize that I had been bruising my knuckles on a cast-iron jaw and shifted my attack to O'Toole's beer belly. This time, O'Toole hit the deck. Arising with a big grin, he came toward me, hand outstretched. "Now, me bye," he said, "we are friends." From there on, O'Toole took over and made the gang work as it had never worked before. There was nothing more for me to do but to watch admiringly. Long after I had left the B. & O., O'Toole and I exchanged Christmas cards. Upon his, O'Toole invariably scrawled: "Keep your chin covered," while I wrote on mine: "Watch your fat belly!"

The final episode in my short career as a railroader occurred when I was working in the office of the vice president in charge of traffic. (The title was a euphemism for the road's chief business-getter and press agent.) I had been assigned the job of drafting an advertisement for the Baltimore & Ohio passenger service between Washington and New York which had steadily lost business after the Pennsylvania Railroad had tunneled into the city, while the Baltimore & Ohio still discharged its passengers in Hoboken, New Jersey. The slogan which I proudly conceived and suggested very nearly got me fired. It read:

"Take the B. & O. and avoid the crowds!"

CHAPTER VII

Clipped Wings

A MONTH LATER, I was a cadet flyer at the newly established naval air station at Hampton Roads, Virginia. Although the station had been in operation for only a few days, many of us already had our civilian pilot's licenses. A group of Yale students had spent several weeks training at H. P. Davison's place on Long Island. Among them were Harry Davison, Jr., Robert A. Lovett, Kenneth MacLeish, and Artemus ("Di") Gates. Our Harvard group had learned to fly at the Curtiss Aviation School at Newport News. Among its members were my friends, Westmore Willcox, Moseley Taylor, Charles Fuller, and Mike Murray. It was Willcox who had written me while I was working at Baltimore, telling me that the Harvard unit was in the process of formation and suggesting that I join it.

The United States was not yet at war, but its entry seemed inevitable and, to most of us, desirable in the interest of preventing an otherwise almost certain German victory. Allied losses had been appalling, and Britain apparently faced starvation from the depredations of the German U-boats. It was the submarine menace that had led us to seek to enlist as naval flyers.

Immediately upon receipt of Willcox's letter, I had gone to Washington to talk things over with my parents. The discussion had been long and painful.

Both of my parents loathed militarism. My father was a quiet, judicial-minded, scholarly man with a strong sense of duty to his country—originally Germany and then the United States—but he was essentially more pacifist than patriot. My mother was more emotionally American, but there was little if any militancy in her patriotism. Both at first reacted almost angrily to my desire to enlist.

My father drew a sharp distinction between doing one's duty if called up for military service and needlessly volunteering for what he called "the horrible business of killing people." Also, he could see no point in deliberately choosing a branch of the service in which even the training period was extremely hazardous. (The danger of learning to fly could not at that time be denied; it was only fourteen years since the Wrights had made their famous first flight at Kitty Hawk.) Although amply endowed with moral courage, my father was inclined to look down upon physical bravery as a form of stupid vanity.

My mother, on the other hand, had physical courage and respected it in others. She probably understood better than I the compulsion to conquer physical fear by doing precisely what one is most afraid of doing. In the end, it was she who persuaded my father to withdraw his objections. And so, in early March, I had gone off to Newport News, handsomely equipped by my Baltimore girl friends with quite useless knitted mufflers, wristlets, and helmets.

My first flight had been with Victor Carlstrom, one of the early civilian stunt flyers. The plane was a single-motored, open-cockpit Curtiss JN4, known as a Jenny. After climbing to about 5000 feet, Carlstrom had shut off the engine and shouted: "Now I'll show you what this plane can do so that you'll have confidence in it. First, I'll do a loop, then a stall, then a sideslip, and then a tailspin. Ready?"

After about ten minutes, during which I found myself either hanging by my seat belt or crushed down by gravity into the cockpit, feeling alternately scared to death and exhilarated, Carlstrom once more shut off the engine's roar, told me to put my feet on the rudder bar and my hands on the dual control to get the feel of what he was doing. Shortly after, he held his hands up in the air to let me know that I myself was now flying the plane. Then he took over and made a perfect three-point landing. Turning around in his front seat, he grinned and said: "Think you can take off and land? Okay? Then open the throttle and be sure to hold her nose down until she's got flying speed. I'll tell you when by putting up one hand."

Taking off an airplane for the first time is a sensation no one is likely to forget—like the first time one jumps a horse over a five-foot fence. At a thousand feet, Carlstrom motioned to me to do a wide circle, corrected me when I banked insufficiently, and then pointed downward for a landing. As the plane hit and bounced, Carlstrom cut the ignition switch and let the Jenny roll to a stop. "Okay, kid, you'll do. See you tomorrow."

I never did fly with Carlstrom again. Before my next turn came, a few days later, Carlstrom was killed. A wing came off the new JN4 he was testing, and I sadly helped to carry his shattered body from the wreckage.

My next lessons were with Ted Hequenberg in a flying boat. The F1 was heavier and not nearly as maneuverable as a Jenny. It had a bad tendency to sideslip on a turn and then to go into a spin from which recovery was next to impossible. As I was awaiting my turn, after having had about three short lessons with Hequenberg, such an accident occurred. The F-boat sideslipped, spun into the water, and crashed. Hequenberg's back was broken (he died later in the hospital) and his student, my friend, Larry Curtis, was fished out of the sea with a broken jaw and a thigh so badly fractured that his leg had to be amputated. Later, he became a distinguished congressman from Massachusetts.

Hequenberg's place was taken by a gruff navy lieutenant, named Harry Cecil, one of the earliest U. S. Navy flyers. In contrast to the gay and carefree civilian instructors who had preceded him, Cecil was deadly serious. He also had an unpleasant habit of jamming his elbow into the stomach of a student when he made a mistake. (Teacher and student sat side-by-side in F-boats, not fore-and-aft as in the JN4 land planes.) After two or three none too enjoyable short, dual-control flights, I was happy when Cecil turned me loose for my first solo. I had now had, in all, forty-eight minutes of instruction!

Lieutenant Cecil's orders were to take off, do a right-hand circle around Hampton Roads, land, and taxi in to shore. I did my circle, but suddenly and unaccountably terrified to make a landing, I went around the bay for a second time. Having done so, I was still too scared to land. On my third circuit the engine sputtered, and I thought that I was running out of fuel. Forced to come down at last, I landed neatly enough and taxied in to the beach, expecting to be chewed out for having stayed up so long. Instead, Cecil merely said: "You've wasted enough time and gas for two other flights, so you'll miss your next two turns." I saluted and turned away, thinking: "He doesn't know that I'd still be up there if I hadn't thought the gas was running out."

Later, it turned out that he had known exactly what had happened. In fact, he told me that, on his own first solo flight at Pensacola, he had done precisely the same thing.

Late in March, the Navy was ready to take over the two privately trained units. Cecil and his cadets were ordered to the new air station at Hampton Roads. The cadets were sworn in as seamen second class. In place of the easygoing life at Newport News, discipline now took over. Cadet uniforms replaced civilian garb.

On April 6, the United States declared war. What for most of us had been nothing more than an exciting adventure now became grim business. The chief topic of conversation was: "When do we get sent overseas?"

The newly appointed commandant of the Naval Air Station was Lieutenant Commander E. O. ("Eddie") McDonnell, a former lightweight boxing champion at the Naval Academy and already the holder of the Congressional Medal, awarded for exceptional bravery at Vera Cruz. Since there were few qualified instructors, McDonnell assigned the more advanced students to teach the more recent arrivals. I was taken in hand by Harry Davison and Kenneth MacLeish, each with a few more hours of flying time. Before long, I, too, was assigned to instructing, a task I enjoyed until I had a frightening experience.

A student whom I was teaching suddenly froze onto the controls in the forward cockpit. At an altitude of not over 3000 feet, the plane went into a spinning nose dive. It was impossible to shake loose the controls. For a few seconds, which seemed like eternity, a crash seemed unavoidable. Then, in the nick of time, I remembered the pyrene extinguisher under my seat, yanked it out, and, standing on tiptoe in the rear seat of the open cockpit, slammed it down on the student's head. In spite of his leather safety helmet, the blow knocked him out, enabling me to pull out of the dive barely in time to make a safe landing. I insisted upon the boy's taking the plane up again. This time he flew like an angel. He did equally well on two subsequent flights with another instructor. A week later, he was killed on his first solo flight.

Had it been wrong not to recommend that he be washed out?

Brooding over this incident, I wondered whether perhaps my judgment had been affected by a secret fear of being washed out myself. I knew that my eyesight was somewhat defective. In order to gain admission to the Curtiss Aviation School, I had thrown away the glasses I had worn since childhood and, by memorizing the eye card, had faked my way through a rather primitive eye examination. The only time my lack of binocular vision had bothered me since learning to fly was in landing on glassy water, but I had soon learned that, when I lost clear sight of the water, I had about fifty feet in which to level off. This slight difficulty had seemed of no importance so long as I was risking only my own neck, but, after this incident, I began to have qualms about teaching students.

I was afraid to ask to be relieved from instructing for fear that a re-examination of my eyes by a navy doctor would lead to disqualification. The same risk would be involved in asking for a transfer to the Army Flying Corps in which I would not have to make landings on water. For the time being, I decided to leave well enough alone.

In many respects, World War I was a strange war. One morning at inspection, we were confronted by an unfamiliar British sergeant, recently invalided out of combat duty, who introduced himself as follows:

"Do any of you chaps know Mrs. T. E. Scruggins of 'artlepool, England? No? Well, this is 'er son and yer'd better mind yer pee, pips, and ques! Nah, then, I'm 'ere ter teach you blokes bay'net drill."

And so he was, although no one could figure out why aviators should be trained in the use of a bayonet. It seemed as though the higher-ups had forgotten which war they were directing.

By this time, we had a number of new recruits, some of them interesting characters. One, by the name of Steve Stone, was a former racing-car driver who had volunteered for service in the British Army. Seriously wounded in France, he was sent back to England on the ill-fated *Sussex*, which was torpedoed in the Channel. Not having had enough excitement, Steve had decided to become a flyer. Incongruously, he always referred to himself as "Clara's Boy," Clara being his mother's name.

One day, Secretary of the Navy Josephus Daniels arrived on an inspection trip, wearing his customary black suit, ten-gallon hat, and black string tie. Clara's Boy was ordered to escort him. Looking at our row of planes neatly lined up on the beach, the Secretary asked Stone: "How fast do these things fly?"

Stone: "About ninety miles an hour, sir."

The Secretary: "My God, how do you breathe?"

Stone (sotto voce but quite audibly): "Through your ass, of course!" (The Secretary was a good sport and pretended not to have heard.)

Eventually, my defective eyesight led me to make an invention that, to my disgust and disappointment, deferred my hopes of becoming a combat pilot overseas. The navy planes were equipped with old-fashioned boat compasses, placed on the cockpit floor so that the pilot, by looking down at them, could take a reading. This made it difficult for the pilot's eyes to adjust to the comparative darkness of the cockpit and then back again to the bright sky. Having twice nearly got lost at sea through my inability to take an accurate compass reading, I hit upon the idea of floating a compass card with reversed markings in an inverted tumbler and mounting the latter on the cowling of my plane so that, by looking straight ahead, I could read the band suspended from the edge of my compass much as one reads a speedometer. Commander McDonnell, seeing this device, at once took a trial flight with me and, greatly pleased, ordered me to perfect and patent the instrument for the Navy. To my dismay, I was detailed to Washington in charge of getting the new compass mass-produced for all naval aircraft. It was later used on army planes as well.

Thereafter, until the end of the war, I was to fly only occasionally as a test pilot.

Toward the end of the war, three giant seaplanes were built by the Naval Aircraft Factory at Philadelphia with the idea that they might accomplish a flight across the Atlantic. I went on a test flight in one of these machines with Lieutenant Commander David McCulloch and two other officers. The plane was so nose-heavy that it took the three of us tugging with might and main on the controls to lift it off the water. It was nose-heavy in the air too—a truly horrible craft to fly. Nevertheless, I was to get a vicarious thrill some years later, when this very machine became the first lighter-than-air craft to span the Atlantic. All three of the N.C. planes took off from Newfoundland for a flight to Europe via the Azores. Two were forced to drop out or turn back, but the third, under command of Lieutenant Commander A. C. ("Putty") Read, reached the Azores and then completed the flight to England. This was eight years before Charles Lindbergh's famous non-stop flight from New York to Paris.

At the time, I felt that my war experience had been frustrating. I had gone through most of the hazardous training of a combat pilot only to end up as procurer of navigational instruments. I envied those of my comrades who were sent overseas and felt rather like a child who, at the last minute, had been left out of a promised party.

If I had been more mature, I might have been grateful to have been spared the duty to kill or be killed. I might also have realized that, no matter how short and unsatisfactory my career as a flyer, the experience had changed me from a boy into a man. Since those days in 1917, I have often known physical fear, but I have never again felt that worst of all fears, the fear of being afraid.

CHAPTER VIII

Sex, Puritanism, Love, and Marriage

MY COMMANDING OFFICER in Washington was an easygoing retired navy regular, who left me free to come and go as I pleased in carrying out my work. This involved numerous visits to the Sperry Gyroscope Company and the Arma Engineering Company, both near New York City, and to the Taylor Instrument

Company at Rochester, New York. I missed the companionship of my friends, but the new assignment had one advantage; it permitted me to live at my parents' home in Washington and, in the course of the next few months, to enjoy the privilege of meeting many of my father's friends on the Federal Reserve Board and in President Wilson's cabinet.

One evening when I came home from work, I found Supreme Court Justice Oliver Wendell Holmes sitting in my father's study. The Justice arose from his chair as I entered, saying, "Young man, I, too, once had the honor of wearing the coat you are wearing. Give me your hand."

Taking my hand and placing it over the small of his back, Justice Holmes said: "Feel those?" I felt what seemed to be a bunch of marbles. "Those are Minié balls," the Justice said. "Collected at Antietam."

Later, I could recall only this part of the conversation. I still remember my sense of awe at meeting the great man and the impression of a ramrod-straight, tall figure, a beautiful white mustache, and a pair of twinkling blue eyes.

On another occasion, I was introduced to Secretary of the Treasury William G. McAdoo, who had married one of President Wilson's daughters. Frederic Delano, the uncle of Franklin Roosevelt, was a frequent visitor at my parents' home. He and Adolph C. Miller were my father's closest friends on the Federal Reserve Board. And while I did not meet them, I heard my mother speak of the Franklin Roosevelts as the most attractive young couple in Washington, an opinion to which my father, with an unusual lack of prescience, added: "Yes, but he is not very bright." (F.D.R. was then Assistant Secretary of the Navy.)

On one of my trips to New York on government business, I went to a dance and met a girl about whom I had already heard much enthusiastic comment from my mother and sister. Her name was Katharine Swift. She was a student at the Institute of Musical Art and had recently met my mother and sister in the Adirondacks. Her father had been the music critic on the New York *World,* and her widowed mother, an Englishwoman, supported herself and her two children as an interior decorator, helped out by Katharine's earnings as a piano teacher.

Katharine was fun to dance with and even more fun to talk to. She had a lively sense of humor, brown hair worn in a chignon, brown eyes, and a provocative little figure. I liked her and was highly pleased when she invited me to stay at her mother's apartment the next time I came to New York. I did so, not once but several times during the next few months.

The idea of marriage never entered my mind. "This," I thought, "is going to be my girl until I go overseas." (My hope of being sent abroad was still very much alive. I was completely unaware that months earlier my father had spoken to Secretary of the Navy Daniels, asking that, unless absolutely necessary, I should not be sent overseas where I might have to drop bombs on my own relatives.)

There was no doubt in my mind that I liked Katharine Swift better than any girl I had known. When I found that she reciprocated my feelings, I told her that if I felt free and ready to marry, I would ask her to become my wife, but that I did not feel ready for marriage and, in any case, I couldn't think of becoming engaged so long as I might at any moment receive orders to go overseas. Katharine respected this feeling, although she did not altogether share it.

I had every reason to feel unready for marriage. My generation had been raised according to the taboos and moral concepts of the late Victorian age. Boys were taught that the sex drive, though necessary for the survival of the race, was actually one of man's baser instincts to be indulged in only if associated with "true love." True love, in turn, meant that lovers, in order to be "decent people," must enter into a contract of companionship for life, accepting each other "for better for worse, in sickness and in health" until death did them part. Divorce was considered a disgrace.

Premarital sex experience was strictly forbidden for girls and frowned upon for young males. ("If you expect some day to marry an innocent virgin, you should come to her as pure as you expect her to be.") Contact between the sexes was carefully chaperoned. "Nice girls" did not permit boys to "take liberties." "Nice boys" would not attempt anything more adventurous than a chaste goodnight kiss. One did not hold hands in public. In fact, one was supposed to act as if the sex instinct did not exist.

At home I gained the impression that sexual activity was something men unfortunately desired and to which a woman who loved her husband submitted reluctantly, partly in order to satisfy his desire but chiefly in order to have children. Without ever discussing the subject of sex with me during my adolescence, my father managed somehow to give me the feeling that his ideas were not essentially different—that a man should be grateful to his wife for fulfilling a carnal requirement, the existence of which was, on the whole, regrettable.

Frederick Winsor's weekly lectures in "Hygienics" to the graduating class at Middlesex—known to the boys as "Smut One"—had embodied a few elementary facts of life that most of the boys already knew and thrown heavy emphasis upon the desirability of premarital continence. This admonition was fortified by a few frightening details concerning the various venereal diseases a promiscuous male might contract.

Among the men I knew best at Harvard, similar backgrounds had produced something like a consensus to the effect that no decent man would "take advantage of a nice girl," that if a man had to be a "woman chaser," he ought to satisfy his desires—not with a prostitute, because then he might get syphilis or gonorrhea—but with some "chippie," meaning some little working girl whom he might pick up and seduce.

Of course, by no means all Harvard undergraduates adhered to this code. There were a few lusty males of my acquaintance who made no secret of their sexual adventures and who had no feeling of guilt; but, unless such an individual happened to be an outstanding athlete, he was looked upon with disapproval by the prep-school elite. The elite itself was absurdly immature and smug in its puritanical innocence.

Any reasonably intelligent boy in his late teens, especially one with a half-European background, could not fail to entertain at least some doubt as to the validity of this "Anglo-Saxon" middle-class morality. Why, for example, was it reprehensible to seduce the daughter of a State Street bank president or college professor while it was, if not commendable, at least far less sinful to seduce the janitor's daughter? Why was it permissible to explore the breasts of a little working girl on a dark street corner, but "going too far" if one took her to bed? Was chastity a purely technical matter which permitted one to reach orgasm by "petting," but forbade the more natural consummation of passion in the act of intercourse?

There had, of course, been various girls in my life ever since, at age fifteen, I had had a bad case of puppy love for the twenty-year-old daughter of a Swiss landscape painter at Sils Maria in the Engadine. Then there had been the young French governess of one of my German cousins, who might have treated me with kindly French tolerance and taught me something about love, had I not been too timid to make any advances.

At Baltimore, I had flirted with the pretty daughter of the B. & O.'s general counsel, engaging with David K. Bruce (later to become a lifelong friend) in a friendly rivalry for her favor. Another attractive Baltimore girl with a taste for poetry had inspired a few romantic lyrics from my pen; and, on occasional visits to Washington, I had gone out with the slightly more sophisticated daughter of one of my father's colleagues on the Federal Reserve Board.

Here and there, I had messed around a bit with a few compliant females but these half adventures had invariably left me with mingled feelings of disgust and unsatisfied desire.

At the Naval Air Station, things had been different. The group was older and more heterogeneous. Sex was a major topic of conversation among the regular enlisted personnel and also among many of the cadet flyers. A few of my friends were engaged and intended to get married as soon as possible.

Close association with two wholly disparate groups—with those who enthusiastically sought, found, and talked about promiscuous adventures and those who were in love with girls whom they intended soon to marry—produced conflicting thoughts and emotions. I envied the carefree individuals who were apparently quite uninhibited in seeking sexual pleasures. I also envied those of my friends who were headed toward marriage, but wondered whether it was right for a man to get married at a time when he was about to go off to war.

The evening after the episode in which I had felt death breathing down my neck as my plane spun earthward, I got into my car, drove to Norfolk, and, in the most sordid manner possible, made certain that I would not die as an innocent. The experience left me with mingled feelings of disgust and satisfaction. Driving back through the night toward the air station, I thought I could hear Frederick Winsor's voice, saying: "It would serve you right if you caught a venereal disease." But another louder and more jovial voice seemed to be saying: "Congratulations, old man. It was about time for you to grow up and shuck off all that Puritan nonsense!"

Was it nonsense? Were so-called morals hypocrisy? Obviously it would be wrong to seduce a virgin or to father an illegitimate child, but what could be wrong—whom did one injure, except possibly oneself, by going to bed with a harlot? Was it a betrayal of one's future wife? But how did a man know that he would ever have a wife?

A wave of nausea swept over me as I recalled the cold professionalism of the writhing, naked body on the bed.

Suddenly it dawned upon me that the disgust I felt was not over what I had done but over the utter lack of anything beautiful in the experience. It was the ugliness, not the "immorality" of the act that had left me with a feeling of emptiness. Why had I not been told that the act of love should be a thing of beauty, rather than an act of sordid ugliness? Why should parents make a mystery of sex, making their sons feel that there was something shameful about it, thus practically driving them into the arms of a prostitute?

"If I am ever lucky enough to have a son," I thought, "I am certainly not going to let him grow up in ignorance or be burdened with a ridiculous and unnecessary sense of guilt . . ."

By the time I got back to the air station, disgust had vanished, replaced by a sense of accomplishment. I had now become a man who could swap experience with other men. I went to sleep that night dreaming of a little French-Canadian waitress in Boston whom I had disappointed by not going to bed with her . . .

When I met and fell in love with Katharine, these things were still very much on my mind. I did not think that I knew enough about sex to make a good lover, yet I certainly did not now want to make love to any other woman. Nor did I want my awakened but unsatisfied sexual desires to trick me into an ill-considered marriage. What I needed was time.

In a way, I think that Katharine understood all this. She put no pressure upon me, but her mother made it clear that she would like our engagement to be announced and in various subtle ways tried to make me feel that I was committed. Torn between my love for Katharine and Mrs. Swift's pressure on the one hand, and, on the other, by my strong feeling that neither the time nor the circumstances were right, I decided to consult my parents.

By them, I was told in no uncertain terms that, at barely twenty-one, I was too young to know my own mind; that a man had no right to ask a woman to marry him until he could support her; and that I was emotionally too immature to think of marriage. All this was probably true, but it was hard to take. To make matters worse, I now learned for the first time about my father's intervention with the Secretary of the Navy. This infuriated me and would long remain the one thing for which I could never quite forgive my father.

The elimination of the probability of being sent overseas, which had served as my rationalization for a strong inner resistance to committing myself, plus the resentment aroused by my parents' attitude, tipped the balance. The next day I went back to New York, proposed to Katharine, and was accepted.

When I told my parents of my now definite engagement, I said that I was sorry that they felt as they did, but I intended to show them they were wrong—I *did* know my own mind; I was not immature; and I would be quite capable of supporting a wife without any further parental assistance.

My mother understood my resentment of my father's secret intercession about which she, too, had not known. Partly because of this, she persuaded my father to accept my engagement with good grace; even though she probably shared his misgivings. "After all," she said, "he couldn't have chosen a nicer girl." My father, too, liked Katharine. He merely felt quite sincerely that I was making a mistake.

If either of my parents harbored any strong feelings about their son's marrying a gentile, they kept their thoughts to themselves. Not so the self-appointed family patriarch. Upon the announcement of my engagement, I received a telegram from Jacob H. Schiff:

I wish you joy to your happiness but cannot refrain from telling you that I am deeply disturbed by your action in marrying out of the faith in view of its probable effect upon my own progeny.

Now I can chuckle over this message. At the time, it infuriated me.

Had it not been for that unfortunate interview with my parents

I would almost certainly not have wanted to get married until the war was over and I could see more clearly what I would do after being discharged from the service. Now, however, my Dutch was up. On my recent twenty-first birthday, my father had generously set up a trust fund which gave me an independent income amounting to about $4000 a year. This, plus my flying pay as a lieutenant, junior grade, would be more than enough to support a wife who was not accustomed to luxury. My inner doubts as to the wisdom of this course were now submerged in a state of infatuation fortified by revolt against parental authority.

Katharine and I were married on June 1, 1918 at her mother's small West Side apartment. The ceremony was performed by a civil magistrate. Katharine's sole attendant was her friend, Louise Homer, junior, daughter of the well-known Metropolitan contralto. Westmore Willcox was my best man.

After spending my ten-days' leave at Lake Mohonk, we settled down in a two-room apartment in Washington. Katharine's piano occupied most of the little living room and most of her time while I was at work. In the evenings, unless we went for a walk with Michael, our Irish terrier, Katharine gave me lessons in harmony and I taught her to drive a car. Most weekends we visited my parents, who greatly enjoyed having Katharine play for them.

Before the war ended, on November 11, 1918, I learned of the death of several of my friends. Among my flying companions, Ken MacLeish, Ben Lee, and Mike Murray had been lost. Alan Clark and Randolph Brown, two of my classmates at Middlesex, had been killed in France, as had a number of my friends at Harvard. Bob Lovett and Di Gates were distinguishing themselves with the Northern Bombing Group; Fuzzy Blaine was in France with the field artillery; Johnnie Morgan was serving on a destroyer. I heard of these remote happenings with sadness and a rueful sense of the inadequacy of my own wartime service.

On December 18, the Navy Department placed me on inactive duty in the reserve, on condition that I would remain in Washington for a few months in case I should be needed in connection with winding up procurement contracts.

Katharine was five months pregnant. We would soon have to look for a larger apartment. It was time for me to get started on a career.

CHAPTER IX

Learning a Profession

EVER SINCE my freshman year at Cambridge I had harbored a secret ambition to become a writer—secret because I took it more or less for granted that I would become a banker. I had written poetry and a few plays and short stories and had translated French and Greek poetry into English verse. The various verse forms fascinated me. Katharine, a newspaperman's daughter, would have liked me to become a writer but I was by no means sure that, as such, I would be able to support a wife and children. Above all, at this time, I wanted to stand on my own feet.

The decision to follow in my father's footsteps would have been easier if I had been able to foresee where my father's footsteps were likely to lead. His future seemed uncertain. He had declined reappointment to a second term on the Federal Reserve Board and had embarked upon writing the history of the Federal Reserve System—a massive, two-volume work it would take him several years to complete. So far as I could make out, my father had no intention of going back to Kuhn, Loeb & Company, although his former partners, and especially his brother Felix, were urging him to do so.

Since the Navy had stipulated that I must remain in Washington for six months, I decided that, during this time, I would learn what I could about the workings of a bank. At a salary of twenty dollars a week, I became a sort of odd-job handy man to Mr. George W. White, the president of the National Metro-

politan Bank of Washington. I worked as a messenger and in
the various teller's cages as well as in the bookkeeping department. The advantage of working in a small bank was that one
could learn about every aspect of its not very complicated operations. But I think I actually learned more about banking and
finance from listening to my father and his friends.

Meanwhile, our daughter was born and named April. My parents were delighted. Shortly thereafter, we moved into a
slightly larger apartment.

In the spring of 1919, my father began talking about forming
a new kind of banking institution in New York—a sort of bankers'
bank, to be owned by leading American and European banks
and also by private bankers, which would specialize in financing
international trade by means of bankers' acceptances issued under letters of credit. (A bank acceptance is a draft drawn upon
it and "accepted" under a letter of credit, then sold to and endorsed by another bank. Prior to the establishment of the Federal
Reserve System single-name thirty-, sixty-, or ninety-day promissory notes, known as "commercial paper," and stock-exchange
"call loans" formed the chief liquid reserve of American banking.) In this contemplated venture, my father was motivated
by two considerations.

First, he wished to give his brothers in Hamburg a closely
affiliated commercial banking institution in New York to help
them in reconstructing the shattered German economy. (Kuhn,
Loeb & Company did not engage in commercial banking.) This
led to the idea of including as shareholders in the new institution not only M. M. Warburg & Company, but the Hamburg
firm's old-established correspondent banks in Britain, France,
Switzerland, the Low Countries, and Scandinavia.

A second and equally important motivation was to introduce
two-name bank acceptances, instead of single-name promissory
notes, into the American discount market, thus strengthening the
liquid reserves of the banking system.

As the project began to take shape, my father talked about
my joining him. I was enthusiastic about the project but felt
that first I should get a job in some commercial bank, learn
about foreign and domestic financing, and come to work with
my father only after I had established myself on my own feet.
I was determined that whatever position I might occupy in my

father's bank should be earned on merit, not handed to me because I was my father's son. This determination on my part, plus the fact that I rather ungraciously refused to accept any financial help beyond the trust income my father had already provided for me, caused him some unhappiness at the time. Later, however, he told me that he thought I had been right.

In June 1919, with the understanding that my father would do nothing to facilitate my getting a job, I went to Boston and applied at the First National Bank. The president, Daniel G. Wing, a gruff, cigar-chewing Nebraskan, who had come up through the ranks as a bank examiner and earned the not-easily-won respect of patrician State Street, granted me an interview on the strength of the Warburg name. But that was as far as the magic of the name carried. Wing asked me to outline my past experience. I began by stating that I had graduated *magna cum laude* from college.

"What college?"

"Oh, Harvard, sir."

"You know, young man, there are a lot of other colleges beside Harvard. None of you Harvard men ever seem to realize that. How long have you had to get over Harvard?"

Eventually, after some shrewd questions about my work on the Baltimore and Ohio and in the Washington bank, he asked why I wanted to be a banker, why I didn't go into the bank my father was establishing, or into Kuhn, Loeb & Company, and how I had happened to come to him. I said that I hoped eventually to work with my father but not until after I had proved my usefulness elsewhere. I had come to him because I liked New England and because my father had told me that the First National Bank of Boston was likely to become a shareholder in the new bank; and I thought working in a shareholding bank would be a good way to learn what sort of services my father's shareholders would expect.

Mr. Wing grunted, rang for his secretary and told her to put me on the payroll as a bookkeeper. That same afternoon, I found a small apartment in Cambridge and telephoned my wife in Washington to tell her to get ready to move North.

Three days later, I was sitting on a high stool, working at a fiendish bookkeeping device known as a Boston ledger. (No one who has not had to post accounts on such an old-fashioned ledger can appreciate what Thomas Watson and his International Business Machines have done for the banking profession.) After a few months, I was shifted to the credit department, taught how to analyze financial statements and sent out as a credit investigator.

In those days, many of the most respected business concerns still refused to disclose their financial condition and obtained large amounts of credit on nothing more than their reputation. Cullman Brothers, an old, established firm of tobacco merchants, had a credit line of $500,000 with the First National. One day I was told to call on the senior partner to see whether I could obtain a balance-sheet or at least a statement of net worth. When, after some desultory talk about business conditions, I delicately broached the subject, Joe Cullman said: "So Dan Wing sent you to see my statement, eh? All right." He opened the middle drawer of his desk, pointed to a folded document, slammed shut the drawer, and said: "Go back and tell Wing you saw it." And that was that. When I reported to Mr. Wing, he merely nodded. Cullman Brothers' credit line remained unchanged.

Studying the list of clients, I realized that a large part of the bank's business consisted in financing wool, cotton, and leather manufacture. Accordingly, on my travels as a credit investigator, I made a point of learning how to sample raw wool, cotton, and hides and familiarized myself with the rudiments of the processes through which these raw materials were turned into woolens, worsteds, cotton sheets, and shoes. I became so interested in these trades that I wrote a pamphlet about each, all three being published by the bank as a means of promoting business. A fourth pamphlet, *A Clerk's Eye View of the First National Bank of Boston*, was published by the bank as an aid to new employees and a morale-builder. Thus, I found my ambition to write was not altogether incompatible with a banking career.

At about the same time, my first successful effort to publish verse resulted in the sale, for ten dollars, of a sonnet to the *Century Magazine*. I was prouder of that ten dollars than of any other money I had earned to date.

In 1920–21, there was a panic in the wool and cotton markets, with a considerable number of business failures. My specialized knowledge turned out to be helpful in liquidating some of the bank's frozen loans. In fact, I became Mr. Wing's chief trouble shooter in my particular field. My reward was to be appointed assistant cashier with a generous raise in salary. Having arrived at this point, I began to feel that I had proved I could stand on my own feet and it would soon be time to join my father in New York. The International Acceptance Bank had opened its doors for business and my father's letters kept urging me to come.

With a certain sadness Katharine and I contemplated leaving New England for New York. Life in Cambridge had been pleasantly variegated and peaceful. We had many friends with whom we played tennis, skated on the river, and occasionally played bridge. Some of them were my classmates taking courses in one of the graduate schools. Some were my former teachers. As treasurer of my class, I kept in touch with as many of its members as I could locate for our triennial reunion.

Katharine had been studying composition with Martin Loeffler, a charming old gentleman who, besides being a distinguished violinist and composer, was something of an authority on Asian cultures. Loeffler's house in Medfield was filled with Indian, Chinese, and Japanese art treasures. Occasionally, we spent an evening there. The old gentleman showed a kindly interest in my translations of Greek and French poetry and, to my surprise and delight, asked me to try my hand at writing a libretto for an opera with a Hindu setting he was then composing. Many evenings of labor went into the attempt to fulfill this assignment. Loeffler liked my libretto, but unfortunately the opera, *Karma,* was never finished. The composer died before he could complete the score.

Shortly before we pulled up stakes to go to New York, a curious episode occurred. I received a telegram from Herbert Hoover, who had just become Secretary of Commerce in the Harding administration, asking me to come to Washington on a certain day. I had no idea what this was about but, naturally, presented myself at his office at the appointed hour. Outside of the Secretary's door, I found Chris Herter (Christian A. Herter, later a congressman, then governor of Massachusetts and later Secretary of State under President Eisenhower), whom I had known as an upperclassman at college. I asked him why I had been summoned. He had time to tell me only that this was "a terrific opportunity," when Hoover buzzed and I was shown in.

I knew nothing about Hoover except that he had done a

magnificent job in postwar food relief. I knew even less about
the functions of the Department of Commerce, so that, when he
asked without preamble whether I would like to become Assistant Secretary of Commerce, I was completely flabbergasted.
Later, I was to discover that Buck Hallowell, one of the First
National Bank's directors, had recommended me for the job on
the strength of my trouble-shooting activities.

The recollection of the interview makes me shudder even
today. I asked Hoover what my duties would be. He replied
laconically: "Helping me." Then, quite inanely, I asked: "But
what do you do?" With the faintest of smiles, the Secretary said:
"You'll find out if you take the job." I mumbled something about
having embarked upon a banking career and about wanting to
consult my father, thanked him, and departed. Chris Herter
couldn't understand why I had not jumped at the opportunity.
Neither could I, except that I had an instinctive negative reaction to both the proposition and Hoover.

My father supported this. In the first place, he said, I was
much too young to fill a junior cabinet post; accepting a political
appointment would merely interrupt my career unless I wanted
to make politics my profession; and Washington was "a soul-
destroying place, especially for a young man." I wrote to Hoover,
thanking him for his most flattering offer but declining it on
the grounds that I wished to enter my father's bank. In retrospect, I am not sorry. Had I accepted, I might out of loyalty
have become a Hoover Republican.

In the autumn of 1921, Katharine and I and our two-year-old
daughter, April, moved to an apartment on Riverside Drive in
New York, and I entered the International Acceptance Bank as
a junior officer.

The International Acceptance Bank, quickly to become known
in Wall Street as the IAB, was a success from the day of its
launching. This was due primarily to three factors: Paul Warburg's reputation; a small but expert staff; and a unique list of
shareholders.

My father was chairman of a board of directors comprising a
number of prominent bankers and business leaders. F. Abbot
Goodhue, a former vice president of the First National Bank of
Boston, became president of the IAB. Two experienced German-
Americans, Lucien Nachmann and P. J. Vogel, were the vice

presidents, and Fletcher Gill, a talented bond trader, was treasurer.

Among the IAB shareholders were the leading banks in many American cities, such as the Corn Exchange Bank, the New York Trust Company, and Kuhn, Loeb & Company of New York; the First National Bank of Boston; the Cleveland Trust Company; the First National Bank of Chicago; the Wells Fargo National Bank of San Francisco; the First National Bank of Los Angeles; the Philadelphia National Bank; and the Kansas City Trust Company. Among the European shareholders were: in London, the National Provincial Bank and N. M. Rothschild & Sons; in Paris, the Banque de Paris et des Pays Bas; in Amsterdam, the Nederlandsche Handelsmaatschappij and Hope & Company; in Switzerland, the Crédit Suisse of Zurich and the Swiss Bank of Basel; in Belgium, the Banque de Bruxelles; in Scandinavia, the Svenska Handelsbanken and the Skandinaviska Kreditaktiebolaget of Stockholm, and R. Henriques, Jun., of Copenhagen; in Vienna S. M. von Rothschild; and, in Hamburg M. M. Warburg & Company.

These initial connections had, of course, to be exploited. My father assigned me the job of developing the bank's business at home and abroad. During the next ten years, I was destined to make at least one trip to Europe a year and to travel extensively in the United States and Latin America. In the course of this work, I would not only get to know the officials of our shareholding concerns at home and abroad but call upon the finance ministers and central bank authorities in most of the countries I visited.

Katharine and I were soon to discover that life in New York was very different from life in New England. Boston and Cambridge had been as yet scarcely touched by the postwar revolution in customs, manners, and morals that had overtaken New York and was spreading throughout most of the country's major cities. The Sacco-Vanzetti case had not yet stirred the relatively placid New Englanders out of their complacent provincialism, but New Yorkers were acutely aware of the Bolshevik scare and of Attorney General A. Mitchell Palmer's witch-hunt. They knew about the unrest in the French-occupied German Ruhr and about Mussolini's having come to power in Italy, though very few as yet understood the significance of the birth of fascism. New

York newspapers carried news dispatches from all over the world, such as were rarely to be found in the Boston newspapers, except perhaps in the *Evening Transcript*. People on subway trains talked in many languages and on many subjects. In fact, New York seemed like another country altogether.

CHAPTER X

The Gay Twenties

THE WAR accelerated and dramatized the change in mores and value standards that had been taking place almost imperceptibly during my childhood and adolescence. I first became acutely aware of this while living and working in New York during the early 1920s.

The altered relationship between men and women, now so evident in every walk of life, had, for example, been coming about quite gradually while I was growing up. Women had sought the suffrage in Britain and the United States long before the war and had obtained it in some of our Western states. (No such thought had yet entered the minds of German women.) Within my memory, the bicycle had started a change in women's clothes, away from the long, bustled skirts and puff-sleeved blouses worn over petticoats, camisoles and tightly laced corsets. Women's bathing suits consisting of short black skirts worn over bloomers and long black stockings, such as my mother wore when she first took me into the ocean, had given way to one-piece suits known as "Annette Kellermans," which my father thought indecent. A few daring "nice" women had begun to smoke in the presence of men, and, at Harvard, Charles Eliot Norton had given up smoking, declaring that, if women were going to smoke, men should give up tobacco because "it is necessary that one sex be more refined than the other."

The turkey trot and the bunny hug had, before the war, taken the place of polkas and waltzes at young people's dances and caused raised eyebrows among worried mothers and chaperones. Vernon and Irene Castle had introduced the fox trot and the machiche to polite society; they had, in fact, somewhat surprisingly given an exhibition dance for some charitable cause in my parents' house and my parents had afterwards argued as to whether or not the new dances were "vulgar."

I remember being told that President Fallières of France, observing society couples dancing in London, had been heard to remark: "*Ah, les Anglaises' elles ont le derrière si gai et le devant si serieux!*" Had he known the truth, he would have realized that "*le devant*" of the sweet young things in Britain was already becoming quite as *gai* as the *derrière*, though not as unashamedly so as in France.

During the war women had served as nurses and Red Cross drivers overseas; many of them began to have their hair bobbed, originally not out of a reoriented sense of vanity but for the sake of cleanliness. Now they were taking office jobs and wearing clothes better adapted to work, to rapid movement, and to sports.

The war had also given rise to an easy comradeship between the sexes. Among the upper-income groups in Britain and along the eastern seaboard of the United States moral standards were relaxed—perhaps originally in an atmosphere of "Eat, drink, and be merry, for tomorrow we die." For the lower-income groups there was not much to eat, drink, or be merry about during or immediately after the war. Prices were high and wages low, causing widespread dissatisfaction and unrest.

War profiteering and the fact that war seemed to sanction murder and violence left a residue of lawlessness and disregard for the rights of others that might have been of shorter duration had it not been for the wartime enactment of Prohibition.

But the war had at the same time helped to level class distinctions in the United States and even in Britain. Social, racial, and religious prejudices were temporarily subdued; in their place had arisen an almost hysterical hatred of the Germans and—after the war—an equally hysterical fear of Bolshevism.

Although the war had scarcely touched America, anti-German feeling on the eastern seaboard was perhaps more extreme than in Britain or even in France. Friends in New York and Washington had warned my parents against keeping on their faithful German servants. A usually sensible friend of my mother's, who lived in New Jersey, told her that the Hoboken ferries were full of German spies; the lady knew this for a fact, because, she said: "One can tell them by their faces!" Beethoven's music could not be performed in New York, while even in London an established English family changed its name from Battenberg to Mountbatten.

The postwar fear of Bolshevism was far more irrational and hysterical in the United States than in European countries, where a real threat of communism existed. (The raids of Attorney General A. Mitchell Palmer should have conveyed a sobering warning of worse outbursts to come, if Americans did not learn to immunize themselves against hysterical demagoguery.)

So, too, the failure to make a just peace created greater disillusionment in the United States than in Britain or France. This seemed to me understandable. The British and French had fought for their lives and, in a sense, had achieved victory by their mere survival. Americans had been indoctrinated with the belief that they were fighting to achieve a peace that would end all wars, abolish "autocracy," and, in President Wilson's famous phrase, "make the world safe for democracy."

The disillusioned, idealistic youth of America in the nineteen twenties did not become pacifists except in the sense that they wanted no further part in the quarrels of the Old World. They did not reject war. They rejected ever again being drawn into "other people's wars." Nevertheless, most of my friends and most of the people I knew supported Woodrow Wilson's plea for American membership in the League of Nations. When that failed, many of us became interested in a revision of the harsh Versailles Treaty. We began to wonder whether the Kaiser or the Germans had really been solely responsible for the war. A number of writers, like John Dos Passos and Walter Millis, were looking carefully into the influences alleged to have been exerted by the "munition makers," the international bankers in Wall Street and the pro-Allied propagandists. Before long, Senator Nye's committee would be making a study of these questions.

Quite a number of my friends lost all interest in international affairs. Some retreated into the Scott Fitzgerald world of wild parties, bathtub gin, and sexual promiscuity.

Prohibition probably had a more pernicious influence on this so-called "Lost Generation" than disillusionment over the outcome of the war. Wilson's failure had at least been a noble failure, due only in small part to his own shortcomings, less as a statesman than as a domestic politician. The peace had been wrecked by Clemenceau, Lloyd George, and Orlando—by the shortsighted greed and vengefulness of the European leaders, and, to some extent, by the isolationists in the American Senate whom Wilson had failed to carry along with him. The resentment the war generation felt because of its disillusionment was directed externally—at Europe, which had started the war and then wrecked the peace.

The Volstead Act, on the other hand, undermined the foundations of the American society. The almost absent-minded wartime enactment of a law that did not command the support of the majority of the American people led to widespread disregard of the statute. Even such law-abiding citizens as my parents seemed to see nothing wrong about serving wine at dinner. In the New York area, there were few adherents of the temperance movement.

Through the highly profitable business of bootlegging, Prohibition led to gangsterism and corruption. New words entered the American vocabulary: speakeasy, pay-off, hijacking, protection, and kickback. Eventually, corruption reached into the highest places and the words "Teapot Dome" became a symbol.

Oddly enough, the age of lawlessness and disorientation produced a remarkable flowering of the arts. The theater flourished as never before. Edwin Arlington Robinson, T. S. Eliot, E. E. Cummings, Edna St. Vincent Millay, Robert Frost, Archibald MacLeish, and a host of minor poets blossomed. Art galleries were giving more one-man shows of American artists than ever before. Sinclair Lewis, Thomas Wolfe, Ernest Hemingway, Willa Cather, George Jean Nathan, H. L. Mencken, and countless others, including F. Scott Fitzgerald, appeared on the literary scene. *The New Yorker* magazine was born. Walter Lippmann was writing for *The New Republic*. Franklin P. Adams' "Conning Tower" appeared in Herbert Bayard Swope's New York *World*.

"Modern" composers, such as Ravel, Debussy, and Mahler, broke into the stately programs of leading American orchestras. Tin-pan alley produced such immortals of American jazz as George M. Cohan, Irving Berlin, Jerome Kern, Vincent Youmans, Richard Rodgers, and George Gershwin.

Although, throughout this period, I was working hard in the bank and often away from New York, I came to know many of the men and women who contributed to the intellectual and artistic renaissance of the twenties. Among the playwrights, Robert E. Sherwood and Marc Connolly were my old friends. Franklin P. Adams (F.P.A.) had been a close friend of Katharine's father. Through him and his wife, Esther, we were initiated into the sophisticated circle of which Alexander Woollcott the drama critic of *The New Yorker,* was the central, patriarchal figure.

Woollcott, who knew and had strong opinions about practically every playwright, actor, singer, poet, and writer of that time, did not suffer fools gladly. One poor lady became permanently known to all and sundry as Bella Birdbrain, because Woollcott so named her after some display of ignorance that to Woollcott seemed inexcusable. Sarcastic, mordantly humorous, but at heart a very kindly man, Woollcott had the gift of inspiring loyal and devoted friendship. The favorite hangout of his court was the Algonquin Hotel, where he was frequently to be seen lunching with one or more of his cronies.

Evening parties, often after a first night at the theater, took place in various private homes and usually ended with everyone playing backgammon, poker, or the latest parlor game. The Game varied over the years from various forms of imaginary crime and detection to charades of the most complicated sort. In all this semi-serious play, the one unforgivable sin was to be found slow or dull-witted.

In the summer, Woollcott and some of his cronies repaired to a place in Vermont, mysteriously referred to as The Island. Here croquet was played with great skill and passion. The printed letterhead on Woollcott's stationery read: ROARING TOILET, VERMONT.

An offshoot of this group, known as the Thanatopsis Club, met at irregular intervals exclusively to play poker. Usually there were three or four regulars and one or two guests, the latter hopefully invited as victims. As one such putative victim, I played one night with Adams, Woollcott, Connolly, Swope, Harold Ross, and Raoul Fleischmann, the two latter respectively editor and founder of *The New Yorker*. Fleischmann and I were, it seemed, to be led to the slaughter. I was a far from expert poker player. My experience was limited to friendly games of penny ante. The stakes were high and, as the evening progressed, grew higher. Fortunately, it was one of those evenings when a mediocre player has such fantastic luck that he can hold his own against experts. As midnight approached, I found myself the big winner. Fleischmann was not doing badly either, and the faces of the regulars became more and more elongated until all four of them looked like ravening wolves.

None of these people ever got up in the morning, but I had to be at the bank at nine o'clock. In the circumstances, it was, of course, impossible for me to go home. For the next three hours, I tried my best to lose; and the more I tried to lose, the more I won. Finally, the game broke up in the early hours of dawn. I went home loaded with I.O.U.s and was never invited again.

Most of the men and women in this intellectual group were distinguished in their various fields, but there was almost never any talk of shop or, for that matter, of national or world affairs. They met after working hours to amuse each other and to play games against each other with often passionate fervor. Among my favorites were Frank and Esther Adams and the Baragwanaths. Adams encouraged my efforts at writing verse; few people ever had a keener sense of form and of the exact meaning of words. Jack Baragwanath was a mining engineer and a most entertaining soldier of fortune. His wife, Nysa McMein, was a well-known illustrator and a most attractive woman. When Jack and I became Sunday painters specializing in nudes, Nysa let us use her studio and provided us with the most delectable models. We were chaperoned by Nysa's Siamese tomcat, who watched over the proceedings, accurately choosing a crucial moment at which to tickle the model and thus to destroy the pose.

Another and quite different group centered about the Walter Damrosch family. Musical evenings at their home brought together composers, virtuosi, orchestra leaders, teachers, and mere amateurs. Occasionally, Frank Damrosch, with whom my parents and my uncle, James Loeb, had founded the Institute of Musical

Art, came to his more renowned brother's soirees. Almost always, one or more of Walter Damrosch's three striking daughters were there, as were their first cousins, Marya and Leopold Mannes.

At the Damrosch house we became acquainted with the Gershwin brothers—George and his lyric-writing brother, Ira—and the rival team of Dick Rodgers and Larry Hart. Eventually, this was to lead to serious complications in our married life.

Katharine was a first-rate pianist and had already composed a number of excellent more or less classical pieces. She now became completely fascinated by popular music, especially with song-writing for musical comedy. After getting the amiable Dick Rodgers to give her a job as rehearsal pianist for *A Connecticut Yankee* (which became one of Rodgers and Hart's first big hits), Katharine determinedly set out to write popular songs of her own. Partly because her interest was contagious and partly because I feared that our lives might otherwise drift apart, I became her lyric writer. Our first big hit was a torch song, "Can't We Be Friends?" sung by Libby Holman in Dwight Wiman's highly successful *Little Show* of 1928. Later we had songs in the *Garrick Gaieties*, the *Nine-Fifteen Revue* and finally we wrote the entire score for *Fine and Dandy*, a musical comedy starring the comedian, Joe Cook.

Writing for the theater was hard work, sporadically entailing long evenings of auditions and rehearsals, not to mention the hours spent at home preparing material. It was particularly exhausting for a lyric writer whose banking career demanded that he get to his office at nine in the morning when most of the theatrical world was still in bed.

Also, for a young man trying to make his mark in Wall Street, show business seemed a somewhat incongruous sideline. For this reason, and out of deference to my father, we wrote our songs under the pseudonyms of Kay Swift and Paul James.

During rehearsal for *The Little Show*, I met the later famous comedian, Fred Allen. We had no sooner been introduced than Allen asked: "Do you play drugstore golf? No? Well, come on, let's go get a soda, and I'll show you."

At a nearby Liggett's, Allen ordered two milk shakes, an open-face Swiss cheese sandwich, and two aspirin tablets. Drugstore golf, Paul James discovered at a cost of six nickels, consisted in snapping the aspirin tablet into successive holes in the Swiss cheese. The snap was accomplished without touching the sandwich, by sliding the middle finger off the thumb. Allen was an expert at this sport—a most lovable man with a childlike and very original sense of the ridiculous.

A producing firm called Green and Gensler, operating on a shoestring as it turned out, hired Donald Ogden Stewart to write the book for a Joe Cook musical comedy. Stewart was a rather successful professional humorist whose sophisticated wit had very little in common with Joe Cook's well-established slapstick comedy and his penchant for incredibly complicated machines. As a result, most of *Fine and Dandy* was rewritten in rehearsal, with Stewart's favorite lines passing one by one into oblivion.

Casting the show presented certain difficulties. Cook refused to have a leading lady who made him look old or who sang better than he, which was not very well. The result was a rather brassy leading lady whose range was not much over one octave. In addition, there was a chorus, a juvenile, and an ingénue. Finally, there was Dave Chasen, Cook's extremely skillful feedman.

Kay Swift and Paul James were hired to write the score. Among half a dozen song hits, we produced two—"Fine and Dandy" and "Can This Be Love?"—which, along with "Can't We Be Friends?" from *The Little Show* were to continue to earn us royalties for over thirty years.

Just before the Cook show was ready to open, the producers went broke. Two of my Wall Street friends, Marshall Field and Averell Harriman, had seen and liked the play in rehearsal. They and I put up a substantial sum of money, with the understanding that it would be returned out of profits. *Fine and Dandy* was hailed as a "smash hit" and ran for well over a year, grossing more than $1,000,000 at the box office, but not one cent was ever repaid to its backers. The producers insisted that there had been no profits! There was no way to prove the contrary from their casually kept records. Fortunately, I was able to repay my two friends and to recapture most of my own investment out of our royalties.

I concluded that there could be no crazier business than show business; an "angel" could lose his money in backing a successful play, while a lyric writer could earn more from a single song written in a few hours than a junior bank officer earned in an entire year.

After *Fine and Dandy* had become an established success, Joe Cook invited a group of cronies, all male, a few newspapermen, and his lyric writer to come out to his place at Lake Hopatcong in New Jersey. The group arrived late one afternoon in two large limousines provided by Cook and was met by one of Joe's innumerable hangers-on, immaculately dressed as a butler. This impressive individual collected our hats and coats and, having made sure that he had them all, heaved them unceremoniously into the bushes.

Cook appeared and asked whether anyone would like to see his kids. We trooped upstairs to the nursery where we found nine children and a nurse, all standing on their heads. Joe spoke to the littlest one, Leo, and asked: "Say Leo, can you stand on your head?" Leo, upside down, replied: "No, Pop." End of scene.

Next, Joe asked me whether I would like to shoot a hole of golf. Once more I was taken upstairs, this time out on a balcony with grass growing on it and a golf ball already teed up. About fifty yards away was a green. Joe handed me what was then called a niblick and said: "Your honor!" My shot went high in the air and landed on the far edge of the green—a real duffer's shot. To my amazement, the ball began to roll, at first slowly, then faster and faster in the direction from which it had come, until it dropped neatly into the cup. Loud cheers from everyone. Cook told me to get the ball so that he might autograph it. We walked over to the green. I looked in the cup. No ball!

"Look over here," said Joe, descending some stone steps about thirty feet from the green. There stood an old-fashioned roll-top desk with a pipe opening in its front, and below the opening of the pipe—my ball, resting on a certificate of my membership in the hole-in-one club!

There followed a barbecue prepared by Cook and served by two midgets.

Cook apologized for serving only beer but said that he could take us to a nearby speakeasy where they served really good liquor. By this time it was getting dark.

The group piled into the cars and drove off, following Cook over country roads for about half an hour. Eventually, we arrived at a dimly lit house. Cook gave a special knock on the door. A face peered through a barred peephole. Cook said a few words and the door was opened into a pleasantly furnished taproom. A waiter took orders for whatever drinks were desired. The whiskey was excellent, real imported scotch and well-aged Kentucky bourbon.

After about an hour of this, Cook announced that he was tired, paid the bill and said: "Let's go. I've got a couple of bottles to take along. Come on, we'll go out this way." So saying, he opened a door through which we passed to find ourselves in the front hall of Cook's house!

(Later, I was told that once one of Cook's guests somehow caught on to the fact that the alleged speakeasy was actually in Joe's house and that Cook never spoke to him again.)

Many years later, when Cook died after a long illness, I could only hope that the angels in heaven would never fail to laugh at his jokes. He remains in my memory as not only one of the funniest but also one of the kindest and most generous men it has been my good fortune to know.

So far as I was concerned, *Fine and Dandy* ended the adventure into the strange world of Broadway, the Algonquin and tin-pan alley. By this time, my work at the bank and my travels abroad left me no time for extracurricular activities. However, Kay Swift, as she was henceforth to call herself, continued industriously writing popular songs.

CHAPTER XI

Febrile and Ostentatious City Life Redeemed

NEITHER my wife nor I realized for some time the effect on our marriage of the life we were leading during the twenties, or its influence on our children.

In September 1922, when April was three and a half, our

second daughter, Andrea, was born. We were still living modestly and quietly in our Riverside Drive apartment. The following summer, spent in a rented house in Rye, New York, gave us our first taste of suburban social life—an endless round of cocktail and dinner parties, dances, and treasure hunts. I made up my mind then to acquire a summer place of our own, if possible near enough to New York for commuting purposes but rural enough to be remote from the unhealthy effluvia of metropolitan sophistication. That autumn, I took Katharine to Havana as a sort of rest cure from a dizzy summer.

With two little children, a nurse, and a general houseworker, the Riverside Drive apartment was crowded to capacity. By the time a third daughter (Kathleen—later shortened to Kay) was born, in 1924, I had made enough money to be able to remodel an old brownstone my father had given me at 34 East Seventieth Street, opposite the red brick Presbyterian Hospital which then occupied the entire square block between Seventieth and Seventy-first streets and Madison and Park avenues.

Because of my success in developing the bank's business, I was by this time earning a respectable salary as a vice president and, in addition, had been able to accumulate a modest capital by shrewdly or luckily investing the substantial annual bonuses resulting from my participation in the officers' profit-sharing plan. By 1926, I was able to buy the small adjoining brownstone, to install a private garage in its basement, and to join the upper floors of the two houses together.

Looking back in later years, especially after I had read Veblen's *Theory of the Leisure Class*, I would consider our way of life in the latter part of the twenties as a most unattractive period of "conspicuous consumption." Like many of my contemporaries who also "struck it rich," I lived like an obnoxious parvenu. In place of the one servant, we now had five. A chauffeur drove the children to school. In a way, our mode of life was no different from that of my parents, who also maintained a large establishment; but the tasteful, quiet manner in which they had always lived was very different from the life that developed at my home.

Thirty-four East Seventieth Street became one of the places where cafe society, artists, and musicians foregathered, and a sort of pub for young doctors and nurses from the hospital across the street. Coming home from work in the late afternoon, I never knew whom I would find there or what plans were afoot for the evening.

On one of the more amusing occasions, I found a number of musicians gathered around the two grand pianos at the end of the living room. Sigmund Romberg was at one piano, George Gershwin at the other. Romberg had just finished a rendition of his recent song hit, "Lover, Come Back to Me," and Gershwin was saying: "I'll show you where you swiped that melody, Siggie." He then proceeded to play several bars from one of Liszt's Hungarian Rhapsodies. Romberg, mock-furious, said: "You're absolutely wrong, George! I'll show you where I got those eight bars!" And he played eight bars from a different Hungarian Rhapsody.

While Kay greatly enjoyed this sort of thing and I at first found it entertaining, I grew more and more to dislike it. Coming home to act as bartender or to get ready to be host at a suddenly arranged more formal party, or else having to go out to a similar affair at someone else's house, I scarcely saw my children and was almost never alone with my wife. No one could say that this sort of existence was dull or uninteresting, but it was restless, frenetic, and tiring.

The one redeeming feature was that, in 1925, I found exactly the sort of summer home for which I had been looking. Nine miles from the center of Greenwich, Connecticut, and thirty-six miles from New York, I discovered a pre-Revolutionary homestead in what the local people called "the back country." The place had once been a prosperous farm, named Bydale because it nestled in the valley of the West Branch of the Byram River. There was an ancient dam, a millpond, and a small cottage, once the home of a pre-Revolutionary gristmiller. Below the dam, the river flowed through a gradually steepening gorge in the midst of a virgin forest of hemlock, beech, oak, and ash. A maple-shaded house, built in 1741 by Silas Mead, one of the early settlers, snuggled into the side of a hill at the top of which was a windmill and a barn surrounded by pasture land.

The house was uninhabited and belonged to a recently widowered elderly gentleman, Benjamin Fairchild, who lived not far away. He had bought Bydale some years earlier because he and his wife loved the trees; it was not on the market, but I thought there was no harm in finding out whether it could be bought.

Fairchild first said that he had no wish to sell and affectionately discussed the various trees, shrubbery, and wildflowers. After a thoroughly pleasant half hour of this, he suddenly turned to me and asked: "Don't you think a carload of rhododendrons would improve the place?"

Surprised and shocked, I blurted out: "Good God, no!"

"Very well," he said, "you can have the place. I just didn't want to see Bydale turned into a Long Island estate."

I said that I would like to buy immediately the ten acres comprising the pond, the house, and the other buildings and that eventually I would very much like to acquire the forest and the gorge. Fairchild asked a price so extremely reasonable that I had to say I thought it was too low.

"Do you want the place or don't you?" asked the old gentleman.

"Of course I do. But I want to pay a fair price."

"I have named a fair price," he said. "Give me a dollar to seal the bargain, and I'll give you the key."

When I went to look at my acquisition, I found the rather tumble-down house full of early American furniture. I called Fairchild to ask where he wanted it sent.

"I don't want it sent anywhere. You've bought it, you young idiot."

Over the years, the old gentleman became a cherished friend and neighbor, frequently consulted about the renovation of the house, the installation of a tennis court, and, finally, the building of a swimming pool. With the help of Russell Jones, Fairchild's handy man, an aged and wise Negro whose ninety-year-old mother grew her own pipe tobacco and remembered being a slave, I built a spring-fed pool in what had been a swamp. Russell was an expert in the mixing and use of cement which he called "roton." As he and I troweled the "roton" on chicken wire laid against the sloping clay walls of the irregular-shaped pool, Russell would keep up a constant, low-voiced admonition to the mix. "Now then, roton," he would say, "you be good. You be good and lay there for a long, long time."

(It was thirty years before the first serious cracks appeared in Russell's "roton.")

In the course of time, I acquired some eighty acres in all, including the virgin forest and the land along one side of the Byram gorge. Although at first Bydale served us only as a summer place, often visited on winter weekends, it was eventually to become my year-around home.

To me, the acquisition of this lovely place was psychologically important. To plant a garden, to raise chickens, dogs, and horses on one's own soil was the fulfillment of an unconscious dream. The authentic Americanism of Bydale, with its historic house and its age-old trees eliminated the last vestiges of an only half-conscious sense of homelessness.

During the summers I now saw much more of my wife and children, except when business all too often took me abroad. Even at Bydale, however, Broadway occasionally intruded in the shape of visitors from the theatrical world.

George Gershwin was a frequent guest. Most of his *Rhapsody No. 2* and much of his opera, *Porgy and Bess,* were composed in the guest cottage. At the first performance of the *Rhapsody No. 2* in Carnegie Hall, we were invited to sit in the Gershwins' box. Father Gershwin—a source of never ending entertainment to his family—sat immediately behind his son. As deafening applause broke out at the end he leaned forward, stop watch in hand, touched George on the shoulder, and remarked in his heavy Jewish accent: "Judge, only twelve and half minutes."

The fact that the old gentleman always pronounced George as "Judge," once got him out of a speeding ticket when he told a policeman that he was on his way to see his son, "Judge Gershwin."

George was a fascinating but disturbing element at Bydale. His exuberant vitality and many-sided zest for life knew no bounds. He wanted to learn and experience literally everything that he had not known in a childhood on Manhattan's Lower East Side. He wanted to learn to ride a horse, to buy and wear the right country clothes, to play with young children, and, most of all, to acquire from Kay the techniques of orchestration. He would sit for hours at the piano, experimenting in contagious excitement with a new melody or rhythm while Kay suggested harmonic treatment. Day turned into night and night into day when George was in the throes of creation. I found his visits stimulating but tiring. I liked Gershwin but resented the way in which our whole life was taken over by this completely self-centered but charming genius whose premature death was all too soon to end a brilliant career. I still consider him our most authentically American composer.

While Kay was for the most part absorbed in the world of music and the theater, I spent almost all of my leisure time outdoors, exercising horses, teaching the children to ride, fishing with them in the pond, cutting trails through the woods, or rebuilding tumble-down stone walls. Usually I had some major project under way.

The little girls thoroughly enjoyed everything about the place. They loved riding with Daddy, watching the grooming and occasional shoeing of horses, and climbing on the rocky ledges of granite outcrop near the house. Unfortunately, there were no nearby neighbors with children except my old school and college friend, John Morgan, who lived three miles away and would quite often bring his wife and three children to play and swim while he and I went fishing, played tennis, or worked around the place. Occasionally the girls would visit their Lewisohn cousins in Harrison.

The one feature of Bydale life that really aroused my wife's enthusiasm was my accidental acquisition of a one-horse racing stable. A big, raw-boned Irish three-year-old named Rhosil, which I had bought to use as a hunter with the Fairfield Westchester Hounds, had run away with me on his first outing, showing such speed that I suspected he might be a first-rate steeplechaser. After training the horse over timber for a few weeks, I won a local steeplechase. In the following year, while I was in Europe, Rhosil won a number of important four-mile races, thanks to Kay's finding a capable "gentleman jockey." During this summer, Kay followed the horse eagerly from one race meet to another, taking great pride in his winning trophies under the Bydale silks.

But in spite of the distractions of winter life in New York and the pleasant activities during the summers, my major interest during the whole decade of the twenties centered upon my work at the bank. This work, and the people connected with it, did not greatly interest Kay. I enjoyed it chiefly because it threw me into such close contact with my father. During the winter months, once we had moved to the East Side of New York, I regularly walked ten or more blocks with my father and then drove with

him the rest of the way to the bank. I cherished these half hours
and used them to discuss not only business problems but whatever else happened to be on my mind. Sometimes I would get
my father to talk about world affairs, especially the problems
faced by postwar Germany under the onerous Versailles Treaty;
he was at this time working for a revision of reparations with
Dr. Vissering, president of the Netherlands Government Bank,
and with Professor J. Maynard (later Lord) Keynes who was
then in the process of writing his famous *The Economic Consequences of the Peace.*

I visited Germany twice during the runaway inflation of
1922–23 that completely destroyed the purchasing power of the
German mark. This experience taught me how insidious and
ill-understood by its victims such a catastrophe could be. Most
of the bankers I knew tried to protect themselves and their
clients by buying gold, commodities, or foreign exchange. (In so
doing, of course, they heaped fuel on the inflationary flames.)
A few fortunes were made during the inflation by ruthless men
like the coal baron Hugo Stinnes and a Viennese speculator
named Castiglione. The vast bulk of the German population knew
only that prices were rising and that their wages and savings
daily bought less and less.

During these first postwar trips to Europe, I was aware of
the economic chaos left by the war, especially in Germany and
Austria, and of the impoverishment of France and Britain. I was
acutely conscious of the harsh injustice of a peace treaty that had
saddled Germany with sole guilt for the war and imposed an
impossible burden of reparations. But it was not until some time
later that I realized the full implications of the peace treaties.

Whatever their faults, the Romanov, Turkish, and Hapsburg
empires had provided supranational structures for most of the
Continent within which a wide mixture of nationalities and
ethnic groups had been governed and had lived in relative peace
for most of a century. Franz Josef's Dual Monarchy had provided what in later years would be called a "common market"
for most of Central Europe.

Woodrow Wilson's doctrine of self-determination, which at the
time had seemed to me unimpeachable, broke up the Russian,
Austro-Hungarian, and Ottoman empires, destroying all vestiges
of regional supranational government and giving rise to new

chauvinistic nationalisms in more than twenty newly created or liberated European states. The Danubian "common market" was destroyed.

Moreover, while old injustices had been largely remedied, new injustices had been created. The 250,000 Austrian Tyrolese had been placed under Italian rule. The 2,000,000 Sudeten Germans had had their homeland subtracted from Germany and added to the new Czechoslovak Republic. Other parts of Germany and Austria, inhabited by German-speaking people had been added to a newly independent Poland. The peace treaties of Versailles, Lausanne, and the Trianon had created not only a host of new nationalisms—some, like rump Austria, totally unviable—they had also created new irredentist chauvinism.

In Asia Minor, the Turkish peace treaties had destroyed the Ottoman Empire, created new rivalries between Britain and France, and sown the seeds of dissension between Arabs and Jews.

Most of these errors might have been remedied if Woodrow Wilson had not made the fatal mistake of tying his lofty and wholly admirable dream of a League of Nations to the by no means admirable peace settlements, in the making of which he not only compromised with European nationalistic greed but also sought to realize his own idealistic dogmas. The League was stillborn primarily because it had been made inseparable from the peace treaties.

Moreover, autocracy, which Wilson had sought to abolish, was far from dead. The Soviet Union was a communist dictatorship and the threat of communism was destroying democratic development in much of Central Europe. Jósef Pilsudski's Poland was a military dictatorship. Mussolini was organizing a new kind of totalitarianism in Italy. In Hungary, after Béla Kun's short-lived communist revolution, there was a military dictatorship. I myself witnessed communist riots in Hamburg and Berlin and saw how, under the threat of Bolshevism, the feeble Weimar Republic was drifting under the dominance of the generals. Throughout Europe, except in Great Britain, the Low Countries, and Scandinavia, the destruction of the old order and the weakening of the middle class had opened the door to dictatorships of the right or left.

Like most Americans at that time, I knew very little about the

Russian revolution, except that it was bloody and that it had caused Russia to drop out of the war. I had read neither Karl Marx nor Lenin. Adam Smith's *The Wealth of Nations* seemed to me an almost wholly satisfactory rationalization of a capitalist society whose general beneficence I as yet saw no reason to question, even though I recognized the need for a certain amount of social reform. Except for my brief experience on the railroad, I had scarcely come in contact with the underprivileged. I was a young banker trying to build up a profitable business between the United States and Europe. As such, I knew businessmen, financiers, bankers, and diplomats. I had not yet learned to know people. My social education had scarcely begun.

CHAPTER XII

Adventures of a Young Banker

THE International Acceptance Bank developed rapidly, not only in its highly specialized form of commercial banking. My father had agreed with Kuhn, Loeb & Company that his new institution would not go into the field of issuing securities. Nevertheless, through my contacts abroad, I developed a highly profitable sideline of originating such issues for Kuhn, Loeb and, later, for other issuing houses. Thus, we were paid a commission and given a share in the underwriting of American loans for Hamburg and Copenhagen and for various national and provincial European governments. Eventually, this business extended to Latin America. Frequently we arranged for the participation in such loans by some of our European friends.

These financial rather than commercial banking activities brought me into close contact with Mortimer Schiff, now the senior partner of Kuhn, Loeb, and with a number of my Wall

Street contemporaries engaged in similar activities, sometimes
as associates and sometimes as competitors. Among those who
became my lasting friends were W. A. Harriman and Marshall
Field, each of whom had founded his own investment house;
Robert Lovett, who had become a partner in Brown Brothers;
James Forrestal and my old friend Westmore Willcox, at Dillon
Read & Company; and Gilbert Browne at White Weld & Com-
pany.

To augment the older staff of our growing institution, I brought
in a number of my friends, all of whom became valuable officers. Graham Blaine, my former colleague on the Harvard
Crimson, came from Kidder, Peabody & Company in Boston.
Hugh Knowlton, erstwhile Cambridge neighbor, joined the firm
that was handling the bank's law business and eventually became vice president of the bank's securities affiliate of which I
was president. John Milholland, another college friend, became our specialist in municipal, state, and government bonds.
John Morgan, my school and college classmate, who had worked
for two years in Mexico, became head of a subsidiary company
organized to keep abreast of new industrial developments. Somewhat later, Lewis Stuyvesant Chanler, Jr., a graduate of Eton
and Harvard who had served with Knowlton overseas, became
the bank's vice president in London.

With this congenial and efficient group augmenting my father's older team and backstopping me in New York, I was free
to devote most of my time to the development of the bank's
business in Europe and Latin America.

Before we established Lewis Stuyvesant Chanler, Jr., in London as a resident vice-president, we had arranged most of the
bank's business in that important financial center through Messrs.
N. M. Rothschild & Sons, the firm that had for many years been
the London correspondent of M. M. Warburg & Company. The
Rothschild offices were in New Court, the original founder's
mansion in St. Swithin's Lane just off King William Street. The
fourth generation of partners consisted of two brothers—Lionel
and Anthony—who occupied a spacious partners' room containing, besides their handsome antique French desks, a number of
easy chairs and two couches. A glass-paneled door opened into
a long, loftlike room in which clerks sat before their desks on
high stools.

The firm's more important affairs were usually discussed with visitors over lunch—a four-course meal served in a special dining room by a one-eyed family retainer. Toward the end of a sumptuous repast, the surfeited guest or guests would witness the ritual of ordering the next day's lunch which, after some discussion with his brother, the senior partner would write down in a black patent-leather book.

Guests were not expected to stay after they had finished their armagnac. The partners retired to their room and pulled down the shade over the glass-paneled door, signifying that they were not to be disturbed during their siesta.

Lionel de Rothschild was a portly gentleman whose chief interest was in charities and in raising exotic plants. He was also an ardent lepidopterist, whose collection of butterflies was eventually purchased by New York's Museum of Natural History. His brother Tony was a friendly sort of person, with a curious habit of abruptly asking almost any question, no matter how personal, that happened to come into his head. He was fond of sports and maintained a racing stable.

On one of my earliest visits to London for the bank, Tony invited me for Sunday lunch and tennis at Gunnersbury Park, one of the family's country seats. There were a number of other guests and, according to British custom, no introductions. I was invited to play tennis with a man whom Tony called "Bobbety," who turned out to be Lord Cranborne, son of the Earl of Salisbury, whose ancient title he would one day inherit.

The Rothschilds, along with Baring Brothers and the Schroeder banking firm, had what amounted to a monopoly in the issuance of important securities on the London market, and Lionel and Anthony looked down somewhat upon later arrivals in London's financial world. They teased me about my friendship with two junior partners of the Johnny-come-lately firm of Lazard Brothers, Hugh Kindersley, the oldest son of Sir Robert, later Lord Kindersley, and Tommy Brand, (later Lord Hampden) a nephew of Robert Brand, a friend of my father's and an economist of remarkable prescience. These two young Englishmen had attractive, gay wives and I enjoyed their company. All of us have remained friends ever since.

Two other good friends of mine were London representatives of two Morgan-controlled New York banks: Dan Grant of the

Guaranty Trust Company, and Reggie Foster of the Bankers Trust Company who was married to the charming daughter of Senator Hoar of Massachusetts. (A friend had once greeted her famous father as follows: "Hello, Senator Hoar, how are Mrs. W. and all the little W.s?") When I went to the Fosters' for an evening, I never knew whether I would find such fellow guests as George Bernard Shaw and H. G. Wells, a cabinet officer, or a group of musicians and theatrical people. If Reggie and Fran took me to the theater, we were quite likely to end the evening at Rosa Lewis' Cavendish Hotel in Jermyn Street.

As Rosa liked the Fosters, she would usually provide free champagne, charging it to the account of some other habitué who had fallen out of her good graces. In her younger years, this delightfully bawdy old lady had been the mistress of a famous English peer and had taken the reward for her services in magnificent Sheraton and Chippendale period pieces. At Rosa's, the Edwardian age overlapped modern times. No one asked, though everyone knew, what went on upstairs, but Rosa's living room had become an after-the-theater rendezvous for the respectable elite of Mayfair.

One night, Reggie, who loved to play the piano and played it well, ran his fingers over the keyboard of Rosa's Bechstein grand, remarking that it was a beautiful instrument.

"It ought to be, dearie," Rosa said. "I've just spent five quid 'avin' the cigarette stubs tyken out of the wires."

After the International Acceptance Bank opened its own London office—a move not too gladly received by the Rothschilds —the most pleasant part of my trips to Europe became my visits to London, where I stayed at the Chanlers' home in Hyde Park Street, and the visits to Paris Chanler and I frequently made together. In both places, we usually managed to combine business with pleasure.

One summer evening when Chanler's wife and children were in the country, he and I were walking along Piccadilly on our way to Kettner's, a restaurant at which we intended to find out whether the Elizabethan two-bottle men really could and did each put away two bottles of port with their dinner. (This experiment when eventually carried out on another occasion, resulted in our giving up after each drinking not quite one bottle.

1. The medieval town of Warburg.

2. Moses Marcus Warburg.   3. Gerson Warburg.

The Founders of the Firm. (1798–1836)

4. Sara Warburg (1831–64).

5. *(Left)* The original banking house on Marktstrasse.

6. *(Below)* M. M. Warburg & Co. as it looked in the 1930s.

7. Moritz Warburg and his family, about 1893. The author's father is at extreme right.

8. The seventeenth-century farmhouse at Kösterberg.

9. Paul Warburg's house at Kösterberg, where the author spent his early summers.

10. Felix, Paul, Aby, and Max Warburg, about 1910

11. Grandmother Loeb and the author in his cradle.

12. Young James with his parents.

13. James Warburg aged two.

14. Mother and son (1900).

15. James Warburg aged six.

The next day, we were unable to see anything at all except black spots dancing before our eyes.)

Before we reached the restaurant, we met a man in full evening dress with a black patch over one eye who was introduced to me as Mike Wardell. The name registered vaguely as that of an intimate friend of the then Prince of Wales, later to become King Edward VIII. Wardell asked what Chanler and I were doing and then said, "Oh, you can go to Kettner's any time. Why not come along with me to what ought to be an amusing party? It doesn't matter that you're not dressed."

Characteristically, Chanler accepted without asking a single question. As we proceeded down St. James's Street, I thought that we were probably headed for some stag affair at White's Club or Boodle's. Our host, however, led us straight to the bottom of St. James's Street and, to our utter surprise, past the saluting guard into St. James's Palace.

We were left for a moment in a small anteroom to which Wardell presently returned with no less a personage than the Prince of Wales, who cordially bade his unexpected guests welcome to what he described as "a small family party." The party, as it turned out, consisted of the Prince, his brother the Duke of York (later to become George VI), the Duchess of York (later Queen Elizabeth), and, of all people, Fred and Adele Astaire —then currently appearing in one of George Gershwin's musical comedies. The Astaires, whom I knew well, were as surprised to see me in these surroundings as I was to see them.

One never knew what would happen with Chanler as a companion.

I had always loved London and had never felt particularly at home in Paris, but going to Paris with Stuyve Chanler invariably led to some unexpected form of delightful adventure. One Sunday morning, for example, Chanler decided that it would be pleasant to drive to Fontainebleau, hire a pair of horses, and go for a ride in the forest. No sooner said than done. An hour or so later, jogging along through the forest, we suddenly heard the sound of hunting horns and galloped off to see what was going on. Presently we came upon a procession of eight ladies, dressed in bottle green and riding sidesaddle, accompanied by eight gentlemen similarly attired, each with a round hunting horn. The ladies wore hats with ostrich plumes; the gentlemen hunting caps. The group proceeded at a hand canter, punctuated by occasional cacophanous soundings of the horns. Naturally, we fell in behind and were welcomed with polite smiles. After about ten minutes, the procession emerged upon a clearing where stood two vans, accompanied by hunt servants in livery. At the procession's approach, the two vans were opened. Out of the one emerged, rather reluctantly, a venerable antlered stag who was urged by loud cries of, *"Va-t'en, Guillaume!"* to take off into the forest. Out of the other van there came, with an equal lack of enthusiasm, four couples of staghounds who were induced with some difficulty to take off after Guillaume. The ladies and gentlemen now resumed their hand canter. The hunt was on!

We proceeded thus for perhaps half an hour with our quarry never more than a hundred yards ahead. The hounds bayed with mock excitement. The horses pranced. The gentlemen blew their horns. The scene might have served as a model for a stylized nineteenth-century French painting of *La Chasse*.

Now we came to a second clearing. Here stood the same two vans, plus a third out of which servants were taking food and bottles of wine, which they placed upon an enormous linen tablecloth spread out upon the grass under the trees. Guillaume contentedly trotted into his van, the stags into theirs; the doors were closed, and the two vehicles were driven off. We two intruders were invited to join the "peekneeque," consisting of a delicious *pâté de foie gras*, chicken in aspic, salad and cheese, fruit, and green champagne. No one asked who we were or where we came from. Neither Stuyve nor I ever saw any of these charming people again.

Business itself was not without its humorous moments. On my first trip to Copenhagen in 1921, I visited the firm of R. Henriques, Jun., bankers to the King of Denmark and for generations correspondents of M. M. Warburg & Company. The active partner was Carl Otto Henriques, a man in his thirties; but his father, a bearded patriarch, still maintained a lively interest in the firm. I was in the old man's office, receiving instructions about how to talk to the Minister of Finance with whom an appointment had been arranged, when I became aware of an urgent need. In response to my request to be permitted to use the facilities of the office, Henriques said: "Of course, my boy. Here you are." And he took out of a cabinet in his desk an old-fashioned chamber pot, not entirely empty, which he handed to me.

On another occasion, my father suggested that I try to get the New York account of Gerlats & Company in Havana. Don Narcisso Gerlats was known as the J. P. Morgan of Cuba.

Entering the firm's small but impressive white marble building in Havana, I saw an elderly gentleman in a bowler hat, clipping postage stamps off envelopes. I said good-morning and asked whether I might see Don Narcisso. The old gentleman scrutinized a stamp, threw it in the wastebasket and asked why I desired to see Don Narcisso. I gave him my card and explained my mission.

"I see," said the old gentleman, "but Don Narcisso does not require another New York bank account. He keeps his money where it is safe and he never borrows."

"Well," said I, "couldn't I at least see him and pay my respects?"

"You *are* seeing him," was the reply. "You may pay your respects and give mine to your famous father."

(Two weeks later, Gerlats & Company opened a courtesy account with the International Acceptance Bank upon which not a single check was drawn for years.)

Most of the bank's business consisted in financing commercial transactions between exporters and importers in various countries. Many of these transactions were arranged with or through M. M. Warburg & Company, necessitating not only frequent visits to Hamburg but a steady flow of cables and correspondence.

My two Hamburg uncles were of widely differing natures. Max was a lively, quick, hard-working go-getter. He ruled the roost not only at home and in the bank but also in the town of Hamburg, which accepted him as a sort of uncrowned, wise, and benevolent king. He was warmhearted and generous, making money easily and spending it with equal ease. Fritz, the youngest of my father's brothers, who had intended to become a lawyer but became a partner when my father settled in the United States, was homely, good-natured, long-winded, shrewd, and lazy.

Dr. Carl Melchior, originally the firm's legal counsel, was the first non-Warburg in over one hundred years to become a partner of the firm. He was a bachelor, punctiliously correct in behavior and pleasant, if formal, in his human relations. The two junior partners were Max Warburg's son, Eric, and Siegmund Warburg, a Swabian cousin who was later to found his own banking firm in London.

Most of my dealings were with my Uncle Max, in whose house I usually stayed and whom I loved almost as much as I loved my father, enjoying the function of acting as a link between the two mutually devoted brothers.

Since there were only one or two secretaries on the firm's staff who could write English, I either dictated my voluminous reports to my father to a German secretary or typed them out myself in English. I still have the carbon copies. My use of a portable typewriter caused considerable comment. Typewriters had only recently been installed in the Hamburg office, it having been the firm's traditional belief that letters should be written by hand, if not by a partner then at least by a clerk with a good handwriting. For a similar reason, the firm had been reluctant to install adding machines; they were thought to interfere with the development of accurate arithmetic.

Throughout the years of almost constant transatlantic travel, I used to look forward to each sea voyage as a period of rest, relaxation, and occasional adventure. Nowadays, in the age of air travel, I have often thought nostalgically of the old *Mauretania*, the *Aquitania*, the *Bremen* and the *Europa*, the *Ile de France*, and the many other liners on whose decks I played shuffleboard and deck-tennis or danced at night, in whose smoking rooms I sat with friends; and of the many ship's officers and stewards who became old friends. There was a marvelous sense of disconnection from the world during the days at sea, with time to savor the always fresh excitement of a change of language, custom, currency, food, and wine.

I remember when ships were first equipped with Marconi wireless and the first ship's-news bulletins were published for passengers. Then came the ship-to-shore telephone. The latter had just been experimentally installed on the *Homeric* when I came home in her during the late twenties. Reasonably sure that my father had not yet heard of this latest device, I called him from mid-ocean at his office in New York. Much surprised, my father said: "What happened? Did you miss the boat?"

"No, Father."

"You mean you're in New York already?"

"No, Father."

"Well, where the devil are you?"

"I'm in the middle of the Atlantic, Father."

"You're drunk!"

"Yes, Father, a little—but just the same I really am in the middle of the ocean."

Sometimes an embarrassing situation could arise on shipboard. One day I was walking the deck with an attractive lady, working up an appetite for lunch, when a man in the conventional steamer attire of that time—plus fours, cloth cap, and sweater—undid his rug, got out of his deck chair, and said: "Aren't you Jimmy Warburg?"

I said I was. Thereupon the man extended his hand and said: "I'm John D. Rockefeller."

Thinking it was a joke, I replied: "Well, I'm really Henry Ford." No sooner had I said this than I realized that it actually was Rockefeller, whom I knew to be a good friend of my father's. In my embarrassment, I asked him if he would join us for a drink before lunch. (Rockefeller was a well-known teetotaler.)

There could also be reverse twists to the identification of fellow passengers. One evening, returning from Europe on the *Europa*, I was quietly dining alone, when the headwaiter brought me the largest engraved visiting card I had ever seen. On it was inscribed the name of a well-known Russian emigrée princess, and, written by hand: "I know your Papa. Won't you join us after dinner for coffee in the lounge?"

The headwaiter pointed to a distant table to identify the source of the message. I sent back word that I would be very happy to accept. (What else can one do on such occasions?)

"Us" turned out to be four people: the lady herself, a rather used-looking brunette with bedroom eyes, who, I felt sure, had never known my father; her husband, who looked as if he had been recently exhumed; and two highly perfumed, wavy-haired, youngish men whom she introduced as her brothers.

After coffee and liqueurs, during which there were frequent references to the late Tsar and Tsarina, the lady said: "Come down to our sitting room and let me show you my photograph album."

All five of us trooped down to a private parlor, where a bottle of iced champagne stood in a bucket. The lady motioned me to a seat beside her on a small divan and proceeded to show me pictures of her parents, almost invariably in the company of royalty. "There is Mama. There is Papa. There is the Tsar and there is the Tsarina." While this was going on, her husband quietly left the room, followed first by one brother and, a little later, by the other. At this point, I thought it wise to shift my seat from the divan to one of the vacated chairs. The lady protested. When I declined to resume the seat beside her, she jumped up, ripped her dress from one shoulder, and let out a piercing scream.

At this not altogether unexpected development, three doors opened, and the three men reappeared.

I burst into laughter and said that I was a poor subject for the old badger game. The group took this as implying that there had been something wrong about their performance and demanded to know why it had been unconvincing. I told them that the performance had been superb but that they happened to have chosen the wrong victim. As I made my departure, the lady's husband said with the utmost seriousness: "Can you suggest anyone among the passengers with whom we might be more successful?"

Not all my shipboard experiences were incidents without sequel. Some resulted in lasting friendships. On one of my 1930 crossings I met Alfred Knopf, the publisher. A discussion of poetry led, quite casually, to my showing Knopf a little black book containing some recently written light verse and a few bits of serious poetry written over the years. Knopf took the book to bed with him and the next day, to my surprise and pleasure, offered to publish it. A slender volume entitled *And Then What?* was published in 1931, followed a year later by a second—*Shoes and Ships and Sealing Wax*. Both appeared under the *nom de plume* Paul James.

Because of my father's participation in the consultations over the stabilization of the German currency after the inflation and in the negotiations leading up to the Dawes and Young Plan loans granted to the German Government, the International Acceptance Bank was appointed American agent of the German Reichsbank and its newly created subsidiary, the Gold Discount

Bank. Thus, the famous and later infamous Dr. Hjalmar Schacht became one of the International Acceptance Bank's most important clients.

Dr. Schacht was one of two world figures of the time about whom I violently disagreed with my father. For some reason which I found difficult to explain, I disliked and distrusted the German wizard of finance, while my father and Uncle Max both admired and trusted him. Fortunately, my father did not live to see the day when Hjalmar Schacht became Adolf Hitler's financial adviser.

The other man about whom we disagreed, but for wholly different reasons, was the Swedish match king, Ivar Kreuger. One of my first assignments in Europe had been to get to know the fabulously wealthy Kreuger and, if possible, to obtain a share of his business. The Kreuger & Toll account was then considered one of the prize plums in the banking world. After I had met Kreuger several times and found him a most agreeable and amusing man, he offered me a very important piece of business: the arranging of a $50 million American loan that would enable him to acquire control of the entire Swedish pulp industry. Somehow, this transaction did not seem quite sound. Kreuger had recently acquired the great Boliden gold mine in the north of Sweden and had expanded in many other directions. The idea of acquiring the pulp industry—and the way he talked about the venture—struck me as megalomaniacal. I politely turned down the business. This had never happened to Kreuger before, but, although surprised, he took no offense. The deal was made shortly thereafter with Lee Higginson & Company.

My father was furious, and I was given a most unpleasant dressing down by my usually gentle parent.

Kreuger's own reaction was characteristic. Within about a month of my return to New York he opened an account at the International Acceptance Bank with a deposit of $1 million! I returned his check with a letter saying that I appreciated the gesture but that, so long as my bank had been unwilling to lend him money, it could not in decency accept his. This caused another, though less violent row within the International Acceptance Bank.

The next time I saw Kreuger in Stockholm at a dinner party, he was as friendly as ever. In fact, our refusal to do business with him became something of a joke in the Swedish community, a joke Kreuger himself seemed to relish.

Kreuger, of course, turned out to be the most spectacular swindler of the postwar period. When he shot himself some years later, it was discovered that he had for years falsified his companies' balance sheets, even going to the extent of including among his assets some $70 million of forged Italian Treasury Notes. The bankruptcy of his empire wrecked innumerable private fortunes and very nearly destroyed his Swedish, English and American bankers. No one was more surprised than I at Kreuger's turning out to be a crook; I had never suspected his honesty—only his common-sense intelligence.

Being one of the very few bankers who had done no business with Kreuger, I was asked by one of my close friends among the Swedish bankers to help in trying to untangle the complicated ruins of Kreuger's fortune. (For whatever small service I was able to render, the King of Sweden decorated me with membership in the ancient Order of the Knights of Vasa.)

There was not much in the way of comfort for Kreuger's creditors. His ability to perpetrate so gigantic a swindle illustrated the inability of many bankers who had grown up in the prewar age of relative decency and mutual confidence to adjust their thinking to the decay of postwar morality. It is true that Kreuger's was an exceptional case. Nevertheless, it called attention to the need for greater caution and skepticism on the part of bankers and underwriters of securities.

In the period from 1926 to 1929 American bankers went hogwild. On the domestic American scene, there was an insatiable demand for speculative securities—a demand the investment bankers proceeded to satisfy with flotations of every sort, from blue-chip securities to the scandalously watered stock of pyramided holding companies. Excessive equity financing created a scarcity of fixed-income senior securities, so that the demand for bonds, plus the capital needs of the rest of the world, brought about an orgy of foreign-bond emissions on the New York market. At first, these foreign issues were cautiously and selectively issued on behalf of a few reputable foreign governments or industrial enterprises, but, before long, American bankers were competing with one another for bond issues of foreign cities and provincial governments the very names of which had hitherto been unknown to them. German cities, provinces, and industries obtained the largest slice of these capital issues, with South American borrowers not far behind.

The State Department, under the Coolidge and Hoover administrations, did nothing to halt this reckless financing, nor did the United States Government apparently recognize any more than did most American bankers, that the great stock-market boom rested upon quicksand.

The basic, unrealized trouble was that, from having been a prewar borrower, the United States had become the world's great creditor nation. The billions of war debts incurred by the Allies in America were clearly uncollectible, unless Germany could be forced to make them good through reparations. But, as everyone knew and refused to admit, Germany could not possibly pay the bill imposed at Versailles; in fact, Germany could for a time meet even the reduced reparations, as scaled down under the Young Plan, only by borrowing from Peter to pay Paul.

In these circumstances, the United States should have canceled the war debts and reduced its protective tariff structure. Instead, President Coolidge issued his famous dictum, "They hired the money, didn't they?" And, during the Hoover administration, Congress enacted the Smoot-Hawley Act raising the American protective tariffs to an all-time high. As a result, the United States kept on draining the world's gold supply into its coffers and lending its debtors the money with which to meet their maturities and even their interest payments.

In March 1929 my father issued a public warning against a continuation of the inflationary boom. He was denounced as a pessimist. Six months later, the stock market collapsed, and the gloomy period of the Great Depression set in.

As a matter of fact, both my father and I had begun thinking some years earlier that the international situation was becoming dangerous—quite apart from the growing stock-market inflation in the United States. I feared that a bank such as ours, with most of its credit facilities issued to foreign debtors and without any substantial domestic deposits, might some day find itself in difficulties. Therefore I had for some time urged my father and my other associates to consider merging the International Acceptance Bank with a domestic banking institution not heavily engaged in foreign lending. Several merger possibilities were explored, and finally, in 1928, an agreement was reached to amalgamate the International Acceptance Bank with the old-established Bank of the Manhattan Company. This proved an advantageous arrangement for both institutions, giving the one a substantial foreign business with unique connections and the other the advantage of diversified risk.

Nevertheless, difficult times lay ahead. Gold kept draining out of Europe into the United States. The stock-market collapse all but dried up the American capital market, and foreign borrowers found it more and more difficult to meet their interest payments and maturities.

During the stock-market collapse, we worked day and night, trying to save as many of our clients as possible. Day after day, brokerage houses became insolvent. Twice, I saw men jump out of Wall Street windows. Others shot themselves or had nervous breakdowns and heart attacks. Eventually, the acute panic subsided, but the prices of securities continued to drift downward in spite of all efforts to support them.

Even with the benefit of hindsight, it is difficult for me fully to understand the orgy of runaway capitalism that took place in the nineteen twenties. Greed and irresponsibility, of course, played their part, but by no means all of the participants were greedy or irresponsible. Many of the securities issued during this period and later defaulted were issued in good faith, and, if viewed as individual loans or investments, had been perfectly sound. The trouble was that *all* securities, no matter what their individual intrinsic worth, were rendered unsound by the fact that the entire postwar capital market rested upon false political premises.

Were the bankers to blame? Only in part. Individual bankers were clearly guilty of unscrupulously taking advantage of a speculation-mad public. Other individual bankers lacked the strength of character to resist falling in with the procession. Bankers as a whole were to blame for not making their governments realize that their political and economic policies were leading to international chaos and financial disaster; bankers after all were in a position to know this, but only a tiny minority had spoken out.

Governments, particularly the government of the United

States, seemed to me more responsible for the disaster than the bankers. Governments had created and maintained the fatal fiction of war debts and reparations upon which the house of cards had been erected. Governments, more than bankers, had fostered the notion of inevitable progress and automatic prosperity. Even in the face of imminent disaster, President Hoover had talked about "a chicken in every pot," at a time when hunger was beginning to stalk the land.

The people, too, had been responsible—or the part of the people that had become bedazzled by the idea that one could get something for nothing.

In a way, almost everyone was partly to blame and partly a victim of the times. The decade of the twenties was a period in which a people cut loose from its traditional moorings had not yet found a new anchorage. Religious belief had been weakened. Old moral standards had been discarded. The past no longer seemed any guide to the present or the future.

No matter how hard or how conscientiously he might have worked during this dizzy decade, no banker could in retrospect be proud of having participated to even the slightest extent in an era of disgraceful irresponsibility. Yet I must confess that I thoroughly enjoyed working hard and playing hard in these carefree, irresponsible years. I enjoyed building up my father's bank and the old family firm. I enjoyed climbing the ladder to personal "success," even though it was achieved in a context I now utterly deprecate.

CHAPTER XIII

The Brothers Karamazov

THE ONSET of the Great Depression was not solely an American disaster. In the elections of September 1930, Hitler's National Socialists won their first substantial block of seats in the German Reichstag. Several years earlier, I had heard Hitler speak at a rally in Bremen and had shuddered to see how his screaming gibberish had inflamed his listeners with enthusiasm. I had read *Mein Kampf* and had vainly tried to persuade my German relatives and friends to take the Nazi threat seriously. Almost none of the German bankers and business leaders were alarmed by Hitler; few had read his book, and the few who had refused to recognize in it a seriously conceived plan of action.

When I returned to New York after the 1930 German elections, I told my father that I felt almost certain Adolf Hitler would come to power in Germany; and that, if he did, he would, within five years, either let loose a second world war or conquer all of Europe without firing a shot.

Albert Wiggin, then head of the Chase National Bank, invited me to lunch the next day to hear what I had to say about Germany. Afterward, he called my father on the telephone and said, "Your son is crazy. You ought to have him locked up."

The storm broke in 1931. First, the Austrian Kreditanstalt, the Rothschild bank in Vienna, was forced to close its doors after the gallant Baron Louis von Rothschild had yielded, against his better judgment, to the Austrian Government's plea to have his bank take over another Viennese institution that was in trouble. The Bodenkredit Anstalt's trouble turned out to be too great for even the Rothschild bank to master. It was widely believed that the Austrian crisis had been deliberately precipitated by French withdrawals of funds aimed at blocking an Austro-German customs union.

The Brüning government in Germany was pursuing a policy of trying to bolster its weak internal position by an aggressive, nationalistic foreign policy that would appeal to President Hindenburg and the military leadership upon whose support it depended. This foreign policy had two aims: the establishment of a customs union with Austria, eventually leading to political union; and the canceling of any further reparation payments.

To make a case for the revision of reparations, the German Government played up the weakness of the German economy, following a deflationary policy and exploiting the resulting shortage of foreign exchange earnings. This was intended to frighten the British and American bankers as to the soundness of their German loans and win their support for Berlin's revisionist aims. Paradoxically, the Wilhelmstrasse and the German Reichsbank simultaneously tried to obtain further British and American loans and credits.

This curious policy was successful in winning the support of the Bank of England, whose governor, Montagu Norman, greatly admired Dr. Schacht and, for reasons of his own, favored the elimination of reparations and war debts. But Brüning's nationalistic foreign policy alienated France. Having failed, after World War I, to obtain an Anglo-American guarantee of French security, the French were understandably determined to cling to the provisions of the Versailles Treaty. Hence they opposed and intrigued against a German-Austrian union and refused even to consider a discussion of reparations.

After the failure of the Austrian Kreditanstalt, the Bank of England extended a large credit to Austria, but the sole result was to weaken Britain's own position without appreciably helping the situation in Central Europe.

Withdrawals of foreign funds from Germany and Austria now assumed such proportions that a collapse seemed imminent. In June, President Hoover finally decided to act, suggesting a one-year moratorium on all payments by Germany. The French were furious because they had not been consulted. Long, wearisome negotiations ensued, during which the situation grew steadily worse.

I had for some time suspected that the family firm in Hamburg was overextended. With some difficulty, I persuaded my father to ask his brothers to let me look into the firm's affairs. This was an extremely delicate mission.

The position of the firm turned out to be worse than I had suspected or the Hamburg partners had realized. At first, my father found my cabled and written reports difficult to believe, especially as the German partners were convinced and insisted that the situation was not as alarming as I thought it to be. It was a most painful experience for all concerned.

In a quick trip back to New York, I persuaded my father and Uncle Felix, a partner in Kuhn, Loeb & Company, that their own reputations were at stake and that drastic action on their part was required if M. M. Warburg & Company was to be saved from bankruptcy. I suggested that they immediately guarantee all of the Hamburg firm's rather heavy direct and contingent obligations to the International Acceptance Bank-Manhattan, and, secondly, they make up their minds, if they wished to save the firm, that a substantial infusion of capital would be required. Paul and Felix Warburg were shocked but reacted nobly. The guarantee of M. M. Warburg & Company's obligations to the New York bank was given immediately; I was authorized to return to Hamburg and to draw upon the American brothers up to an amount of several million dollars if this should prove necessary.

In Hamburg I learned that another smaller banking house was in trouble and decided that the best way to put to rest the rumors about M. M. Warburg & Company would be to make a show of strength, by coming to the assistance of the other firm. This relatively inexpensive venture accomplished its purpose; it caused rumor to subside and halted the withdrawal of funds from the Warburg bank.

But this was only the beginning. For the next eighteen months, a close watch had to be kept in order to liquidate frozen commitments and prevent new engagements without setting afloat new rumors. After two more trips to Hamburg, I was able to report to my father and Uncle Felix that things were not going badly, although the reorganization of the firm was costing them a fabulous amount of money.

The Hoover moratorium and a one-year Standstill Agreement on German commercial debts had gone into effect in July, but

Germany's internal situation was still rapidly deteriorating. There were a number of commercial failures that affected the solvency of the big banks, and there was a continued flight of German capital.

Having learned from the experience of the previous year how easily confidence could be restored by confident action, I returned to New York and presented to my father a proposal that —had it been carried out—would surely have had far-reaching effects.

The idea was to persuade a number of American banks with frozen deposits in Germany to convert a part of these into capital with which to clean up and reorganize one of the four big German banks. (These banks, the Deutsche, Dresdner, Darmstaedter and Diskontogesellschaft, known as the D banks, had branches all over Germany and controlled a large part of German industry.) I proposed to find out which of the D banks was the weakest and to pick that bank for reorganization.

My father and Abbot Goodhue helped me sell this idea to a group of American banks and to line up a fund of 50 million marks (the equivalent of about $12½ million). Max Warburg and I went to Berlin to see the German Chancellor, Heinrich Brüning, a quiet, intelligent, and sorely harassed man, who listened intently, instantly grasping the potentialities of the proposal. As he listened, the eyes behind his spectacles filled with tears. Finally, he said, "Gentlemen, this is like manna from heaven. I should like you to talk about this to Luther (Hans Luther, then president of the Reichsbank) without delay."

Luther, a typical stout, bald-headed functionary, with rolls of fat on his neck, was also not slow to see the possibilities. He squirmed uncomfortably when asked which of the D banks was, in his judgment, most suited to the carrying out of the American plan. Eventually, he reluctantly named the Darmstaedter Nationalbank.

Now the real trouble began.

A cursory examination of the bank's books revealed a ten-million-mark asset labeled "Account X." The condition of the bank appeared to be such that this amount might make the difference between solvency and insolvency. The officials of the bank declined to give any information as to the nature of this mysterious account, saying only that it was unquestionably a good asset.

What to do? Max and I went back to Luther, who sent us back to Brüning. The Chancellor said he would look into it. A week passed. Finally I called up the Chancellor and was told by the ineffable State Secretary, Otto Meissner, (who later served Von Schleicher, Von Papen, and Hitler) that the Chancellor was unavailable. I left a message saying that if I did not hear something definite within forty-eight hours, I would have to pack up and go home, since my principals in New York would not keep their offer open indefinitely.

Later that day, the Chancellor asked me to come to his office. He did not invite me to sit down but told me, without preamble and again with tears in his eyes, that there was nothing he could say or do. He was immensely grateful to the American banking group but could neither take advantage of its offer nor explain why it was impossible for him to do so.

Years later, I learned the answer to this enigma: "Account X" had represented a worthless asset, resulting from an injudicious loan granted to President Hindenburg's ne'er-do-well son, Oskar, whose speculations had gone awry. Rather than involve the Hindenburg name in a scandal, it had been decided to decline the American offer.

Had the proposed reorganization been carried out, the failure of the Darmstaedter Bank and the subsequent collapse of the entire German banking system might quite possibly have been averted. Had the banking collapse been prevented, it would have cut one leg out from under the Nazi drive for power.

In choosing the name National Socialist for his revolutionary movement, Adolf Hitler had recognized that its strength derived from two major sources: frustrated nationalism on the part of the Junker-militarist-industrialist power elite; and anti-capitalist sentiment on the part of the masses suffering from the loss of jobs and savings. Without the collapse of the banking system, it is at least doubtful whether the anti-capitalist sentiment of the masses would have been strong enough to energize the "Socialist" part of Hitler's appeal. The result might have been a "Nationalist," rather than a National Socialist revolution, quite possibly a fascist revolution, somewhat similar to Mussolini's seizure of power in Italy. I still believe that, unless the right-wing Junker-militarist-industrialist clique had needed Hitler to gain mass support, it would never have financed him and brought him to power in the foolish belief that he could be used and controlled.

Would a Nationalist, rather than a National Socialist revolution in Germany have been any less obnoxious? Only in the sense that it would almost certainly have been less likely to disturb the world's peace and less likely to carry endemic German anti-Semitism to the barbaric extremes of mass murder and persecution. In foreign policy it would very likely have pursued much the same aims, but its actions in pursuit of those aims would have been dictated by conservative generals and diplomats. In many ways, a Mussolini-type revolution might have re-created a pre-Weimar monarchist Germany, playing off East against West in search of its "place in the sun." But even this would have been better than the holocaust let loose by Hitler in his mad dream of world conquest by a German "master race."

With the German economy collapsing and the solvency of London's commercial banks threatened, Britain became the target of the exchange speculators. In September 1931, the Bank of England, unable to sustain the continued withdrawal of foreign funds, was forced to suspend gold payments. This was an event psychologically equivalent to the sudden crumbling of the Rock of Gibraltar. London had traditionally been the world's banker; the pound sterling, convertible into gold, had been the keystone in the arch of the system of international payments. With the keystone shattered, the entire structure of international finance crumbled into anarchy. International economic co-operation ceased, with each nation pursuing a *sauve qui peut* course of self-protective economic nationalism that was to lead eventually to the almost complete strangulation of international trade and to the deepening of the worldwide depression.

The clumsy and typically German Machiavellism of the German Foreign Office, the vengeful intransigence of fear-ridden France, and the irresponsible absenteeism of Britain and the United States from European affairs had combined to complete the breakdown of the Versailles system in such a way as to set the scene for the rise of Hitler and the economic conquest of Central Europe by Dr. Hjalmar Schacht.

At this point it may be appropriate to insert for those interested a brief explanation of what happened to the gold standard in 1931 and what its breakdown meant.

The Traditional Gold Standard

Being a relatively scarce and therefore valuable as well as handsome metal, gold had long been the chief medium of exchange in and among the great trading nations of the world. Silver had served as subsidiary coinage and, in a few countries, as the chief medium of exchange. Paper currency had come into use for reasons of convenience, originally in the form of warehouse receipts for gold or silver.

It soon became evident, however, that it was not necessary for a government or a note-issuing bank to hold 100 per cent of metal cover against its outstanding paper currency, just as it became evident in the early days of banking that a bank did not need to hold 100 per cent of ready cash against its deposit liabilities. Experience, both good and bad, had given rise to various laws and customs that, in their respective countries, fixed the percentages of metal cover to be held against currency issues and later (in some countries) the percentage of liquid assets to be held by banks against their deposit liabilities.

In international affairs, the shipment or earmarking of gold became the accepted method of settling balances of payment due from one nation to another.

Until the upheavals caused by World War I, any holder of paper money in any of the gold-standard countries could at will exchange his paper money for gold coin or bullion. Since each of the gold-standard currencies had a fixed value in terms of a certain weight of gold of an agreed standard of fineness, the holder of any gold-standard currency could readily exchange it for another.

The fact that the over-all supply of gold was limited and that each nation had to maintain certain gold reserves against its outstanding currency acted as a brake upon both overexpansion of the currency (inflation) and allowing excessive imports to exceed a nation's capacity to earn foreign exchange through its exports.

This automatic machinery worked well so long as the world's gold supply increased roughly in proportion to the growth of world trade and as long as the over-all balance of international trade was not upset by major upheavals. It ceased to work when currency and credit inflation in some countries and the deflationary policies pursued by others after World War I created a chronic imbalance of payments, magnified by the war-debt-reparations tangle and by the failure of the United States to adjust its foreign economic policies to the fact that it had become the world's largest creditor.

In other words, the gold standard broke down because it could not cope with the permanent disequilibria following upon the war. (In addition, the advent of check money as a growing medium of exchange had an effect in many countries similar to currency expansion without any increase in gold reserves.) Thus, a system which had been convenient and useful could no longer fulfill its traditional purpose, actually becoming a drag upon postwar recovery in countries where the maintenance of gold convertibility demanded deflationary policies.

The breakdown of the gold standard in 1931 created a vicious circle. To escape from the deflationary drag and to protect their gold reserves, nations adopted a course of economic nationalism in the interests of their domestic economies, forgetting that in so doing they were strangling international trade and preventing the world recovery without which their domestic aims could not ultimately be realized.

World economic recovery demanded the free movement of goods and capital among nations. There could be no such free movement without an international medium of exchange. A reliable medium of exchange could not be re-established without an end to economic nationalism.

When I returned from Germany in November 1931, my father, as was his invariable custom, met me at the dock. One look at his drawn face was enough to arouse the deepest concern. My sister and I begged him to have a physical check-up. It revealed nothing. Yet both my sister, who was now through medical school, and I had the feeling that in some strange way the life had gone out of him. We knew that the anxiety felt by all responsible bankers at the time was not sufficient to account for his condition. Nor did it seem likely that his inexplicable lassitude and depression were caused by the fact that more than half of his already severely shrunken fortune had been sunk into saving his brother in Hamburg from failure. He was not a man to whom money meant power or potency.

My father died on January 24, 1932, after lying in a coma for several weeks. During his lucid moments, he spoke to me about many things but never once mentioned his brother Max or the Hamburg firm. I am convinced that what had destroyed his will to go on living was that Max, for whom he had throughout his life felt a younger brother's slavelike devotion, had let him down.

Yet Max Warburg was anything but a scoundrel. He was a man of great gaiety and charm—a benevolent despot, hard-hitting, ambitious, but extremely generous and uncritical. As Max saw it, his younger brothers, Paul and Felix, had grown rich in America while he was left to hold the family fort in Hamburg. Hence, what was his brothers' was also, in a sense, his. He would have felt the same way had the roles been reversed.

Together in the same firm, the two brothers had been ideal partners—the one adventurous and expansive, the other cautious and far-seeing. Left to himself in sole command of the Hamburg firm, Max had overextended himself.

During the last years of my father's life, a curious and rather painful reversal of roles had taken place in our relationship. Temperamentally more like my Uncle Max than like my father, I had originally supplied the adventurous and my father the conservative element in our working companionship. However, where the Hamburg firm was concerned, my father's natural caution had been overridden by his subservience to his older brother's ambition, and my role had become that of the restraining influence. Oddly enough, on the occasions when I balked one or another of the Hamburg firm's ambitious schemes, my father resented it far more than his brother Max.

Later, when Max got into trouble, it was my lot to insist that he be given the extremely costly help required to keep the old family firm afloat. In a strange sort of way I was forced to become the protector of both my father and his brother. It goes without saying that this was not a happy relationship.

Much as I missed my father during the year that followed his death, I was grateful he had not lived to see the utter collapse of the banking system he had done so much to strengthen, or the rise to power of Adolf Hitler in Germany.

My father's death made me realize how greatly the desire to work with him had motivated my decision to enter the banking profession. Had it been possible, I would probably have given up banking there and then. For a number of reasons, this was out of the question for the time being. I felt a strong obligation to remain with the bank until more of its German commitments were liquidated. I wanted to see M. M. Warburg & Company into safe waters, not only for the sake of the people in Hamburg, but because I felt that I owed this to my Uncle Felix who had loyally stood by, matching dollar for dollar the money that my father had poured into the rescue operation. I had my father's decimated estate to manage and, if possible, to rebuild, and my mother's and sister's welfare to look after. Finally, I had a wife and three children to support, and, unless I drastically changed my mode of living, I could not afford to give up the handsome salary the bank paid me as vice chairman of the board and president of its securities affiliate.

In addition, I had been elected to succeed my father on several boards of directors. The two which interested me most were the Juilliard School of Music and the Union Pacific Railroad.

In 1927, the Institute of Musical Art, founded by my parents and my Uncle Jim, had been merged with the Graduate School of Music founded somewhat later by the trustees under the will of A. D. Juilliard, a wealthy textile manufacturer. In 1932 there remained much work to be done in consolidating two quite disparate institutions into a harmonious whole. This was a task to which I addressed myself with enthusiasm and which was to remain one of my major interests for the next thirty years.

On the Union Pacific System's boards of directors and executive committees, I happily found myself in the company of a number of old friends. Averell Harriman was chairman of the board. Bob Lovett, now a partner in Brown Brothers, had recently taken the place of his father, Judge Lovett, one of E. H. Harriman's original associates. Other directors were Newcomb Carlton, the humorous and kindly president of the Western Union Telegraph Company and a former director of the International Acceptance Bank; Gordon Rentschler, president of the National City Bank; James Perkins, president of the Farmer's Loan

& Trust Company; and Fannin W. Charske, the able chairman of the executive committee.

During my years as a director, the railroad was to face many interesting problems. Oil was discovered on its California property and was soon to produce as much revenue as the road itself. The Union Pacific was to pioneer the use of Diesel engines in place of steam and to introduce the first lightweight, streamlined trains. Later, on the initiative of Averell Harriman, an enthusiastic skier, it was to create the famous resort of Sun Valley.

A combination of luck and daring brought success to my efforts to rebuild my father's estate. With security prices at or near what turned out to be their all-time lows in 1932, I converted what was left of my father's holdings from tax-exempt bonds into common-stock equities. Having done this, I followed the maxim of my Grandfather Warburg and sat on what I had bought.

Grandfather Warburg had been wont to say: "It is easier to make money with your behind than with your head." His advice proved spectacularly rewarding and enabled me to fulfill my father's anxious deathbed wish that his wife should always be able to live in the comfort to which she was accustomed.

Before the end of 1932, it also became possible for me to achieve an arrangement with another old, established German bank that, so far as I could then foresee, would guarantee the survival of M. M. Warburg & Company. No one could know at the time that all the costly efforts to save the old firm would be in vain, since it was destined within a few years to be taken over by the Nazis and its partners driven into exile.

In April and May 1932, I undertook what turned out to be my last business trip to Europe and my last visit to Germany for many years to come. In the course of two months, I succeeded in liquidating a substantial number of my bank's loans and investments in Germany, Austria, Czechoslovakia, and Hungary.

During this trip I made a last effort to arrest the economic decay in Germany. Entirely on my own initiative, I proposed to the Brüning government a scheme for funding the floating foreign debt by allowing those German debtors who were able to meet their obligations but unable to obtain foreign exchange (because of the government's currency restrictions) to pay off their obligations to the German Government in Reichsmark. The government would then issue to the foreign creditors its five-year-dollar treasury bills. The foreign creditors would be able either to hold these obligations to maturity or, if they preferred to liquidate at a loss, to sell them at whatever price they might bring. From Germany's point of view, the scheme would require no transfers of funds and would let fresh air into the economy by relieving the banks and the government from carrying concerns that were insolvent only because of transfer restrictions.

The new State Secretary of the Treasury, Count Schwerin von Krosigk, looked upon my proposal with favor. So also did a number of German, Dutch, Swiss, and Swedish private bankers whom I consulted. President Luther of the Reichsbank had his usual doubts and misgivings. Whether for this reason or because of the sterile immobility of the Brüning government, nothing came of the proposal. In any case, it was probably too late.

Although I was unaware of it at the time, the Brüning government was on its last legs. While the Chancellor himself was at Lausanne and Geneva, apparently at last making real progress toward a friendly understanding with the Western powers, he was being undermined at home by the court intrigues of the ambitious and unscrupulous General Kurt von Schleicher, who had the ear of the senile President von Hindenburg. At the last moment, Von Schleicher managed to convey to Paris the suggestion that Brüning's days were numbered; this was enough to prevent the French Government from proceeding with the almost completed negotiations. Brüning was forced to return to Berlin without having achieved the long sought success in foreign policy upon which he had staked his political life. That was all that Von Schleicher needed. On May 29, Hindenburg brutally asked for Brüning's resignation. Von Schleicher's tool, Franz von Papen, became Chancellor, with Adolf Hitler standing in the wings.[1]

Had Brüning succeeded at Lausanne, the course of world his-

[1] For the best account of this period, see John Wheeler-Bennett's *Wooden Titan*, Morrow, 1936, pp. 389–94. In addition to this excellent biography of Hindenburg, see also the more recent work of Edward W. Bennett, *Germany and the Diplomacy of the Financial Crisis, 1931*, Harvard University Press, 1962.

tory might yet have been changed. In one sense, his failure was his own fault. A man of scrupulous honesty and great courage, he had lacked two essential qualifications: the ability to make up his mind, and a gift for making friends. Loyal to those whom he conceived to be his friends, he was unable to inspire a corresponding loyalty. An ardent believer in the democratic process, he had been forced by history into a position in which he had no choice but to rule by decree, without a parliamentary majority and in dependence upon the support of a senile and undependable chief of state. In a more fundamental way Brüning's failure and the fall of the Weimar Republic were due to the intransigence of France, which, in turn, was closely related to the isolationist withdrawal from world affairs of the United States and, to a lesser extent, of Great Britain.

A dinner in Berlin, at which I met General von Schleicher, confirmed my worst fears. When I said good-by to my Uncle Max and my Hamburg friends, I did so with a feeling of sad foreboding. I knew that a chapter in European history had ended. I was not yet aware that my career as a banker had also come to its end.

Part Two

CHAPTER XIV

The First Hundred Days of the New Deal

IN NOVEMBER 1932, Franklin D. Roosevelt was elected President of the United States. I returned from Europe just in time to cast my vote for him.

While I was abroad, the domestic situation had worsened. Farms and homes were being foreclosed. Railway cars rusted on sidings. Food was rotting in warehouses, while increasing millions of hungry men were walking the streets in search of employment. Veterans were selling apples on the street corners of New York. Businessmen had lost confidence and business had come almost to a standstill. During the ensuing winter, hunger-marchers descended upon Washington and, under President Hoover's orders, were fired upon by troops under the command of General Douglas MacArthur. The President appeared to have lost his grip and had definitely lost the confidence of the people.

No one knew what policies Roosevelt would pursue as President. Hoover vainly tried to draw him out and to enlist his cooperation during the interregnum (which, since the Twentieth Amendment to the Constitution had not yet been enacted, lasted until March). But the President-elect took the position that the crisis was not of his making and that the situation was deteriorating so rapidly that it was impossible to foresee what actions would be desirable or practicable when he took office.

Bank failures increased alarmingly, and people began to hoard both currency and gold. As an executive of one of the big New York banks, I worried about what the future would bring. My associates in the bank felt it was impossible to plan an intelligent course of action without having some idea of what the policies of the new Administration would be.

It so happened that I had known the President-elect's eldest son, James Roosevelt, for some years, because he had been living in one of the cottages on my Uncle Felix's estate in White Plains. At my invitation, Jimmy Roosevelt brought Professor Raymond Moley to lunch with me at the bank. I had gained the impression that Moley was Roosevelt's most intimate adviser, and hoped he might give me some idea of what Roosevelt and his so-called Brain Trust were thinking. The Brain Trust was the name newspapermen had given to the largely anonymous group that had assisted Roosevelt in planning his campaign strategy. This strategy had in many respects been conservative. Roosevelt had denounced deficit spending and come out strongly for "a sound currency." Like many others, I wanted to know whether these ideas would be adhered to or whether, in view of the deteriorating situation, inflationary remedies would be sought. After my lunch with Moley, which lasted about two hours, I concluded that, so far as banking and currency matters were concerned, no very definite ideas had as yet crystallized.

A few days later, I met Moley again at a dinner given by Paul Mazur, a partner of Lehman Brothers. As we were walking home together, Moley asked me whether I would be willing to be one of a group of three to work out the agenda for discussion with the British, French, and other nations in preparation for the forthcoming World Economic Conference. The other two men he mentioned were Walter Stewart, an economist I knew and liked, and Professor Ernest Minor Patterson of the University of Pennsylvania. I said I would be glad to explore the situation to see whether the three of us thought enough alike to be able to tackle such a complicated assignment together, and I asked whether this was Moley's idea or Roosevelt's. Moley said the request came from Roosevelt and that the selection of the three men had been made by Roosevelt and himself.

Stewart, Patterson, and I had several meetings at which we tried to find out from Professor Rexford G. Tugwell and Charles Taussig, both of whom had been with Roosevelt during the campaign, upon what basic assumptions we should base our study— especially whether or not we were to assume that the new Administration would adhere to Roosevelt's campaign pledges of maintaining a "sound dollar" and a balanced budget. We pointed out that one could hardly prepare an agenda for talks with other nations without knowing whether the United States intended to persuade the off-gold countries to go back on a gold standard or to go off the gold standard itself.

When we failed to obtain any indication of Roosevelt's thinking, I wrote to Moley. In reply I got a telephone call saying that the three of us must see Roosevelt as soon as he got back from Warm Springs. This was in the first week of February. A week later, we were told we were to meet Roosevelt at his home on East Sixty-fifth Street.

Some ten or a dozen men, mostly unknown to each other, were in the narrow front drawing room when the governor was wheeled in. I vividly remember my first impression of F.D.R.'s massive shoulders surmounted by his remarkably fine head, the gay smile with which he greeted his guests, and the somewhat incongruous, old-fashioned pince-nez eyeglasses that seemed to sit a little uncertainly on his nose.

Consulting a slip of paper in his hand, Roosevelt asked: "Which one of you gentlemen is Ikes?"

A figure detached itself from the wall and came forward saying: "Ickes, Mr. President."

"Oh," said F.D.R., "so that's how you pronounce it." Thus the future President first met the man who for years was to be his Secretary of the Interior.

When he came to my name on the list, Roosevelt spoke with charming warmth of my father's work on the Federal Reserve System and, with admiration, of the warning he had issued in March 1929.

"Ray Moley tells me," he said, "that you are the white sheep of Wall Street." I replied that this flattering distinction more appropriately belonged to my father and that, so far as I knew, a white sheep did not necessarily beget white lambs. At this F.D.R. chuckled and said: "I didn't know you were a farmer like me. Anyway, I want you to work with Ray Moley on the banking and currency situations."

This began my association with the New Deal, from which I was to learn more in a few kaleidoscopic months than I would ever learn thereafter in any remotely comparable period of time.

Franklin Delano Roosevelt's inaugural address, with its later famous "We have nothing to fear but fear itself," won the confidence of a badly shaken people. From that moment panic subsided. The next day, President Roosevelt declared a "national bank holiday," closing every bank in the country. No one, no matter how large his bank balance, could now withdraw a cent! (The choice of the word "holiday" was felicitous. Herbert Hoover, I am sure, would have used the more gloomy and technically more appropriate term "moratorium." This was my first lesson in the Rooseveltian psychology of popular leadership.)

What had happened to make this drastic and unprecedented action necessary? During the five years preceding the 1929 crash, American banks had been steadily investing more and more of their funds in securities or loans against securities, and less and less of their funds in commercial turnover loans. As a result, "bank money" was outstanding largely against transactions of a capital rather than a commercial nature—transactions that should have been financed in the investment market.

The whole country had been seized by a speculative mania. Merchants bought shares when they should have kept their money working in their own businesses. Industrial corporations bought stock of other corporations. Widows sold their bonds and bought stocks. The elevator boy bought stocks—so did the bootblack, the dentist, and the college professor. All they had to do was to pay down a small proportion in cash—the broker loaned them the rest—and wait for the boom to make them rich.

The brokers in turn went to the banks to be carried, and the banks, when they had loaned all their available funds, went to the Federal Reserve Banks to rediscount their commercial bills and lend out the proceeds in still more broker's loans.

Stocks went higher and higher, because everyone was scrambling aboard the get-rich-quick wagon, and those who had profits refused to sell out and take them because that would mean paying taxes.

When the inevitable crash came, customers of brokers could no longer put up their margins and were sold out. Brokers went "broke" because they could not sell fast enough. Banks suffered heavy losses not only on their own holdings of securities (which were too large) but through the insolvency of many of their customers. And still the market went down.

After a time people began to realize that this was more than just a "technical setback." In the sober light of a new dawn they looked at their battered financial position and realized—most of them—that they had been on a gigantic financial drunk. They also realized the part bankers had played, or failed to play, in this debauch, and they began to wonder whether, after all, bankers were as wise as they were supposed to be. When people begin to wonder about bankers, it is only a short step before they begin to distrust them and, when they distrust banks, they draw out their money.

That is exactly what happened in the period preceding Roosevelt's inauguration. At first it was a slow seepage of withdrawal. Here and there a man or woman would go to the bank and draw out currency. Then they told their friends, and their friends went. By and by it became known that such and such a bank was suffering heavy withdrawals. Then there was a run, with queues forming out in the street. Meantime, the bank was frantically calling its loans, selling out collateral, borrowing where it could borrow—anything to get cash.

Eventually the cash gave out, and the bank closed its doors. More often the bank was closed without all this happening, because the bank examiner, seeing that the bank did not have enough liquid assets to meet the probable demand, would close it in the hope of saving more for the depositors and of seeing that all got equal treatment.

Bank failures or closings increased steadily throughout 1930, 1931, and 1932. By the first of March 1933, nine out of forty-eight states had closed their banks or issued orders to permit only restricted withdrawals. By the night of March 3, similar action was being taken in every state of the Union.

In their mad rush to get out of the banks the people of the United States took out more than $2 billion of currency—over $700 million of it in the last week!

They had taken it out of the banks so fast that at the end, the Federal Reserve Banks were unable to supply the banks with currency. It could not be printed fast enough!

During this same time, the American people had withdrawn $563 million in gold, more than 17 per cent of what gold there had been in the vaults of the Federal Reserve Banks when the rush began. That was the situation when Franklin D. Roosevelt took office.

On March 7, Moley summoned me to Washington to help with the task of reopening as quickly as possible those of the nation's banks that were sound. During a week of frantic day and night activity, I worked with Treasury Secretary William H. Woodin and three able outgoing Republican Treasury officials—Under Secretary Ogden Mills, Assistant Secretary Arthur Ballantine, and Assistant Secretary James H. Douglas (not to be confused with Roosevelt's first Budget Director, Lewis W. Douglas). The Treasury was overrun with bankers from all parts of the country, most of whom I knew.

Parts of a plan I submitted to Woodin and Moley were adopted, but I fought unsuccessfully for what seemed to me its most important provision: a provision that would have brought the reopening of non-member state banks and trust companies under federal control. I pointed out that unless this were done, the federal government would assume a moral guarantee for every bank opened under state authority—a commitment that would probably lead, as it later did, to a federal guarantee of deposits.

In the same week, the steps were worked out and put into execution by which gold was withdrawn from circulation and exports of gold were embargoed.

On Monday, March 13, the nation's banks began to be reopened under license. By the end of the month 90 per cent of the 18,000 banks in the country were in operation. Many of them should, in my judgment, have been kept closed.

On Friday, March 17, I went to New York, hoping for a quiet weekend. On Saturday morning, I was awakened by telegrams of congratulation. Utterly mystified, I sent out for the New York *Times* and, to my complete surprise, saw the following Washington dispatch:

James P. Warburg to be Woodin's Aide

He is Reported Choice of Treasury Head to fill position of Under Secretary Washington, March 17. James P. Warburg, son of the late Paul M. Warburg is Secretary of the Treasury Woodin's choice for Under Secretary of the Treasury. Mr. Warburg has been here recently conferring with President Roosevelt and others prominent in the administration. While there was no confirmation of his selection, the report was believed to be authentic.

Mr. Warburg, who was born in Germany, is 36 years old. He was graduated from Harvard University and was a naval aviator during the World War.

His banking experience includes connection with the National Metropolitan Bank of Washington, the First National Bank of Boston, the International Acceptance Bank of New York, of which he was president and the International Manhattan Company of which he is now president. He is a director of many corporations including the Bank of Manhattan Trust Company.

As Under Secretary, he might complete a musical team with Secretary Woodin, as Mr. Warburg in collaboration with his wife is the author of several popular songs, including "Can't We Be Friends?"

Two days earlier, Moley had half jocularly suggested to me that I take over the governorship of the Federal Reserve Board, and without taking the suggestion too seriously, I had said that I did not think I was old enough or experienced enough to fill a position that should be held by someone in whom the banking world as well as the Administration would have complete confidence. I had suggested Daniel G. Wing.

The Treasury post had never been mentioned. However, the method of floating a newspaper story as a trial balloon was not new. Just in case there should be something behind the story, I spent the day discussing with my associates in the bank what I should do if the rumor turned out to be true.

There were many things to consider, by no means the least of which was my responsibility toward my mother. She came to see me on her own initiative and said she would cheerfully make whatever sacrifice might be necessary if I decided to enter government service. Unfortunately, as matters stood, the question was not quite as simple as that. A large part of the income from my father's shrunken estate was invested in Bank of Manhattan shares. Under my father's will, his wife had a life interest in the estate which, at her death, was to be divided between his two children. Thus, I had a substantial contingent interest in the shares of a bank that, unless disposed of, would, I thought, disqualify me from taking any government position in which I would have to deal with banking matters. At this time, bank stocks were practically unsalable in large blocks.

My associates in the bank placed no obstacles whatever in my path. I told them why I did not think it possible for me to accept the position, if it should be offered, but asked for a six

months' leave of absence without pay so that I might offer to
serve the Administration in an unsalaried unofficial capacity for
that length of time. This request was gladly granted.

The next day Secretary Woodin confirmed to me that he
wanted me as his top assistant in the Treasury. Moley urged me
to accept. I expressed my appreciation and my great desire to
be of service but explained quite frankly what stood in my way.
Neither Woodin nor Moley took my scruples as to a possible
conflict of interest very seriously. I was told that the President
had said: "Why can't he sell his stock?" to which Moley had
replied: "In this market?" A few days later, I had an opportunity
to explain my position to the President. When I offered to serve
without salary or title for six months, the President, using practically the same words as Woodin, said that he wanted me
around and it didn't really much matter in what capacity. He
wanted me to continue working on the agenda for discussion
in preparation for the World Economic Conference to which
the Hoover Administration had more or less committed the
United States. And he wanted me to work with Moley on the
rehabilitation of industry and with Woodin on reform of the
banking system. To all intents and purposes, the Carlton Hotel
in Washington at which Moley and Woodin were already staying, now became my home.

In all the history of the United States—perhaps in all world
history—there has probably never been a period remotely like
the first hundred days of the Roosevelt Administration. Never
had there been such a variety and complexity of problems demanding immediate solution. Never had there been a Congress
that passed so many important acts of legislation in so short a
period. Never had so many ideas been put forward by so many
minds. Above all, never had there been an American President
who so encouraged new thinking, so welcomed new ideas, and
remained, in spite of the immense burden that rested upon him,
so accessible, so gaily confident, and so confidence-inspiring.

Literally overnight, Washington was transformed from a formal, gloomy, fear-ridden citadel of anxious impotence into a
buzzing beehive of confident activity. The New Deal attracted
an amazing array of talent from every part of the country and
from many different walks of life. The result was chaos, but a
creative chaos. Old-line bureaucrats were at first shocked as

newcomers without experience in public service took over tasks and demanded papers without regard to hierarchical procedure. Mandates overlapped. But, somehow, things got done; and eventually the infectiousness of action aroused many of the best of the old-line government servants to new enthusiasm.

During the first hundred days, the two men who probably had the greatest influence upon Roosevelt were Raymond Moley and Lewis W. Douglas, Director of the Budget.

Moley was to a large extent the sieve through which new ideas passed and were funneled through to the White House. He was a strangely complicated man with a gift for seizing upon ideas of potential value but not for thinking them through. His liking for individuals was strong and instantaneous but fickle. A certain suspiciousness made him sooner or later imagine himself betrayed by persons whom he had liked and trusted only a short time before. His devotion to F.D.R. was, in the early days of the New Deal, unquestioned. Later I think, he began to fancy himself as an *éminence grise*. Knowing Roosevelt as well as Moley knew him, one might have expected him to be aware that, so long as Roosevelt was President, there would never be any power behind the throne.

Lewis Douglas gained his influence through the strength of his convictions, his persuasiveness, and his attractive personality. Douglas' influence remained strong only so long as the President adhered to the orthodox principles of fiscal policy he had enunciated during the campaign. Douglas was largely responsible for the President's first budget message and for the Economy Act, which cut government expenses, including the hitherto untouchable veterans' pensions and congressional salaries. Thereafter, his influence dwindled.

The two most important cabinet officers during the early days were Will Woodin, Secretary of the Treasury, and Cordell Hull, Secretary of State.

Woodin, a former industrialist with no experience relevant to the task to which he had been appointed, was a slight, gentle, frail-looking man who loved music and liked to play the guitar. His quiet, unassuming exterior concealed an indomitable courage and an extraordinary ability to master the intricacies of wholly unfamiliar subjects.

Hull was a veteran of many years service in the House of

Representatives and the Senate; a politician versed in all the tricks of political manipulation; deceptively courteous until his mountaineer's ire was aroused; a passionate free-trader with a tendency to preach rather than to argue for his beliefs on a logical basis. Appointed because of his influence with Congress, "the Judge," as his intimates called him, was from the outset a curious misfit in the Roosevelt cabinet, his position made all the more anomalous by the fact that Moley, who had the President's ear, was appointed Assistant Secretary of State and never even went through the motions of acting as if he were Hull's subordinate.

In addition to these four men, my work brought me into constant contact with Herbert Feis, the holdover economic adviser of the State Department, and William B. Bullitt, a personal friend of Roosevelt's, whom he had appointed as a special assistant to the Secretary of State.

Feis had a brilliant mind which, in the years to come, was to shine when he became a historian. At this time, he was a meticulous bureaucrat with a passion for the kind of orderly procedure to which he had become accustomed under the Hoover Administration and which was wholly foreign to the New Deal. I liked Feis because he knew more about most matters under discussion than anyone else in Washington at that time, but I once described him to Moley, whom Feis irritated, as "the Encyclopaedia Britannica, unalphabetically arranged and with no index." His redeeming features, so far as I was concerned, were his profound knowledge and a puckish sense of humor.

Bullitt, one of the few people who called the President by his first name, was a man not much older than I, who already had a checkered career behind him. He had served in a minor capacity under President Wilson at the Versailles Peace Conference and had then incurred the lasting enmity of most Wilsonian Democrats by publicly attacking Wilson's policy. He had also been twice married and divorced and had written a rather scandalous book about his first marriage. For these reasons, he was anathema to staunch, conservative Democrats like Cordell Hull and William Phillips, Hull's Under Secretary of State. He had a brilliant and often original mind, an irrepressible sense of humor, and an inclination toward dramatic, preferably clandestine adventure. These latter qualities undoubtedly appealed to F.D.R. I found him in many ways the most congenial of the people with whom I had to work, although in later years Bullitt and I were to hold widely divergent views.

Others with whom I came into close contact were: Marvin McIntyre, Roosevelt's gentle, sweet-natured appointment secretary; Steve Early, his hard-headed, able press secretary; "Missy" Le Hand, and her assistant, Grace Tully, who handled the President's correspondence; and Louis Howe, the gnomelike and somewhat uncouth familiar spirit that hovered at the President's side during evening conferences in the Oval Study and frequently interjected objections to a course of action on the ground that it wasn't "good politics." Howe was undoubtedly a loyal, shrewd adviser. He irritated me because he often seemed to advocate political expediency at the expense of what to me seemed sound policy. This was probably an unfair judgment.

From March 9 to early June 1933, I was constantly in and out of the White House, the Treasury, and the Department of State. I saw my family only on those weekends when it was possible to get away to New York.

The work was fascinating in its complexity. In trying to prepare for the conversations with other nations, it was necessary to raise at least a few basic questions of United States policy, such as:

1. *Did the President intend to make an effort to reduce the tariffs and artificial restrictions that had all but strangled international trade?* Secretary Hull, in all other respects a southern conservative, was a free-trade liberal. He had one set speech he would deliver on all occasions, irrespective of whether or not it was strictly relevant; it became known in New Deal circles as the "Underbwush Speech" (Hull pronounced his Rs as Ws) and began as follows:

We must hack away the underbwush of artificial westwictions which stwangle the exchange of goods and services between nations and westore the fweedom of twade.

The President seemed to share Hull's basic view, though the Secretary's long-winded expositions tried his patience. Moley, on the other hand, tended toward economic nationalism and exhibited certain xenophobic tendencies, especially toward the British. He and certain others, notably George Peek in the Department of Agriculture, wanted other nations to reduce their tariffs and import quotas, but looked askance at any tariff reduction by the United States.

2. *What steps, if any, would the United States be prepared to take to bring about international currency stability as the foundation for a restoration of world trade?*

This question involved both monetary and fiscal policy. Did the Administration intend to devalue the dollar in terms of gold and, if so, by how much? Was its purpose to bring about a revaluation of all the world's leading currencies, or did it intend merely to adjust its own? Did it wish to maintain the automatic gold standard, to modify and improve it, or to adopt a managed currency system?

Since currency stability, no matter what international medium of exchange might be established, would require some degree of international co-operation in fiscal policy, what steps, if any, would the United States be prepared to take to bring about such co-operation? Would its own policy adhere to the orthodox principles advocated by Budget Director Douglas, or did the Administration consider a departure from these principles in the interests of recovery? Should the latter be the case, what sort of reflationary measures did it intend to take, and how did it propose to co-ordinate such measures with the policies of other nations?

Boiled down, these two major groups of questions amounted to one question: *Did the Administration intend to make international recovery and stabilization its primary aim, or did it intend to subordinate international considerations to the achievement of domestic recovery?*

After a month of vainly trying to obtain the answers to these questions, which would vitally affect the role of the United States at the forthcoming World Economic Conference, I decided the only way to get the answers would be to suggest some of my own and submit them for discussion. In a series of memoranda which were discussed at length I advocated:

That over-all economic policy be based upon international, rather than purely national considerations, recognizing, however, that in the immediate future the exigencies of the domestic economy must in some respects take precedence for a limited period of time.

That the Administration cut loose from gold immediately in

order to put itself in a position to bargain with the off-gold countries (principally Great Britain) for a return to a uniform standard of exchange.

That, in going off gold, the United States clearly state its intention of returning to some form of gold standard at the appropriate time and at a gold ratio that would protect American interests.

That the United States urge all nations to return, not to the old automatic gold standard, but to a more flexible, modernized gold standard in which gold would be permanently withdrawn from public circulation and would be used only in the form of bullion as the medium by which temporary disequilibria in international balances of payment would be settled.

That the United States take the lead in seeking international agreement for the gradual reduction of tariffs and import quotas in order to free international trade from artificial restrictions and thus promote the welfare of all nations. That it be recognized that such an agreement would be meaningless so long as nations undertook individually to "manage" their respective currencies, since currency restrictions provided the most insurmountable of all obstacles to a restoration of international trade.

The arguments for and against these proposals were recorded in detail in the diary I kept during this time, which I later deposited for the use of serious students in the Oral History Research Office of Columbia University.

With respect to fiscal policy, I felt less certain as to what policy the United States should pursue. I did not share Lewis Douglas' unqualified insistence upon a balanced federal budget, being more inclined to accept the Keynes theory of deficit spending in times of depression. On the other hand, I entertained grave misgivings as to whether the American political system was adapted to the intelligent execution of a policy of cyclical, rather than annual budget balancing. Large public expenditures were clearly needed to provide relief and to stimulate private investment and industrial recovery; but it was also clear that the existing pressures were for more drastic inflationary remedies, coupling an unbalanced budget with depreciation and debasement of the currency.

On balance, my position was about halfway between unqualified fiscal and monetary orthodoxy and the extreme radicalism of those who sought some kind of instant panacea. Of these there were many.

A group of prominent industrialists, calling itself the Committee for the Nation, spread ably conceived and well-financed propaganda advocating the devaluation of the dollar by reducing its gold content, on the theory that a rise in the price of gold would bring about a rise in prices.

George LeBlanc, a former foreign-exchange operator for one of the large Wall Street banks, advocated the complete abandonment of the gold standard and provided the ammunition with which the Reverend Charles E. Coughlin composed his fiery radio sermons from the Shrine of the Little Flower in Detroit, fanning hatred among the masses for gold, for bankers, and for the "bonds of blood" with which he said the bankers had enslaved the innocent. Coughlin wanted bimetallism; if not that, inflation of any sort.

In the Congress, there were inflationists of every variety. Some wanted greenbacks, some wanted free coinage of silver; there were almost as many plans for inflation as there were inflationists. Senator Elmer Thomas of Oklahoma was emerging as the catalyst of inflationary sentiment on the Hill.

None of these groups had the power to force an inflationary measure upon the Administration, if the Administration was determined to resist the pressure. Whether the Administration was so determined it was impossible for me to discover.

One thing was clear: the President was determined to raise prices. That, as he saw it, was the key to recovery. In vain I argued that raising prices would do no good unless wages and incomes could be induced to rise in proportion. Higher prices without higher wages and incomes would merely increase the cost of living. When the President said again and again that farmers were getting less for their produce than it cost them to raise it—which was only too true—I tried to make the point that the farmers were suffering not from the fact that *all* prices were low but because farm prices had fallen considerably more than the general price level—there was a discrepancy between the prices obtainable for what they raised and the prices of the things they had to buy. The President said that something must be done about that, too, but insisted that a general price rise must somehow be brought about.

Another fallacy—or so it seemed to me—was the contention that, since creditors were few and debtors many, cheapening money in some way would benefit the many at the expense of the few. I believed the facts indicated the reverse—that creditors were vastly more numerous than debtors. Every bank depositor, every owner of a life-insurance policy, every wage-earner and every pensioner was, after all, a creditor, and, as such, would suffer from cheapening the dollar. The number of individual debtors who would benefit was infinitely smaller. The great bulk of the total debt burden was owed not by individuals but by corporations, government agencies and city real-estate owners. Farmers owed only about 6 per cent of the total debt. For farm owners and the owners of individual homes I contended that debt relief could and should be provided by government loans at low interest.

It was a losing battle.

At a White House meeting on the evening of April 18, the President announced to a group of us that the country had that day "gone off gold" and that he had accepted an inflationary amendment to the Agricultural Adjustment Act proposed by Senator Elmer Thomas.

"Going off gold" meant that the President had decided to cut loose the American dollar from the gold standard—a step I thought wise—but without any statement such as I had recommended, indicating that at the proper time and at the proper rate the Administration intended to re-establish the dollar's relationship to gold.

The Thomas amendment to the Agricultural Adjustment Act authorized the President to issue greenbacks or to take practically any other inflationary measure he might choose. Roosevelt blandly stated that he had accepted this measure because it was not mandatory and, as he put it, "because it gives me a birch rod to stand in the corner."

Among those present, neither Hull nor Woodin raised strong objections. Feis, though thoroughly shocked, merely mumbled some unintelligible misgivings. A little later, Lewis Douglas arrived and backed my hitherto solitary stand against going off gold without a clear statement of intention to return to some sort of international standard, and against accepting the inflationary amendment. Moley remained sardonically silent. Bullitt sat smiling like the Sphinx. The President at first listened with amused tolerance to Douglas' impassioned plea but, gradually losing patience, cut off further discussion. Walking back to the Carlton Hotel, Douglas gloomily declared that this was "the end of Western civilization."

I was thankful that I had not become Under Secretary of the Treasury. The position I had declined had just been filled by Dean Acheson, a close friend of Lew Douglas and Professor Felix Frankfurter, with whom I then had only a slight acquaintance.

Son of an Episcopal bishop in Connecticut, Acheson had graduated from Yale, taken his law degree at Harvard, and served as assistant to Supreme Court Justice Brandeis before becoming a partner in a leading Washington law firm. Tall, thin, with an aquiline nose and a bristling sandy mustache turned up at the ends, he looked more like an English country squire than a Washington attorney. I instantly liked his quick mind and his sense of humor. His wife, Alice, was a talented painter and a delightful hostess.

At the time of his appointment, Acheson knew little or nothing about monetary and fiscal matters, but Lew Douglas, who had suggested his appointment, rightly surmised that it would not take him long to master these subjects. In my judgment at the time, he would have made an ideal Solicitor General and an eventual Justice of the Supreme Court.

Acheson had not been present at the White House conference on the fateful evening of April 18, but the next day he participated with Lewis Douglas and me in a meeting at which we managed to modify the Thomas amendment in such a way as to mitigate to some extent its shock upon the financial community. Basically, however, the die had been cast. It was now clear that there was going to be some sort of inflation and monetary experimentation.

The President's sudden action was taken while the British delegation, headed by Prime Minister Ramsay MacDonald, was at sea on its way to the United States. How would it now be possible, I wondered, to explain American policy? I had not yet seen President Roosevelt in action and did not realize the extent to which his personal charm could gloss over a purposefully maintained ambiguity of purpose.

Prior to the arrival of the British delegation, Moley, Feis, Bullitt, and I had carried on exploratory conversations with the British and French embassies. Moley's method of operation was somewhat strange. At times, he was forceful and brilliant, at other times moody and silent. Usually, he got bored when the conversation turned to technical details and would leave these matters to his assistants, wandering off to use the telephone and occasionally falling asleep. However, he had a knack of waking up at the right moment. Like everyone else in Washington, Moley was overworked. Once, when Feis complained that there never was sufficient preparation—as, indeed, there usually was not—Moley angrily replied: "Since when does an Irishman have to prepare himself for talking to an Englishman?"

The arrival of the British delegation began a procession of visits by representatives of many countries. The French followed the British. Then came the Italians, the Germans, the Dutch, the Swiss, Chinese, Japanese, Canadians, and a number of Latin Americans. With each major delegation there was a formal meeting at the White House followed by working parties that prepared whatever joint statement they would recommend to the President and the visiting chief of mission. With each visiting delegation it was my assignment to discuss monetary and fiscal matters, while Feis discussed tariffs and Bullitt political affairs, with Moley drifting in and out as he thought best. Neither Hull nor Woodin took much part in these meetings. Woodin was ill. Hull appeared at the White House sessions but quite obviously resented having Moley conduct the working party discussions under the direct instructions of the President. Sometimes Hull would complain to me. On one occasion, he plaintively referred to the President as "that man acwoss the stweet who never tells me anything."

Until the middle of April, I had been acting as Moley's and Woodin's deputy in the negotiations with the visiting delegations, and as Moley's assistant in studying numerous industrial recovery plans and proposals submitted to the White House. Each assignment could easily have taken up my full time. At my own request, I was now relieved of the industry study. This left me free to concentrate entirely upon the preparation for the World Economic Conference, the opening date of which had finally been set for early June.

There had been considerable discussion as to where the conference should be held. The decision to hold it in London, rather than in Washington, seemed to me unwise since it was now clear that the President intended to keep the reins in his own hands. How he would be able to do this at long range was as unclear to me as the policy that his representatives in London would be told to pursue.

When it became apparent that I was to be one of these representatives, I decided the only way the instructions to the American delegation would ever be clarified would be to draft for discussion a specific set of resolutions which the American delegation would later be instructed to submit to the conference. The President cheerfully authorized me to proceed with such drafting in consultation with Moley.

This difficult assignment was not made any easier by the experience I had already had in negotiating with the visiting foreign delegations. If American policy in financial matters was unclear, British policy was no less so. Had it not been for the fact that, at the end of each day, I set down in my diary the details of innumerable conversations, it would have been impossible for me to keep in mind the various and often conflicting national points of view that would have to be reconciled at London.

The conversations with the British and, later, with the other delegations, were an exercise in talking without commitment. In the absence of instructions to the contrary, I discussed with my opposite numbers—Sir Frederick Leith-Ross in the case of the British—what might be done to establish international currency stability as the foundation for a revival of orderly international trade. These conversations were a fencing match between two countries that had both abandoned the gold standard and were uncertain as to their future intentions.

The French were still "on gold" and extremely anxious to remain there. This was a more ticklish problem, particularly as the French had defaulted on their last (December 15) debt payment. Bullitt and I prepared a little welcoming speech in French, which the President delivered in an appalling Groton-Harvard accent. The French delegation, headed by Edouard Herriot, was charmed. But subsequent conversations between the so-called experts on both sides were not especially productive. The French agreed to the agenda I suggested as a hypothetical basis for discussion at the Economic Conference but, quite naturally, wanted to know whether the hypothesis had any foundation in official approval. This question had to remain unanswered.

The President did, however, permit one small step toward currency stabilization to be taken. Without committing himself to what he might do after the London Conference, he said that the United States would agree to a currency truce during the life of the conference. Toward this end, it was agreed that British, French, and American treasury and central-bank representatives should meet in London shortly before the opening of the conference to work out a temporary stabilization of the three currencies.

At all the White House conferences, Herriot had held between his knees an extremely fat briefcase, which was never opened. When I escorted the French delegation to their ship in New York, I succumbed to the temptation of asking M. Herriot what had been in the mysterious briefcase.

"Ah, cher ami," said Herriot, "vous voulez le voir?" So saying, he opened the briefcase and disclosed a little traveling pillow! "Voila, c'est tout," he said, "seulement mon petit oreiller."

Dr. Hjalmar Schacht headed the German delegation sent by Adolf Hitler, who had only just come to power. Hans Luther had been appointed as Hitler's ambassador to Washington. Knowing both men well, I was prepared for skullduggery.

Upon his arrival, Schacht announced that the new German Government had just decided to suspend all payments upon German foreign indebtedness and the only reason why this decision had not already been announced was that he had thought it polite to inform President Roosevelt first. I pointed out to Hull, in whose office the meeting took place, that what Schacht had in mind was to make it look as if the German Government's default had taken place after consultation with the United States. With Hull's consent, I immediately went over to the White House to report the matter to the President.

Roosevelt was incensed. "You know this man," he said. "What do you suggest we do? He has an appointment with me tomorrow afternoon."

"I would suggest, Mr. President," I said, relishing the opportunity, "that the first thing to do is to have McIntyre call the

German embassy and ask to speak personally to Dr. Schacht. Then I suggest that Mac tell Dr. Schacht that the President is very sorry to have to cancel tomorrow's appointment because he finds that he has to see the Chinese minister."

Roosevelt began to chuckle. "That will make him mad all right. What then?"

"Then, I suggest that Mr. Hull have his secretary, Hugh Cumming, call Dr. Schacht and tell him—not invite him—to be in the Secretary of State's office at three o'clock." (This was the time of Schacht's appointment with the President.)

"And then," said the President, entering into the spirit of the thing with malicious delight, "then Cordell will not get up from his chair but will simply hand the good doctor a small piece of paper on which he will have written: 'I am directed by the President to tell you that he is profoundly shocked by your proposed action.'"

I was scarcely back at my hotel when Schacht called me on the telephone, exploding with anger at being put off in favor of a mere Chinese. He had not yet received the rest of the treatment. In due course, this proceeded as planned. Schacht did not make his intended announcement. The suspension of payments was announced a month later in Berlin. The American Government was free to express its outraged surprise.

In a subsequent conversation at the German embassy, Schacht tried to convince me that he disapproved of Hitler's anti-Semitism, citing as evidence his retention of Max Warburg (not for long!) on the board of the German Reichsbank. He also tried to give me the impression that he disagreed with some of Hitler's other policies.

A few days later, Roosevelt said to me: "You know, Jimmy, it would serve that fellow Hitler right if I sent a Jew to Berlin as my ambassador. How would you like the job?" This was a joke, but I heard that the President had for a moment actually considered sending Jesse Straus to Berlin.

Among the visiting foreigners, there were several with whom I established close and friendly relations that were soon to stand me in good stead at the London conference. Sir Frederick Leith-Ross, the British financial expert, was a hard-hitting, straightforward antagonist. Charles Rist, the leading French economist, was a charming, wise, and civilized man. Guido Jung, Mussolini's

Foreign Minister, had a mind like the proverbial steel trap. Japan's Viscount Ishii and Governor Fukai of the Bank of Japan had been friends of my father's. I could not make up my mind whether to like or trust T. V. Soong, the affable, Harvard-educated Chinese representative. The whole thing was a fascinating if arduous experience. Most fascinating of all was the privilege of witnessing the way in which the Roosevelt charm captivated all visitors.

The composition of the American delegation to the London conference remained uncertain until the last moment. Bernard M. Baruch, who prided and publicized himself as the adviser of presidents, had hoped to head the delegation. I told Moley that if Baruch were to be the delegation's head, I would have to decline to serve on it. The fact that Baruch had made a fortune as a Wall Street speculator—reputedly on the bear side during the crash—made me unwilling to serve under his leadership. At almost the last minute, the President decided that the mission should be headed by the Secretary of State. I was told that I was to go along as financial adviser.

Repeated vain attempts to find out what the delegation's instructions were to be finally led me to submit to Hull, Moley, and Feis the draft of five resolutions embodying the substance of our preliminary discussions with the foreign delegations. I suggested that our delegation be instructed to propose these resolutions to the conference as the basis of United States policy.

At most, I had expected that the draft resolutions would precipitate discussion and result in clear instructions. What happened was that, at the White House meeting of the delegation, the President made only a few minor changes and then issued the resolutions as the instructions of the delegation. Although this was personally flattering, I had an uncomfortable feeling that the President had, for some reason, lost interest in the conference. There was nothing further I could do, except hope for the best.

On the evening of my departure, I wrote to the President:

Your lunch was getting cold when our meeting broke up yesterday and I did not want to bother you again just to say good-by . . . but before I go, I want to tell you how deeply grateful I am for the many opportunities you have given me to be with you in these strenuous times, to hear and see and, I am afraid, to speak oftener than I should have; and to tell you also how much I appreciate your patience and your never-failing good humor, and how profoundly I admire the indefatigable courage and serene wisdom with which you have attacked all the many problems that form your daily diet . . .

I hope that you will have a well-earned rest and that we shall do you credit on our mission.

Early in June, Oliver M. Sprague, representing the United States Treasury, George Harrison, governor of the New York Federal Bank, and I sailed on the *Olympic* to attend the pre-conference session with the French and British officials which, it was hoped, would arrange for a temporary stabilization of the three major currencies during the life of the London Economic Conference. The United States delegation to the conference sailed a few days later on the somewhat slower liner *Manhattan*.

CHAPTER XV

Fiasco in London

THE DETAILED story of the fiasco at London has been told and retold by many writers and historians of varying points of view. Some considered the negative result of the World Economic Conference a catastrophe; others thought it should never have been held and that Roosevelt was right in bringing about its inconclusive demise.

In 1934, I published a discreet contemporary account in a book, entitled *The Money Muddle*.[1] Many years later I made my voluminous and often indiscreet diary available to Arthur M. Schlesinger, Jr., whose work was eventually to present what I

[1] Knopf, 1934, "The London Fiasco."

consider the most accurate and unbiased account of the episode.[2] In retrospect, I am inclined to think the conference should either not have been held at all or else held in Washington, where Roosevelt might have developed a more serious interest in international co-operation or have been able better to explain his preoccupation with domestic affairs and his sudden turn toward economic nationalism. Better yet, had the conference been postponed for six months, the dangerous futility of unilateral action might have become clear, and real progress made. The premature holding of the conference placed both the President and his representatives in London in an invidious position when the delegation's unequivocally clear instructions were suddenly repudiated.

Even though a vast amount of work went to waste, I found many of the discussions at London illuminating and useful for the future. Quite apart from that, it was a fascinating experience for a relatively young man—I was not yet thirty-seven—to deal at firsthand with many of the world's leading statesmen. What was more, the episode, dismal in itself, was replete with humorous incidents, many of them due to the strange assortment of characters composing the American delegation.

Secretary of State Hull headed the delegation with James M. Cox, a former governor of Ohio, as vice chairman. Cox had unsuccessfully run for the presidency in 1920 with the then youthful F.D.R. as his running mate. Two senators, Key Pittman of Nevada and James Couzens of Michigan; Congressman Samuel D. McReynolds, and Ralph W. Morrison, a Texas businessman, made up the delegation. Bullitt was its executive officer; Feis and I were respectively its economic and financial advisers.

Cox was devoted to F.D.R., even though he himself was very conservative and disagreed with many of the New Deal policies. An old League of Nations man and a sturdy internationalist, the governor's heart and endowment of common sense made up for his rather slight knowledge of the economic and financial aspects of international affairs.

Since Cox was made chairman of the Monetary Commission of the Conference, most of my work in London was done with

[2] Arthur M. Schlesinger, Jr., "The Explosion at London," *The Coming of the New Deal,* Houghton Mifflin, 1958, pp. 213–32.

him. Every morning, before the day's session began, I would either go with him or be sent by him to see Prime Minister MacDonald, the chairman of the conference, to discuss the day's agenda. Before this expedition, Cox would have me brief him while he took his bath and was toweled off by an English valet. He left most of the complicated currency negotiations to me and never failed to give me loyal support. On one rather nasty occasion when I tangled with Britain's Chancellor of the Exchequer, Neville Chamberlain, a less loyal and courageous man might well have disavowed his subordinate.

The two senatorial members of the delegation were both avowed high-tariff protectionists and, therefore, out of basic sympathy with Mr. Hull.

Key Pittman was a colorful character. Tall, rangy, an expert at spitting tobacco juice into a distant cuspidor, he had been the first mayor of Nome, Alaska, before moving to Nevada and becoming one of that state's two senators. His fund of stories was inexhaustible. Ordinarily, Pittman possessed a quick and, on the whole, a reasonable mind, but on the subject of silver he was a monomaniac. This was not merely because he represented a silver-mining state; he had strange theories about the benefits that would accrue to China if bimetallism were adopted, and nurtured an obsessive hatred of gold reminiscent of William Jennings Bryan. Pittman had a "silver speech," which, like the Secretary of State's "underbwush speech," he would deliver on almost any occasion. Apart from this one subject and the tariff question, the senator was a useful delegate, except when, as frequently happened, he was exhilarated. On these occasions almost anything could happen.

One night, I was waked long after midnight by a long-toothed Claridge waiter shaking my bed and saying, "Please, Mr. Warburg, your Mr. Pittman is in my pantry and insists upon taking a bath in my sink. What shall I do?" Another time, Pittman amused himself after dark by quite expertly shooting out the street lights on Upper Brook Street.

The senator's most spectacular exploit while in London, however, had nothing to do with any lack of sobriety. The American delegation had been invited to a garden party by King George V and Queen Mary. This required cutaways and top hats.

Jimmy Dunn, later ambassador to Madrid, was our protocol

officer and, as such, inspected us to see that we were properly attired. Key had on a black cutaway coat somewhat green with age, the proper striped trousers, and an ancient top hat, but —alas!—a pair of bright yellow, bulbous-toed shoes. Dunn suggested that black shoes would be more suitable. Pittman insisted that these were excellent shoes, quite new, and that he had paid six dollars for them. It took about half an hour to get him to take them off.

That was not all. It was raining and everyone wore raincoats. However, when the Americans were about to be brought into the royal presence, an equerry suggested that it was customary to disregard the rain and to be presented to Their Majesties without mackintoshes. We all took off our coverings—except Key, who declared, "I ain't going to get soaked for no king and queen."

And, sure enough, the senator was presented in his raincoat. The extraordinary thing was that Their Majesties detained him longer than anyone else in the delegation, apparently entertained by whatever he said to them. I was told by someone ahead of me in the procession that he had greeted the monarchs by saying: "King, I'm glad to meet you. And you too, Queen."

The other senator, James Couzens of Michigan, had been the original partner of the first Henry Ford. He was shrewd, taciturn, always serious, and being a Republican, frequently critical and at loggerheads with Hull. I got along with him well enough, especially after I had drafted a speech that won him applause at the conference. One day, I asked Couzens why he always seemed grumpy and out of sorts. His reply evoked sudden sympathy. "If you were in constant pain," he said, "you'd be grumpy too." The poor man had some sort of kidney or bladder trouble.

Congressman McReynolds took no interest in the conference and rarely attended meetings of the delegation. His chief concern was to get his daughter presented at Court. In trying to arrange this, Bullitt very nearly caused a major crisis in Anglo-American relations by telling MacDonald's private secretary that, unless Miss McReynolds received the desired invitation, the American delegation would pack up and go home. It fell to my lot to assuage the irate Prime Minister.

Feis, perpetually worried, worked ably at the discussions of tariff reduction but was hampered by the fact that the President had unaccountably failed to submit to Congress the legislation that would have made it possible for Hull to enter into serious negotiations.

Bullitt was to me a constant and highly amusing source of gossip and entertainment who provided welcome relief from the otherwise gloomy atmosphere. One morning, he invited me to have breakfast in his room, saying that he had discovered something extremely interesting. This turned out to be an artfully concealed microphone which Bullitt was quite sure had been placed there by our State Department's secret service. He was infuriated, and as he and I sat at breakfast, he conducted a monologue describing in minute detail the alleged sordid personal habits of the head of this undercover branch, gleefully aware that every word would be reported to the individual in question and that he would be unable to do anything about it.

Apart from the daily grind of the conference, there were innumerable social functions the delegates were expected to attend. Most of them were dull, but at one large reception at the Guildhall, I had a memorable experience. Looking across the crowded hall, I saw a round, pink face which I took to be that of Prime Minister Richard Bennett of Canada with whom I had been working both in Washington and at the conference. I waved my hand. The wave was returned, but, as the portly figure approached, I realized that it was not the Canadian Prime Minister.

"You have made a mistake," the gentleman said. "You have either mistaken me for Bennett of Canada or for Lord Hailsham. We all three look like well-fed pink pigs. I'm Winston Churchill."

Churchill was at that time a back bencher, his career apparently behind him. I knew, of course, of the role he had played in the World War and a little about his earlier life. When I asked him if it was true that he had been a hussar in the Fuzzy-Wuzzy war in the Sudan, the question was like pulling the cork out of a bottle of champagne. I have often wished that I could have made a recording of the conversation that followed during the afternoon, evening, and night.

By the time people were leaving the Guildhall, Churchill was well into an account of the Boer War, in which he had been a newspaper correspondent, and he asked me if I would care for "a spot of dinner." On the way to his club, the story continued.

During dinner, he disposed of the Boer War and the Irish troubles. Over brandy, he launched into a narrative of the World War. All I ever had to say was: "And then what happened?" Whereupon a new chapter would be begun.

The brandy bottle was empty and the lights were being turned out in the club when Churchill reached the Battle of Jutland and said he would walk me back to my hotel. Instead of Claridge's, I suggested the quiet of a private room at Fleming's in Half Moon Street. As we strolled through the moonlight, the story of Jutland was finished and Churchill began talking about the ill-fated Gallipoli campaign. Over another bottle of brandy at Fleming's, the narrative gradually approached modern times. Churchill was deeply concerned about the rise of Hitler and spoke at length and with prophetic vision of the Nazi regime. He was eager to hear all I could tell him about President Roosevelt whom he already admired and considered a great leader. It was nearly dawn when I walked him home across the Green Park.

Never thereafter did I read a book or a speech by Winston Churchill without being reminded of that entrancing evening.

To get back to the business of the conference: In accordance with the President's authorization, Oliver Sprague, George Harrison, and I met with the British and French treasury and central bank officials in order to arrange for a currency truce during the life of the conference. The tripartite discussions were enlivened by the mordant wit of Montagu Norman, governor of the Bank of England, and the utter impossibility of preventing the French from leaking information to their press.

I did not share the widely held opinion that "Monty" Norman was the outstanding wizard of world finance. He was brilliant and, at times, highly entertaining, but I was shocked by his Social Darwinism and his frequently expressed contempt for people on the dole, as well as by his ill-concealed belief that all government officials were fools, especially Americans, and that Hjalmar Schacht was the greatest genius of his time.

Georges Bonnet, the French Finance Minister, seemed to me an altogether unpleasant character. When taxed with his continual leakage to the press, he explained quite shamelessly: "I cannot offend Havas" (the French news monopoly) "because if I do, they will not print my speeches."

One important contretemps in the preliminary stabilization talks at the conference has been insufficiently brought out in Schlesinger's and other accounts. Oliver Spague had been in structed to keep the White House and the Treasury informed as to the course of the pre-conference negotiations for a currency truce. In addition, the President had requested me to cable him whatever comments I might wish to make. As the negotiations proceeded, I urged Sprague to report progress. Sprague preferred to wait until a definite agreement had been reached but had no objection to my cabling the President a preliminary report. On June 13, I sent the President a long personal message outlining the probable basis of an agreement, so that he might suggest any changes he might wish to have made before a final agreement was submitted for his approval. I showed this cable to Sprague, Harrison, and Secretary of State Hull. As it turned out, it accurately forecast the terms of the agreement we reached three days later.

When no reply to my cable was received, we assumed that the White House had no objections. It was, therefore, somewhat of a shock when the President cabled us flatly repudiating the agreement proposed in a subsequent Sprague-Harrison-Warburg message of June 16. This was the beginning of a series of unfortunate developments that eventually resulted in Roosevelt's famous "bombshell" message of July 3, in which he rejected a return to any kind of gold standard and plumped for "a dollar of constant purchasing power," thereby repudiating the delegation's instructions and disrupting the conference.

The President's rejection of a currency truce caused wild speculation in the exchange markets and left the delegations in a state of bewilderment. Nevertheless, the conference proceeded to organize itself. Our delegation introduced the resolutions on tariff, fiscal, and currency matters that it had been instructed to present. Debate was proceeding. The outstanding obstacle to progress was the absence of agreement as to the future of international currency arrangements.

At this point, Moley suddenly decided to come to London. The strange story of the origin of Moley's mission and the President's rejection of the innocuous declaration in favor of eventual currency stabilization has been accurately described by Schlesinger. No one, however, who was not in London when the

President torpedoed the conference could fully appreciate the effect of Roosevelt's now famous telegram of July 3. The American delegation was overrun by other delegates and newspapermen seeking an explanation.

What was the reason for the President's apparent disavowal of the instructions he had given to his representatives? Why had he rejected the advice of the man who was supposed to be his closest adviser? Above all, why the contemptuous tone in which he had couched his message to the conference?

No one on the spot could offer an explanation. Hull was far less upset than Moley, for it was Moley, rather than the Secretary, who had taken the blow. Moley was in despair. Foreign Minister Le Breton of the Argentine Republic came to see me and, in his strongly accented English, made what seemed to me the classic comment: "Ze conference is a failure, but I have learned Eenglish. I now know ze difference between a piss of paper and a shit of paper."

For my part, I was completely at a loss to understand what the President meant by demanding that, in place of any kind of gold standard, he wished to see established "a dollar of constant purchasing power."

After discussing the matter with Hull and Cox, I wrote Hull a letter of resignation and, with the Secretary's approval, prepared to take the next ship back to America:

London, July 6, 1933

Dear Mr. Secretary,

It is clear from the President's messages of the last few days that he now has in mind a monetary and currency program which differs quite radically from that which formed the basis of his original instructions to us. I have carefully studied his cables in an endeavor to find out just what sort of a monetary and currency program he now wants to develop . . .

It is my personal conviction that it will take us more than a few weeks to work out a currency plan better than anything that the combined brains of the world have been able to develop over a period of centuries, and it is for that reason that I have, as you know, urged that we should not oppose a three months' recess but should welcome it in order that we might go home to attempt to work out such a new program.

The President's repeated instructions on this point were, however, that we must at all costs keep the Conference alive, and you have by extraordinary skill succeeded in preventing an adjournment which two days ago seemed inevitable. The result of the continuation of the Conference will be that we shall be asked to define clearly what is meant by the new currency program indicated in the President's message. I do not feel that I can interpret his mind at a distance of 3,000 miles, nor do I feel that the new plan is sufficiently crystallized in his mind to enable him to give us complete clarity by cable or telephone or, for that matter, by letter. No matter how good the plan may eventually be, it will in its very nature be an experiment and I do not feel that we can urge such an experiment upon other nations at the present time and under the present circumstances. For these reasons I feel that I must ask you to accept my resignation as financial adviser of the American delegation, on the very simple ground that we are entering upon waters for which I have no charts and in which I therefore feel myself an utterly incompetent pilot.

If, after I have returned to the United States, I can be of any help, it is needless to say I shall always be glad to do so. I have written you at such length in order to make my position perfectly clear and avoid any misunderstanding or misconstruction which might be put upon my action at this time.

Very sincerely yours,
(s) JAMES P. WARBURG

The Honorable Cordell Hull
Secretary of State
Claridge's
London.

Hull had indeed asserted superb leadership during the tumultuous days following the receipt of the President's message. Almost single-handedly, he had prevented the conference from adjourning and placing the blame for its failure upon the United States. Perhaps the Secretary's sudden confident energy had been fired by resentment at Moley's appearance in London as a *deus ex machina,* presumably sent by the President to save the conference, and by Moley's somewhat extraordinary behavior.

Apparently, Moley had gone to Hull and assured him of his personal loyalty, saying that he intended in every way to respect the Secretary's authority as head of the American delegation. Then, a day or so later, he had sent a cable to the President, not through the delegation's code room but through the American Embassy, stating that the whole delegation was incompetent and that Key Pittman was the only member who made any sense. As might be expected, Ambassador Bingham had at once sent the Secretary of State a copy of this cable.

I knew nothing of all this until, returning to the hotel that night, I found a message on my door asking me to come at once to Hull's room. There I found the enraged Secretary pacing up and down in his dressing gown with a copy of Moley's cable in his hand. In picturesque language he told me his version of what had happened, showed me the cable, and concluded his story with: "Kwyst, Jimmy! That piss-ant came here two nights ago and acted like a houn'dog curled up at mah feet wanting his back stwoked and then, today, he sends the Pwesident this cable biting me in the ass!"

The old man's Tennessee mountaineer blood was up, and it was clear to me that one of his first acts when he got home would be to say to the President: "Either Moley goes or I go." It was impossible to condone Moley's action, yet the loss of either man would be a severe blow to the Administration. Knowing Hull, I thought it was probably too late to save Moley, unless the President would transfer him from the State Department to the White House staff. In making Moley Assistant Secretary of State under Hull and then using him as a sort of personal assistant, Roosevelt had created an impossible situation for both men. My guess was that Hull's knife would soon be sticking out of Moley's back.

When I paid my next visit to Prime Minister MacDonald, the British leader told me, with a haggard expression on his face, that this would mean the fall of his government.

"It is sometimes necessary," he said, "to do a hurtful thing, but it is not necessary to do it in such a hurtful way."

Before sailing for home, I spent four days in Amsterdam with my Uncle Max Warburg and my Aunt Alice. A diary note concerning these conversations reads as follows:

German picture: It is quite impossible to guess what will happen. The internal situation is a great deal worse than it looks from the outside. A cold pogrom is going on, not only against the Jews but against all people with other political convictions than those of the Nazis. Jews are excluded from schools and various professions and are now having their citizenship taken away, which reduces them to the state of serfdom. Even the Jewish blind are being thrown out of homes for the blind. In these circumstances, I told Max that I could see no possible sense in his staying in Germany. He and Alice are quite remarkable and feel that they want to give their country a few more months of grace before they definitely turn their backs upon it; also, Max feels that he can do and, in fact, is doing a lot to help various Jews who are in distress.

(As it turned out, my Uncle did not bring himself to leave Germany until 1938, when the Nazis forced him and his partners out of the old family firm. He and his wife then came to New York, where both lived to a ripe old age.)

Upon my return to London from the Continent, I found two heart-warming letters:

July 12, 1933

Mr. James P. Warburg
Claridge's Hotel
London, England

Dear Jimmy:

It is with much regret that I learn of your separation from our organization and your contemplated departure for home. We have not had a more congenial person or high-class gentleman in our organization than yourself, nor have we had a more highly intelligent financial authority, nor one more attentive in his cooperation.

I am very appreciative indeed of your splendid spirit of cooperation and of your sincere desire to render service, which has not only been exceedingly helpful but offers a splendid example to the young men of our country.

My best regards,

Sincerely yours,
(s) CORDELL HULL

July 14, 1933

My dear Jimmy:

As you are leaving tomorrow, the chances are that I will not see you. May I express my deep appreciation to you for the services which you have rendered to the Monetary Commission. With no intention to indulge in a fulsome word, let me assure you that the economic experts, financiers and bankers of Britain, France, Holland, Italy and other countries have spoken in the highest praise of your extraordinary qualities of mind and the fine spirit in which you have rendered your services. In the future we may or may not want to say much about the Conference because of unpleasant episodes which need not be recounted now; however, in my view of the Conference I shall regard as one of its first compensations the friendship which has developed between us.

Every good wish for a pleasant voyage and for happiness and success attendant upon your future endeavors.

Very sincerely,
(s) JAMES M. COX

During my last days in London, I was deeply touched by the number of delegation heads and assistants who came to say good-by, many of them expressing the hope that there would be an opportunity for future co-operation.

Since Professor Keynes had been one of the few English authorities to hail the President's declaration in favor of some form of money with constant purchasing power, I went to see him in the hope of getting some help in understanding what might be in Roosevelt's mind. Keynes put the matter in these prophetic terms: "Every nation is faced with the choice between being able to control its own price level or enjoying the benefits of international currency stability."

In the absence of close co-operation between the major nations in fiscal policy, Keynes thought that it was more desirable for both Britain and the United States to control their own internal affairs; this meant that for the time being each country would manage its own currency.

Keynes was strongly opposed to our printing greenbacks or adopting bimetallism. He thought my suggested modernization of the gold standard a step in the right direction but said that he would go much further, creating an international clearing house in which the various nations would keep their gold reserves, taking in exchange a new international paper money issued by the clearing house. The clearing house would be empowered to loan to nations requiring assistance, provided that such nations kept their houses in financial order.

This seemed to me an idea well worth exploring. Keynes, as usual, was a decade in advance of the times. The basic idea he put forward to me in 1933 would, some ten years later, be partially embodied in the International Monetary Fund. However,

I doubted very much whether anything of this nature was in Roosevelt's mind. I told Keynes that I thought that the President was playing with the theory of controlling prices by changing the price of gold as advocated by Professor Warren of Cornell. Keynes delighted me by characterizing any such notion as "rubbish." I asked Keynes whether he would be willing to come to the United States for consultation, if the President were to invite him. He said he would be only too glad to do so.

During the four days at sea, I spent most of my time thinking about what I should say to the President. I had seen Prime Minister MacDonald once more just before departing and had found him still deeply hurt. I determined to try to get the President to make some sort of gesture of conciliation before the conference adjourned. On shipboard, I drafted a letter in which, without being apologetic, the President would express regret that necessity had demanded that domestic affairs must, for the time being, take precedence over international considerations. I also carefully drafted a memorandum to the President on the subject of future monetary policy.

I must now deal with some rather technical matters which may not be of much interest to the general reader, except insofar as they reveal some hitherto unpublished sidelights and perhaps provide some slightly new insight into the not always transparent workings of President Roosevelt's mind. I cannot omit this material because it provides the background to an important and not very happy episode in my own life.

CHAPTER XVI

"Gold Standard on the Booze"

WHILE STILL at sea, I received a message through the bank saying that McIntyre had phoned that the President wanted to see
me. Before going to see him, I spent a day trying to find out as
much as possible about what had happened at home to cause
the inexplicable change of signals.

Several long talks with Lewis Douglas and Dean Acheson,
now Acting Secretary of the Treasury because of Woodin's illness, provided only partial answers. Neither had heard of my
June 13 cable. In fact, they said that the President had been
furious because he had heard nothing from Sprague or me until
after the newspapers had carried reports that stabilization of the
three major currencies was about to take place. Upon learning
this, I went to the chief code clerk in the State Department
and ascertained that my June 13 message had been put into the
President's hands at 1:40 P.M. on that date.

Both Douglas and Acheson felt reasonably sure that the battle
for a sound international money standard had not been lost ir-
retrievably. They liked my plan, drafted on shipboard, for the
creation of a monetary commission with instructions to report to
the President within a month, after examining whatever proposals he wished to have considered and after consulting with
whatever authorities he might name. They felt sure that both
Woodin and Moley would back such a proposal.

Piecing together the story of what had happened, the following sequence of events emerged:

On June 16, the newspapers had reported Cox as saying in
London that a temporary stabilization of the dollar, pound, and
French franc was "just around the corner." As nothing had been

heard from Sprague, and the President had apparently not read or else had forgotten my June 13 cable, there was great excitement in the White House. A statement was issued to the effect that there would be no stabilization unless approved by Washington. On June 18, the cable from Sprague and me arrived, outlining the plan on which the London group had in the meantime agreed. Acheson had taken the message to Moley, Baruch, and Baruch's henchman, Herbert Bayard Swope, recommending that the plan be accepted. To Acheson's surprise, all three denounced the idea of temporary stabilization as "crazy."

The President was on his way to go sailing on the *Amberjack* with Henry Morgenthau, Jr., and, before leaving Washington, had seen only the first half of our cable; he had requested that the second half be wired to him. Moley, however, chartered a plane and landed beside the *Amberjack* near Nantucket. He returned bearing the President's definite rejection of the plan and with the President's permission to go to London himself.

Moley and Swope sailed for London. According to Acheson, Moley was in one of his nationalistic moods. The confusion he found in London altered this mood enough so that, shortly after his arrival, he cabled the President the text of an innocuous declaration in favor of *ultimate* currency stabilization. This was to be a substitute for the so-called "gold resolution" our delegation had submitted to the conference in accordance with its instructions. In drafting this mild substitute, Moley had consulted Keynes and Walter Lippmann.

Acheson, Douglas, and Harrison (the latter by this time back from London) approved the declaration. So did Bernard Baruch, whose change of attitude was enigmatic. Acheson had gone to see Woodin at Easthampton, Long Island, and Woodin had fainted during the conversation. Acheson thought for a moment that he had died. After the desperately ill Secretary had recovered consciousness, he fully approved of Moley's declaration.

In spite of the unanimous recommendation of his fiscal and financial advisers, the President had then drafted a message rejecting Moley's declaration, to be followed a day later by the famous thunderbolt of July 2, demanding "a dollar of constant purchasing power."

Douglas, Acheson, and Moley all agreed that the ideas with

which the President had been flirting were those suggested by professors George Warren of Cornell and James Harvey Rogers of Yale.

Having put together this much of the picture, I went to see the President. My diary entry under date of July 24, reads as follows:

1:00 to 2:45 P.M.

Lunched with the President off his desk and had a rather satisfactory conversation. We covered a variety of subjects, the outstanding elements being these:

I told the President that I had been completely at a loss to understand his failure to answer my cable of June 13th and that I had assumed from his not answering that he was in agreement with what was being done to work out a temporary stabilization. In order to refresh his memory, I showed him the cable and he obviously recognized it. He said that he had been so busy with the revolt in Congress at that time that his mind had not been on stabilization. In other words, he had forgotten about the cable altogether. This accounts for the whole series of misunderstandings. Inasmuch as one can hardly scold the President, I proceeded to the next topic.

When I told the President that his message of July 2nd (July 3rd in London) had been most unfortunate both in substance and in tone, this made him quite angry. He said that I should have seen the American press comment which had been universally favorable. I replied that the message had been addressed to the assembled nations of the world, not to the American press, and that its effect abroad had been extremely bad, repeating verbatim what MacDonald, Rist and Jung had said. I strongly urged him to send a final message to MacDonald in order to set himself right. This he agreed to do.

I then read him my draft of a message to MacDonald. He again got angry when I reached the passage in which I had said that domestic considerations had made it necessary for the United States to change its monetary policy. He said that this was not true; that we had never changed our policy. I said that in my opinion we definitely had, particularly with respect to monetary matters, and reminded him of his instructions to the delegation and of his willingness, on May 15th, to enter a temporary tri-partite stabilization agreement. He said that he had never done any such thing and that he had told me to talk to the French purely as an individual and not as representing the Administration. I said that this was not my recollection of the affair and asked him why in that case he had sent Sprague, Harrison and me to London prior to the opening of the conference. We were then (perhaps fortunately) interrupted by Secretary of the Interior, Ickes, who came in for five minutes to get various matters settled.

After Ickes had gone, I told the President that what I would like to discuss with him was not the past but the currency program for the future.

I read him the memorandum I had prepared and he apparently agreed to it. I say "apparently" because I am not at all sure that, upon mature reflection, he will still feel the same way. He takes the whole currency question very lightly.

The memorandum recommended that all monetary ideas, projects and studies be concentrated in the Treasury and Federal Reserve Board; that it be decided immediately what individuals were to be consulted in preparing a definite monetary program; that a study commission be formed of these individuals; and that the commission be given not over a month to prepare a recommendation to the President. Its terms of reference to be: to determine the amount of devaluation desired in order to bring about the necessary price rise; to define the nature of an improved gold standard; and to consider how the purchasing power of the currency could be rendered more stable without resorting to methods so academic and so untried that their adoption would in itself again disturb confidence.

When I had first come in, Warren and Rogers had been with the President and, before they left, the President had asked me to have a talk with them. This request he now reiterated. I said that I would be glad to talk to them; that I thought he should make a list of those who were to take part in formulating the monetary program and have us all meet somewhere in the utmost secrecy to agree upon a single report. I suggested inviting Professor Keynes to participate, with which, to my surprise, he agreed. (Professor Keynes did come to see the President but, while his visit encouraged expenditure for public works, it did not affect the course of Mr. Roosevelt's monetary experimentation.)

The President's instructions to me were to arrange to see Rogers and Warren during the week and then come to see him at Hyde Park.

On July 27, Moley informed me that the President had cabled a message to MacDonald.

The following day, I spent the evening at the Harvard Club in New York with Warren and Rogers and found that their views were not nearly as radical as I had been led to believe. Both realized the danger of uncontrolled inflation. Both felt that the dollar should be revalued at something like two thirds of its former value and that the rate should be determined in the fairly near future. They disagreed with me and also with each other as to the interrelation of the gold price, the dollar-sterling rate and the domestic price level.

Warren contended that the domestic price of gold directly affected the domestic price level; if this should not prove true, then he was certain that the world price of gold would turn out to be the determining factor. Rogers believed that the price of gold was less important than the dollar-sterling rate. Hence, while Warren advocated raising the price of gold, Rogers wanted to push the dollar down in terms of sterling.

I did not think that manipulating the domestic or the world price of gold would affect the general price level at all except in so far as it would cause greater fear as to the dollar's soundness and induce speculative buying of some commodities. Nor would the dollar-sterling rate, I thought, affect the prices of commodities such as vegetables and dairy products, which were not exported in significant quantity; it would affect only wheat, cotton, and other products that had a world market. Moreover, I expressed the view that the dollar was inherently much stronger than the pound and that any attempt to manipulate it downward in terms of sterling would be extremely costly and ultimately result in failure.

On August 8, the President invited Warren, Rogers, and me to lunch at Hyde Park. The President's mother presided over the meal and, at one moment, when the President jocularly used some slightly profane language, said to me: "My son, Franklin, has apparently been associating with his son, Franklin, Jr., who, I am afraid, has been associating with the groom."

Sara Roosevelt was a somewhat frightening old lady, who reminded me of my Hamburg grandmother.

I quote the following passage from my diary:

Rogers, Warren and I spent until quarter to four with the President discussing the monetary problem.

All three of us said that it was necessary to remove the uncertainty about the dollar. The President said he was not ready to remove the uncertainty and could not see what harm it did. I pointed out that businessmen were afraid to make contracts and that, the longer the uncertainty prevailed, the greater would have to be the final amount of devaluation. Warren and Rogers supported this view.

The President said that he wanted to see what the National Recovery Act could do. I said that in my judgment the National Recovery Act could not accomplish much unless a firm monetary foundation were provided. Again Warren and Rogers concurred. What all three of us feared was that the National Recovery Act would so raise the costs of production that, without a strong revival of business, it would prevent rather than aid recovery. We all agreed that there could be no strong business revival unless confidence in the dollar were restored.

Warren now produced his interesting but complicated charts to prove to the President that commodity prices were directly affected by the gold price, quite irrespective of National Recovery Act operations. Rogers and I disagreed, but the President seemed to be quite impressed.

The President then said: "What would you think, if, in order, to put people to work in the gold-mining industry, I should authorize the Treasury, say, for one month to buy newly-mined gold at $29. an ounce?" I raised the question of export licenses. The President said that he could not see why he could not establish a market for newly-mined domestic gold without opening up the question of importing or exporting gold at all. I said that raising the domestic price of gold might be misinterpreted as a move toward stabilization and that, if foreign gold shipments remained embargoed, this would mean a tremendously strong dollar and, if anything, would depress domestic prices. Both Warren and Rogers disagreed.

The President said that he wanted Warren and Rogers to go abroad quite unofficially to "mingle with the hoi polloi," in order to find out the probable effect upon England and France of the various things we might do here.

As the three of us left Hyde Park in a taxi, Warren ruefully remarked: "Well, I guess you ruined my plan."

I replied: "On the contrary, you have won. Wait and see."

When I next saw the President in Washington on August 15, he authorized the formation of the study group and named as its members Woodin, Acheson, Douglas, Sprague, Harrison, Rogers (who had not gone abroad with Warren), Walter Stewart, Eugene Black, of the Federal Reserve Board, and me. However, the President told me that no commission could possibly answer the two main questions: What kind of a dollar? and How big a dollar? When I asked why, he said: "Because I myself can't answer those questions." He further thought it was foolish to try to reach any answers because conditions were so uncertain.

The uncertain conditions to which the President referred were in no small measure due to the unpredictability of his own intentions with respect to the currency. The speculative boom launched by the adoption of the Thomas Amendment had collapsed in July, when it had seemed that there would be no more inflation. The dollar had grown stronger while the prices of equity shares and commodities had dropped sharply. Farm prices—rightly the President's chief concern—had risen during the spring from 68 per cent to 74 per cent of the general price level, partly because of the expectation of increased exports and smaller crops, and partly as the result of speculation in wheat and cotton induced by fear of inflation. By the end of August, almost all of this relative gain in farm prices had been wiped out. Sterling had depreciated almost as fast as the dollar. Doubt had begun to arise as to the effectiveness of the Agricultural Administration's methods of crop control. The National Recovery Administration had swung into action with the imposition of codes which raised the prices of some of the goods in which farmers were interested solely as purchasers. By September, farmers were becoming dangerously restless, seeing not only the loss of their recent gains but the probability that things might get even worse.

It was impossible to convince the President that the farmers' troubles could not be dealt with by monetary measures; that they were not primarily caused by a generally low price level but by the discrepancy unfavorable to agricultural prices within the general price structure; and that this discrepancy could not be cured by manipulation of exchange rates or gold. Further depreciation could increase the prices of wheat and cotton, which had an export market, but only as long as dollar depreciation was not offset by similar depreciation of the pound sterling. By no stretch of the imagination could currency manipulation help the raisers of cattle, hogs, vegetables, and dairy products.

It was even more difficult to demonstrate to the President—although all of us in the study group agreed it was the case—that doubt as to the future of the currency stood in the way of a return to a high level of business activity that alone could restore the economy to health.

My diary for August and September records a succession of conferences in Washington and New York in which the study group wrestled with these problems. As draftsman for the commission, I produced a series of working papers and, eventually, a report that the group submitted.

The President was unimpressed. He was not to be dissuaded from trying out the Warren gold theory. On September 8 he issued an order permitting domestic gold miners to obtain the world price for gold, which was then $29.62 an ounce, as against a previous mint price of $20.67. This had the reverse effect of what the President had intended. Instead of falling, the dollar grew stronger, as I had predicted during the meeting at Hyde Park.

The inflationists in Congress began to hold meetings and to issue statements. The Committee for the Nation demanded a free gold market and a rapid marking up of the price of gold to $41.34 an ounce, which would mean a fifty-cent dollar in terms of gold. Under the influence of this kind of inflationary talk, the dollar again began to fall rapidly.

On September 18 a Cotton Committee went to the President with a demand for the issuance of greenbacks under the Thomas Amendment and the establishment of a minimum price for cotton at twenty cents a pound. (Cotton was then selling at just under ten cents as against five and three quarter cents per pound on February 4, 1933.) When the President barred all talk of currency inflation and instead offered the cotton men interest-free loans at ten cents a pound, his action was optimistically hailed by the anti-inflationists as a stand against further depreciation. Once more, the dollar rose on the exchange markets while the prices of equity shares and commodities dropped as speculators shifted their positions.

During this seesawing of prices Leith-Ross, with whom I had remained closely in touch, arrived with authority to negotiate both a debt settlement and a currency stabilization agreement. The President was now not much interested in either. (In April I had worked out with the French and British a highly complicated but relatively painless method by which the war debts might be settled over a period of years. The President had at the time liked the idea and christened it "Warburg's Rabbit." When Acheson and I sought to revive this project, the President said he had never heard of it! Moley, who could have refreshed the President's memory, had by now disappeared from the Washington scene.)

On September 21 I made a final try to convince the President that further experimentation and depreciation of the currency would do more harm than good. When I entered the Oval Study, the President began by saying that Woodin had just called up to report gleefully that the dollar was stronger and that he had told Woodin he was crazy; we wanted not a $4.85 pound (this was then the rate) but a $5.00 pound. My diary records the following:

I told the President that I had come for the specific purpose of urging him not to let depreciation go any further, but that I could see that my remarks were not going to fall on fertile soil. I asked him whether he wanted a $5.00 sterling rate or a further depreciation of the dollar in terms of gold. He said that he wanted both. I recalled that in March, when the rate was $3.40 he had wanted $3.75; that in April when the rate was $3.75 he had wanted $3.85; that in May when it was $3.85 he would have been satisfied with $4.00; that on June 17th, when we had suggested temporarily stabilizing at $4.00 he had wanted $4.25; that in August, when the rate was $4.50 he had wanted $4.86; and that now, at $4.86 he wanted $5.00. This, I said, could go on *ad infinitum*.

After a long and fruitless repetition of familiar arguments, I said that I was not making a plea for capitalists; capitalists would, by and large, be able to protect themselves against inflation; I was making a last plea for the worker, for the holders of life insurance policies, for the small businessmen, and for the old people who lived on pensions or savings.

The President replied, "If we don't keep the price of wheat and cotton moving up, I shall have marching farmers." He admitted many people would be hurt by further depreciation but believed it was nevertheless the lesser evil.

When I said I knew he was under great pressure from the inflationists, he replied that it was not a matter of pressure at all but of his own conviction. (I noted in my diary: "This is at least clearer than it has been in the past.")

When the President said: "Well, what would you do to raise prices?" I replied that I had no panacea to offer; that removing uncertainty as to the currency would restore confidence and help to promote recovery; that recovery depended more upon the volume of profitable business than upon the price level; and that, in any case, it could not be achieved overnight. The farmers' problems could and should be met by loans, crop control, or, if necessary, by subsidy—not by debasement of the currency. All this left the President cold.

Finally, I asked him point-blank whether he had any objection to having the latent public sentiment against further inflation aroused and explained how this could be done through the savings banks and life insurance companies. The President said very emphatically that he would not like that done; it was too soon and would only create complications. At this point my time was up, and I could merely say in parting: "If it isn't done now, Mr. President, it will probably be too late."

As I left the White House, I thought that I had probably seen the President for the last time. Once more, I was thankful that, not having accepted an official position, I could remove myself quietly, if this should seem to be the best thing to do. Could one, I wondered, disregard the President's wishes and proceed to arouse anti-inflationary sentiment without breaking with the Administration? Would it be possible to act outside of the Administration as a friendly dissenter without going into hostile opposition?

I discussed these questions at length with Douglas, Acheson, and other close friends of mine in the Administration. Douglas and Acheson were both as unhappy as I but were disinclined for the time being to take any action. Woodin was urging the President to accept his resignation because of his rapidly failing health. All three urged me not to give up trying to dissuade the President from his course. I decided to wait a little longer but felt reasonably sure that nothing more could be accomplished unless public pressure could be brought to bear. I began quietly to lay the groundwork for an anti-inflation campaign.

On the evening of October 21, in a nationwide radio talk, the President came out flatly for the Warren program. He announced his intention of raising prices by manipulating the price of gold, of moving "toward a managed currency," and of seeking "to establish and maintain a dollar which will not change its purchasing and debt-paying power during the succeeding generations."

"My aim in taking this step," the President said, "is to establish and maintain continuous control. This is a policy, not an expedient. We are thus continuing to move toward a managed currency."

The inflationists roared their delight. Wheat, cotton, and equity securities soared upward. The dollar dropped in lurches. The program went into effect on October 25, with the gold prices set at $31.36 an ounce as against $29.80 on the previous day. On the last day of October the daily gold-price advances had brought the price to $32.12, making the dollar worth 64.35 per cent of its old par, but only according to Warren's gold thermometer.

In the exchange market, the very thing some of us had foreseen happened. The dollar stayed consistently above Warren's figure. There were now two dollars—a Warren dollar and a foreign-exchange dollar. And there was hopeless confusion in the minds of the people.

Here and there little groups of businessmen foregathered to see if they could help each other understand what was going on. I took part in organizing a protest by a group of Chicago businessmen and economists and urged various friends to take action. Bob Lovett helped the New York newspapers to understand the situation. John Schiff alerted the New York Chamber of Commerce and got it to pass an anti-inflation resolution. Lew Douglas stimulated Leo Wollman to get the American Federation of Labor to declare against inflation. I myself talked to some of the important life insurance company presidents.

All through November, the government's gold manipulation continued. Successive price rises for gold brought the Warren dollar down to 62.92 per cent of parity, but in the exchange market it stood consistently higher. The important thing was that commodity prices had not only failed to go up with the price of gold; they had actually gone down a little since the experiment started.

The Committee for the Nation now clamored for widening the gold-purchase program to include buying gold abroad. Warren himself thought that this was all that was needed to make the program effective.

The results of experimenting with the currency contained equally little cheer for Professor Rogers, who had claimed that the sterling-dollar rate, rather than the price of gold, determined the price level. The pound-sterling ran up to $5.52—

higher even than the President had demanded on September 21 —and yet commodity prices failed to rise.

Acheson, quite falsely accused of spreading criticism of the Administration, was suddenly and summarily dismissed by the President, and Henry Morgenthau, Jr., was appointed Acting Secretary of the Treasury.[1] Those who knew Morgenthau well interpreted this to mean that the President would now be his own Secretary of the Treasury as well as his own Secretary of State.

At the invitation of Professor Ernest Minor Patterson, I made my first public statement on the monetary tangle before the American Academy of Political and Social Science in Philadelphia, choosing this occasion because it offered an opportunity for debate with Professor Irving Fisher, the original proponent of the commodity dollar, and Senator Elmer Thomas, the leading inflationist in Congress. By attacking these two men and their theories, I avoided directly attacking the Administration.

New York's former governor, Al Smith, did not hesitate to make a frontal attack. Wheeling up the heavy guns of his picturesque vocabulary he blasted "rubber dollars," "the crackpots" and "quarter-backs" in Washington who, he said, were "turning 130,000,000 Americans into guinea pigs for experimentation." Up to this point, such demagoguery had been left to the inflationists. Al Smith brought in an element of vindictive personal criticism that bounced off the wall of the President's impregnable popularity.

Wherever I was asked to help in the formulation of anti-inflation protests by various groups, I consistently urged that criticism be kept on a friendly and nonpartisan basis, feeling that outright hostility, particularly of a partisan nature, would only arouse the President's stubborn streak.

Whether because of the mounting criticism or because the gold-buying program was obviously not working, the operation was gradually allowed to taper off.

At this point, Senator William E. Borah of Idaho, a strong believer in "free silver," gave me a welcome chance to state publicly my affirmative views concerning an improved international monetary standard. The senator wrote me an open letter,

[1] See Arthur M. Schlesinger, Jr., *The Coming of the New Deal*, pp. 241–42.

asking what alternatives the critics of the gold- and silver-buying policy had to offer? I replied, outlining my proposals for modernizing the gold standard by reducing reserve requirements and restricting the use of gold to bullion shipments between central banks for the settlement of international balances of payment. I also took the occasion to express the view that no monetary standard, however well conceived, could be expected to do more than provide the means of settling temporary international disequilibria—that permanent imbalances resulting from basic economic causes could be cured only through the abandonment by all nations of the attempt to achieve self-sufficient prosperity at the expense of other nations.

The senator replied with another open letter asking what I proposed to do about silver. I replied that, in my proposal for a modernized gold standard, I had advocated a limited optional use of silver by the various central banks in calculating their metallic reserves against outstanding note issues; but that I flatly rejected the free coinage of silver, or any form of bimetallism.

In spite of its highly technical nature, the exchange of letters received front-page newspaper coverage and aroused considerable public discussion.[2]

On the last day of 1933, criticism of the Administration's monetary experimentation received support from an unexpected source. Professor Keynes, who had in July pronounced Roosevelt "magnificently right," came out with a stinging denunciation of the Warren theory, characterizing as "foolish" the idea that "there is a mathematical relation between the price of gold and the prices of other things."

While I did not agree with Keynes's advocacy of "managed" currencies—at least so far as the United States was concerned—it delighted me to read that Keynes considered the Administration's experimentation "more like a gold-standard on the booze" than an ideally managed currency.

The reason for my opposition to currency "management" was that it required much greater experience and understanding than existed in Washington or, for that matter, in any capital, except possibly London. I was far more attracted to Keynes's idea,

[2] The full texts of the exchange were later reprinted in *The Money Muddle,* pp. 237–57.

privately suggested to me in London, of an international currency issued by an international clearing house. Nationally managed currencies seemed to me too likely to become the instruments of economic nationalism, whereas an international currency would stimulate international co-operation. This view I have continued to hold down to the present time and have repeatedly urged the creation of a new system of international payments.

CHAPTER XVII

A New Dealer Becomes a Friendly Critic

In his state of the Union message, delivered on the opening day of Congress in January 1934, the President disclosed very little of his plans. At his superb political best, he made a brilliant appeal for support of his administration, thereby assuring himself against a congressional revolt.

One phrase, relating to the currency problem, seemed to me significant. "We seek," he said, "a medium of exchange which will have over the years less variable purchasing and debt-paying power than that of the past." This seemed like a considerable retreat from the "dollar of constant purchasing and debt-paying power." To vary less is one thing; to vary not at all quite another. The one might mean an improved gold standard; the other had to mean, if it meant anything, a "commodity dollar."

No sooner had he made sure of the temper of Congress than the President sent along an amazing budget message. Very calmly, he informed the country that the deficit for the current fiscal year would be about $7 billion and that $10 billion would have to be borrowed within the next six months. He said that by June 30, 1935, the national debt would be about $32 billion and from there on, with luck, there might be a balanced budget. Congress and the country gulped for a day or so and then, in an unprecedented vote of confidence, swallowed the pill. Lew Douglas was speechless. I was far less alarmed, feeling that heavy expenditures were unavoidable and dangerous only in conjunction with an unsound currency.

Sure of Congress and sure of the people, and with the bad news of the budget out of the way, the President sent up his long awaited monetary message. In it, he made three major recommendations:

1. That all monetary gold be taken over by the Treasury. (Since passage of the Federal Reserve Act in 1914, gold had been held by the Federal Reserve System.)

2. That the limits of currency revaluation be fixed between fifty and sixty cents of the old dollar.

3. That a large part of the "profit" due to the revaluation of gold be set aside as a stabilization fund to steady the dollar and support the national credit.

This was progress.

Within a short time, however, this message was followed by the President's sending up a Gold Reserve Bill which he wished to have enacted in order to accomplish his three purposes. The bill contained a number of dangerous ambiguities. Both houses of Congress decided to hold hearings. Each invited me to testify.

Before the dates set for the hearings, there was one more job I felt I might usefully do. I had been fairly successful in showing up Senator Thomas at the Philadelphia meeting and again at a dinner of the Economic Club of New York at which I had also taken on Frank Vanderlip, leader of the Committee for the Nation and the inflationist Speaker of the House, Thomas Rainey. Thanks to Senator Borah, I had been able to put an alternative affirmative program of currency reform before the public. There remained among the most vocal inflationists the radio priest, Father Charles Coughlin, whose inflammatory Sunday broadcasts were said to be reaching an audience of twenty million people.

Before attacking Father Coughlin, I took care to make sure, through Monsignor (later Archbishop) McIntyre, that the Roman Catholic hierarchy would understand that I was not attacking him as a priest but only as a self-styled currency expert. Then I wrote an open letter to Father Coughlin, pointing out some of the fallacies in his sermons and challenging him to debate the whole currency question on the air. The letter was prominently published in the press. Coughlin declined the challenge but devoted his next radio sermon to a violent demagogic reply. To this intemperate blast, I again replied by an open letter, published in the newspapers, subjecting the radio priest's false statements and irresponsible proposals to sharp analysis and ridicule while carefully avoiding personalities. I knew, of course, that I had reached only a tiny fragment of Coughlin's vast audience, but I felt that I had at least exposed for many newspaper readers the dangerous absurdities that were being preached from the Shrine of the Little Flower.

Shortly after this, Governor Cox reported that he had seen the President and that Roosevelt, far from being irritated by my activity, had spoken of me in the highest terms. A few days later I received an invitation to spend the evening of January 17 with the President at the White House.

Bullitt was the only other guest present during an evening of relaxed discussion that lasted until just before midnight. When the talk turned to the President's recent monetary proposals, he listened with unusual attention to my warning that too low a rate of revaluation, such as any rate below 60 per cent of the old parity, would be difficult if not impossible to maintain and would very likely cause serious trouble in Europe.

Concerning my own recent activities, the President said he thought I had performed a very useful service. As he put it, "You have squashed some of the worst radicals and, at the same time, brought some of the conservatives nearer to the middle." He was much amused by my battle with Coughlin and said I had handled it with just the right degree of light touch.

I told him I had been asked to testify on the Gold Reserve Bill by both the House and Senate committees, and outlined briefly what I intended to say in my testimony. The President jokingly remarked that he was sorry he could not attend the hearings on the Hill. I promised to leave a copy of my prepared statements at the White House.

In my testimony, I suggested four major changes in the bill as submitted by the White House:

1. Instead of giving the Secretary of the Treasury emergency powers to manipulate the currency without time limit, the bill should provide for the termination of these powers as soon as the United States should find it possible to return to an improved international monetary standard.

2. The bill should include a repeal of the Thomas Amendment authorizing the President to issue greenbacks and should vest the sole note-issuing power in the Federal Reserve System.

3. The bill provided that the Treasury should own the gold and, at its pleasure, should issue gold certificates to the Reserve System as cover for its note issues. I said that the gold reserve should be owned by the Federal Reserve System and not by the Treasury.

4. I suggested that the Federal Reserve Banks should be owned partly by the government and partly by the public—not as in the past by the private banks. Nor should the Federal Reserve System be under political control as proposed by the President's bill.

In addition, I pointed out that, if money lay at the root of the nation's economic troubles—which I thought only partially true—then it must be realized that 90 per cent of the nation's money supply consisted of bank balances and only 10 per cent of currency circulation; therefore, the cure must be sought in a long overdue reform of the banking system rather than in any tinkering with the currency. While banking reform should not be rushed through as part of an emergency bill, I urged the legislators to undertake a serious study of the outmoded system under which some of the nation's banks were under federal control while others operated under the jurisdiction of forty-eight different states, each with its own laws and regulations.

Finally, I said that while I did not believe in the theory of bringing about recovery through currency depreciation, I thought the Congress should now back the President in the course he had chosen to adopt, especially since he had fixed the range within which he intended to stabilize the dollar. I thought this range (50 to 60 per cent of the old parity) too low but did not suggest altering it.

Although the proposed amendments received substantial backing in the Senate Committee, the bill eventually passed without any amendments whatever. The great debate over the currency was now to all intents settled.

It seemed to me that the time had come for a quiet review of what had happened in the monetary and banking field during the first, fast-moving year of the Roosevelt administration. With the consent of my associates in the bank, I took my typewriter and embarked upon the Italian liner *Saturnia,* which was just then sailing on a Caribbean cruise.

Early in 1934, Alfred Knopf, who had published the verse of "Paul James," brought out my first full-length book, *The Money Muddle.* It promptly became a best seller, largely, I think, because it was the first book by one who was considered an "insider."

I sent the President a pre-publication copy, with the following letter:

May 2, 1934

Dear Mr. President:

The first sentence in the foreword of the book, which I am taking the liberty of sending to you, is:

"This book was written with a certain amount of reluctance in the hope that it may be useful."

There is but little that I can add to that statement, except to say that I have tried to avoid anything that might be construed as indiscreet or ungrateful. There will be a general predisposition to regard the book as hostile to the New Deal. It is my hope that any one who reads it through will find that such is far from being the case. It is my hope—perhaps unjustified—that I may contribute in some small measure towards stilling some of the extreme clamor from what Ray Moley once called "the brainless left and the imaginationless right."

In any case, here it is, along with every good wish and the conviction that, whatever is the right way, you will lead us on it.

Sincerely yours,
(s) JAMES P. WARBURG

THE WHITE HOUSE
WASHINGTON   May 23, 1934

Dear Jimmy:—

I have been reading *The Money Muddle* with plenty of interest.

Some day I hope you will bring out a second edition—but will you let an old friend make a special request of you before you do it?

Please get yourself an obviously second-hand Ford car; put on your oldest clothes and start west for the Pacific Coast, undertaking beforehand not to speak on the entire trip with any banker or business executive (except gas stand owners), and to put up at no hotel where you have to pay more than $1.50 a night. After you get to the Coast go south and come back via the southern tier of States. If you start this trip about the first of September you will find the climate charming and the roads passable. Incidentally, you will save money because I am sure that living in New York must cost you a lot more than living in a Lizzie!

When you have returned re-write *The Money Muddle* and I will guarantee that it will run into many more editions!

After the above insulting "advice to a young man"—do nevertheless run down and see me some day.

Always sincerely,
(s) FRANKLIN D. ROOSEVELT

June 4, 1934

Dear Mr. President,

I deeply appreciate your friendly note of May 23rd, and would have answered sooner if I had not been away for the last two weeks fishing in the wilds of Vermont and then attending the Yama Conference.

I do not think that your suggestion is at all "insulting," and I have no doubt that a trip such as you recommend would prove highly instructive as well as most amusing. On the other hand, I doubt whether such a trip would materially alter the second edition of "The Money Muddle," which you want me to write, because what I have tried to do is not to set forth what I think the American people want, but rather to show them that certain things which look alluring are not, as I see it, good for them. Therefore, I doubt whether the second edition would vary much from the first as you would like it to, except that I might learn a good deal about how to present the case more effectively.

I should love to take advantage of your invitation to run down and see you. I know that this is not the time to do so because, until Congress goes home, I have a vivid picture of what your days—and nights —are like. If, when the smoke of battle clears away, you see a little clear time ahead, I should be only too glad to come down whenever you suggest.

Faithfully yours,
(s) JAMES P. WARBURG

The Money Muddle was an attempt to make the complicated and highly technical problems of the supply of money and credit comprehensible to the layman. It endeavored to put forward specific alternatives to the policies criticized. In this book, I remained strictly within the area of my limited competence.

Encouraged by its success, I now branched out into a larger field with which I was far less familiar. My second book, published by Knopf later the same year, bore the title, *It's Up to Us*. It was not, as some reviewers and anti-Roosevelt politicians interpreted it to be, an attack upon the New Deal's assumption of vast new powers, but upon the growing tendency of people, including those businessmen who objected most vociferously to "government interference," to dump all their problems in the lap of the federal government.

Again I sent an advance copy of this book to the President with the following note:

August 29, 1934

Dear Mr. President:
I am taking the liberty of sending you a copy of my second book because of your friendly interest in its predecessor. It is not the "second edition" of the *Money Muddle* that you ordered, nor have I as yet been able to take the Flivver trip you were good enough to prescribe—for which reasons I can scarcely expect you to take the trouble to read what I have written . . .

Faithfully yours,
(s) JAMES P. WARBURG

Hyde Park, N.Y.
September 8, 1934

Dear Jimmy:—
Many thanks for sending me the first edition of the new book. I have glanced through it today and I know you will not mind my saying that you interest me but leave me *freezing* because you do not offer specific alternatives or specific plans.

I still wish you would take that trip in the flivver! You might stop at Hyde Park for luncheon the first day and I think it will take you only three weeks to reach the Pacific Coast and three weeks back. That would be a grand holiday and a grand experience—but remember, you cannot sleep in any hotel that charges more than $1.50 for a room. Most of them have no bathrooms anyway!

Always sincerely,
(s) F.D.R.

The President's kindly criticism was only partly true. I had suggested modifications of the Glass-Steagall Act, the National Recovery Act, and the Gold Reserve Act. On the other hand, I had criticized plowing under crops and killing little pigs without suggesting any alternative to the Agricultural Adjustment Act. In retrospect, I wonder why I did not advocate, as I did years later, the use of our nation's enormous agricultural productivity to feed the hungry peoples of Asia, Africa, and Latin America. This idea might have captured Mr. Roosevelt's imagination and helped to solve the farm problem that caused him such concern.

I did not write the President again until December 21, when I sent him a hand-written note of Christmas greetings. The long hiatus reflected my preoccupation with personal affairs.

During 1930–34, when I had been almost continuously in either Europe or Washington, my wife and I had drifted further and further apart. A growing divergence of interests had led to a situation in which little more than a mutually tolerant friendship was left of a once happy marriage. There had been no quarrels or bitterness, but each of us, with the tacit consent of the other, had more and more gone his own way.

For some years, I had found the slow deterioration of our marriage increasingly distressing, but three considerations had kept me from seeking a separation. Kay had insisted that she was quite happy with things as they were. I feared that a divorce would be bad for the children, at least until they were older. And, finally, I knew that a divorce would have deeply wounded my father's feelings; he belonged to a generation that considered divorce a family disgrace.

Although my father's death had eliminated the latter consideration and my mother's attitude was less old-fashioned, it had taken me two more years to realize that nothing could be worse for three growing girls than to live in a home no longer warmed by love between parents. Having belatedly come to this conclusion, I persuaded Kay to seek a Reno divorce.

April, now almost fifteen and attending Miss Madeira's School in Washington, was not greatly surprised. She decided for herself that she wished to make her home with me. Andy, twelve, and Kay, ten, were both too young to make their own decisions. When I told them that our plan was for them to live in New York with their mother during the school year and to spend their summers with me at Bydale, I remember their instant and very touching reaction: "But, Daddy, who is going to take care of you?"

At the time, with nothing further from my mind than a second marriage, this far from ideal arrangement concerning the children seemed the most sensible. I did not know how very short my bachelorhood was going to be.

For a number of years, I had known the Baldwin family of Mount Kisco and, in particular, the attractive twin sisters, Phyllis and Priscilla, the latter of whom had married a Harvard classmate, William Preston. Phyllis had for a short time been married to my friend, Gilbert Browne. Since her divorce, she had traveled widely, including a trip around the world, and had taken a keen interest in politics. When I renewed my acquaintance with her, she was co-leader with Kenneth Simpson of the Seventeenth, so-called "silk-stocking" Assembly District in New York.

Although Phyllis came of an ultra-conservative family background and was herself a working Republican, she was in revolt against much of her upbringing. Her political ideas were in most respects liberal, especially with regard to labor and the rights of minorities. She admired many things about President Roosevelt, whom her father hated. Eventually, when she had become engaged to me, she rather relished the shock her decision to marry a Jew inflicted upon her parents.

As a matter of fact, "Pops" Baldwin's bark was a good deal worse than his bite. A gay buccaneer who had made and lost a fortune in business, he reminded me in many respects of my Uncle Max. Over the years, he and I became good friends.

During the winter of 1934-35, Phyllis and I saw a good deal of each other and found that we had many things in common. Phyllis shared my love of painting, poetry and music. She was an avid reader of Nehru's *Toward Freedom;* Ortega y Gasset's *Revolt of the Masses,* Sir Bernard Pares's history of the Russian revolution, and other books of that nature. The library in her two-room apartment and her collection of records mirrored both an inquiring mind and a discriminating taste.

My marriage to Phyllis Baldwin Browne, in April 1935, converted many of my hitherto predominantly male friendships into pleasant family relationships. In addition, Phyllis had a great many friends whom I came to know and enjoy.

After a honeymoon in Venice, Paris, and London, we settled down with the children at Bydale. During the summer of 1935, Andy and Kay for the first time in their lives had plenty of playmates. The senior Baldwins had had nine children, and these, in turn, had produced a host of grandchildren. That summer, Bydale was constantly filled with happy youngsters and grownups.

Once we were settled down, I plunged back into political activity. Unhappily, this was soon to lead me into a painful predicament.

CHAPTER XVIII

Apostasy

UP TO THIS point, I had remained a friendly critic of the New Deal. In 1935 and 1936 I fell into a twofold error. My first mistake derived from the success of *It's Up to Us,* in which I had cited the developments in Germany, Italy, and Austria as illustrating what happens when people place too much power in the hands of their government. The chorus of approval that greeted the book led me to develop further a thesis that, as I later realized, was based upon a fallacy.

The rise of totalitarian governments in Western Europe had not resulted from too much exercise of governmental power. Totalitarian governments had come to power in every instance through the failure of democratic governments to do enough— to act decisively and effectively in times of crisis. I myself had witnessed precisely this phenomenon in Germany. The rise of totalitarian regimes had also, to a very large extent, been the product of defeat in war. There was, therefore, no true analogy between the creation of new instruments of public power by the Roosevelt administration and the conditions precedent to the rise of the European fascist dictatorships.

My second mistake flowed from the first and was even more serious. Having adopted the common misapprehension as to the origin of totalitarian regimes, I fell into the error of seeing a potential dictator in Franklin D. Roosevelt. Again, I should have known better. Roosevelt, it is true, represented a one-man, personal government. His tactics were often devious, and even his purposes were not always clear. But anyone who had been privileged to know the President at first hand should have recognized that, while he was a benevolent and sometimes capricious despot in method, he was a solid democrat in ultimate purpose. I was misled into misjudgment of Roosevelt's character by my fear that his nationalism in international affairs would, if continued, inevitably lead to the pursuit of national self-sufficiency, demanding an ever greater centralization of power in the federal government. My inexperience in politics blinded me to the fact that, in expounding this theme, I was by way of achieving great popularity in two quarters with which I was wholly out of sympathy.

The cry of dictatorship was the favorite theme of the ultra-conservative Democrats or former leaders of the Democratic Party whom Roosevelt had eclipsed and disregarded, such as former Governor Al Smith, Governors Ely of Massachusetts, Ritchie of Maryland, and John W. Davis, the defeated Democratic standard-bearer in 1924. On the other hand, there were the Hoover Republicans who were anti-Roosevelt for partisan reasons and anti-New Deal because of their conservatism.

It was my misfortune that I was one of the first to articulate misgivings that, in exaggerated form, found an echo in these anti-Administration quarters, and that I failed to recognize this in time. Before I knew it, I found myself marching in the vanguard of a procession in which most of the other marchers were people with whom I had little, if anything, in common. Most of these people wanted the New Deal to fail. I wanted it to succeed.

Two of my closest friends, Lewis Douglas and Dean Acheson, shared many of my misgivings as to the means by which the President was pursuing ends with which we were in sympathy. Douglas resigned as Budget Director and became an outright opponent of the Roosevelt administration. Acheson and I were reluctant to go into political opposition, but, by the summer of 1935, I, too, felt that it was no longer possible to draw a distinction between the President and the policies he was pursuing. I stated this conclusion in a series of newspaper articles syndicated by the New York *Herald Tribune* and subsequently published as a book bearing the title *Hell Bent for Election*.

In the introductory article, I expressed precisely what I felt:

In spite of what I shall say of Mr. Roosevelt, I have a feeling of affection for him which longs to deny what my reason tells me is undeniable. It is much as if I had a brother who was a locomotive engineer and developed color-blindness. I should continue to love my brother, but I should certainly not feel justified in urging his employers to continue entrusting him with the lives of others.

Having decided to go into opposition, I proceeded to present the case against Roosevelt as strongly as I could. In a chapter called "Words versus Deeds," I cited the platform of the Socialist Party on which Norman Thomas had run for the presidency in 1932, showing that Roosevelt had more nearly fulfilled the Socialist pledges than his own campaign promises. This was fair enough as a political tactic, but it would have been fairer to add that many of the Socialist ideas had been worthy of consideration. The article drew great applause from the conservative press, but Norman Thomas was quoted as angrily saying: "If Roosevelt has carried out the Socialist platform, he has carried it out on a stretcher." Thomas was at this time convinced that the New Deal would lead to fascism. I thought it more likely to lead to something like the centralized socialist state advocated by Mr. Thomas.

The remainder of the book, except the last chapter, consisted, as I see it now, of quite legitimate criticism of the ineffectiveness of some of the major New Deal measures and doubts as to the constitutionality of others. The Supreme Court was, indeed, shortly to declare the Agricultural Adjustment Act and the National Recovery Act unconstitutional.

It was the last chapter of *Hell Bent for Election* I was later to wish I had never written. Here I took it upon myself to analyze Franklin D. Roosevelt's character and motivation. At best, this would have been a violation of good taste. Unfortunately, it was worse than that, for I presented an unfair and distorted picture of a President hungry for power and popular acclaim. Years later I would regretfully understand the unconscious psychological processes that had caused me to do Roosevelt this injustice.

Hell Bent for Election became the favorite piece of anti-Roosevelt propaganda. The newspaper articles reached a nation-wide audience. The book sold almost one million copies.

I would have liked to have seen Roosevelt replaced by another Democrat, but, since the Democrats were certain to renominate Roosevelt, I had reluctantly cast my lot with the Republican Party. Among the Republican aspirants, Senator Borah and Colonel Knox, publisher of the Chicago *Daily News*, were the least hostile to the basic aims of the New Deal. Herbert Hoover, still a great power in the party, stood at the other end of the spectrum; his nomination seemed unlikely, but his influence upon the platform and the choice of candidate would undoubtedly be great. He seemed likely to back the nomination of Senator Arthur Vandenberg of Michigan. Somewhere between the liberal and conservative wings, stood Governor Alfred M. Landon of Kansas. From my point of view, Senator Borah was undesirable because of his high-tariff protectionism and his advocacy of bimetallism. Knox, a former ardent follower of Theodore Roosevelt, seemed to me the most liberal Republican and the most likely to conduct a hard-hitting but fair campaign.

During the spring of 1936, I worked for the colonel, preparing at his request a number of position papers on various issues, especially those involving financial policy and international affairs. Having recently become president of the Economic Club of New York, I invited Colonel Knox to use this forum for his major foreign policy address, in the preparation of which I assisted. At the Republican convention in Cleveland, I worked with the resolutions committee in an unsuccessful effort to liberalize the platform. I was sorely disappointed when the convention nominated Governor Landon, awarding Knox the second place on the ticket.

No one seemed to know very much about Landon except that he had been considered a liberal governor and had been one of the few Republicans elected in the Roosevelt landslide of 1932. Lewis Douglas and I decided to make a pilgrimage to Topeka to size up the Republican nominee. We found Landon a likable, friendly, and unpretentious man, who either had few strong convictions as to national policy or else was unwilling to disclose them. His anti-inflation views were clearly stated, but it was impossible for us to find out where Landon stood with regard to international relations in general or, more specifically, with regard to the recently enacted Reciprocal Trade Agreements Act which Secretary Hull had finally been able to put through the Congress. Douglas came away with the feeling that Landon would be a reasonably good President—better in any case than Roosevelt. I came away with the opposite conclusion, wishing that I had not so strongly and publicly committed myself against F.D.R.

Before long, Landon made a campaign speech against the Reciprocal Trade Treaty program, which settled the matter so far as I was concerned. If elected, Landon would be even more of a nationalist than Roosevelt had been in the early days of the New Deal. Meanwhile, Roosevelt himself had been moving slowly toward international co-operation. A nationalistic foreign policy would not only invite worldwide disaster but would inevitably lead to greater centralization of power in the federal government, no matter how strongly Landon might be opposed to it.

I wrote to Knox expressing my dismay, realizing that I would now have to vote for the President's re-election in spite of all I had said and written. I knew that it would not be right for me quietly to cast my ballot for Roosevelt in November. In view of the public position I had taken, I had an obligation to retract the advice I had given my fellow citizens. In some manner I would have to eat crow.

I could not bring myself to crawl back to the White House. Instead, I decided to state my position fully to the man who, more than any other, had turned the President toward international co-operation. Knowing that the Secretary of State would undoubtedly release my letter to the press, I thought this the best way publicly to state my full position.

October 13, 1936

The Honorable Cordell Hull
Secretary of State
Washington, D.C.

Dear Mr. Secretary:

The recent developments in the direction of stabilization of currencies and revival of world trade are in no minor degree due to your splendid efforts. One who knows the part you have played in bringing these developments to pass cannot refrain from sending you his warmest congratulations.

Ever since the losing fight of 1933 you have steadfastly endeavored to bring this country and the rest of the world back to economic sanity; your loyal adherence to this endeavor is known to many, as are the obstacles, both at home and abroad, against which you have had to contend. That you did drive on to such a successful beginning is a great achievement which I, for one, believe transcends all the many apparent issues, which, no matter how important in themselves, can be met only if we meet the one basic issue squarely.

Your efforts and your achievement help to throw into reverse the present world-wide gravitation toward economic nationalism and illusory self-sufficiency. National self-sufficiency means a permanent government-directed economy; and a permanent government-directed economy means at length dictatorship; moreover, economic nationalism sooner or later means war. This has been and is your view, and those to whom the preservation of the American form of government and the American way of life is more than a mere phrase, share your views and are happy to observe your successful efforts. You have started the world on the way to peace for the first time since 1914. You have held fast to your beliefs and principles and, thanks to your patience and perseverance in the face of frequent opposition within and without the Administration, you have made progress.

You offer a lesson of tolerance for the mistakes of others combined with firmness of conviction—a lesson which cannot help but be enlightening not only to me but to many American citizens who are deeply concerned with the problems which today confront our country and the rest of the world.

During the past three years I have spoken openly and frankly. I have stated my objections and apprehensions. I make no retractions. In the hope that the Presidential campaign would be one of principles and not merely a campaign of ill-advised promises, I expected to support an opposition which would stand four-square against wrong policies and wrong premises, and which would endorse the basic principle for which you stand—for this principle should transcend any partisan considerations.

Unfortunately the Republican platform and the Republican campaign as developed to date openly attack this principle, at the very time when the present Administration is approaching it more closely. To attack this principle is to attack the fundamental basis of all liberty and all liberalism.

While I have always opposed and shall continue to oppose openly and without reservation any policies which run counter to my beliefs and convictions, I am mindful of the fact that the all-important issue is the issue upon which you have made and are making your fight.

The obvious conclusions imposed by these considerations cannot be avoided.

It is impossible for me to support an opposition which either will not or cannot recognize that economic nationalism lies at the root of our great difficulties—an opposition which, clinging to outworn partisan tradition, offers only to repeat the mistakes of the past as a cure for the mistakes of the present. Hence, unless there is a fundamental change in the general alignment between now and November 3rd, I shall cast my vote for the re-election of the President, in the hope that your efforts will continue to bear fruit and that your principles will become more and more the guiding principles of his Administration.

With sincere admiration and warm personal regards, I am,

Faithfully yours,
(s) JAMES P. WARBURG

On the same day I wrote to Frank Knox, enclosing a copy of my letter to Mr. Hull.

Dear Frank:

The enclosure speaks for itself. I hate it just as much as you can possibly hate it—but I cannot help it. The thing that hurts most is what I feel about having to leave you. Some day—when it's all over—let's talk about it.

As ever,
(s) JIM

Knox replied from on board his campaign train somewhere in the Middle West:

October 20, 1936
Dear Jim:

Your note caught up with me enroute and, naturally, I am very much depressed by its contents. I think you are making the wrong choice in the matter, but I respect completely your right of self-decision. I think we are going to win and, in that event, I want the new administration to have your able cooperation in the problems which lie ahead of it and shall count on this.

Yours as ever,
(s) FRANK KNOX

The publication of my letter to the Secretary of State created a minor sensation. I was flayed by the Republican press and received only a chilly welcome from the Democrats, which, I thought, was precisely what I deserved. Some of my closest friends told me that I had committed political suicide. I thought this might well be true but did not regret my action. I did regret having put myself in a position from which there could be no escape from the humiliation of having to eat my own words.

It was not until several years later that I fully understood just where and why I had gone wrong. In retrospect, it seemed to me that most of my substantive criticisms of President Roosevelt's fiscal, monetary, foreign trade, and industrial-recovery policies had been neither invalid nor unfair. I had never been out of sympathy with Roosevelt's objectives but had become increasingly distrustful of the means by which he sought to achieve them. Looking back, I did not feel that this distrust had been unjustified. In fact, by 1939 it was fairly evident that Roosevelt's recovery policies would not have brought the country fully out of the Great Depression and cured mass unemployment had it not been for the stimulus provided during his second term by the outbreak of World War II. I therefore had no reason to regret my opposition to monetary experimentation, to deliberate inflation, to economic nationalism, or to the legislation that was later declared unconstitutional. I did, however, deeply regret the bad taste and lack of common-sense judgment that had marred my privileged relationship to the President, and I determined to find out why I had fallen into this error. As the result of undergoing a most illuminating psychoanalysis, I discovered the answer. My father's death, which had psychologically ended my career as a banker, had been followed within less than a year by my adoption into President Roosevelt's inner circle. Although I was not aware of it at the time, Roosevelt became in many ways a second father to whom I transferred much of the respect and admiration with which a young man needs to endow a father or a father figure.

Unfortunately, Roosevelt proceeded to attack precisely those psychological symbols for which my father had stood: the traditional banking structure, the independent Federal Reserve System, the gold standard and the general concept of "sound money." My participation in banking reform, in a modernization of the gold standard and in a revision of certain aspects of the Federal Reserve System had, without my knowing it, given me an uncomfortable feeling of having taken part in the desecration of my father's life work, even though my conscious reason informed me that these reforms were urgently necessary. When President Roosevelt's actions in the monetary field went beyond what my reason could accept, they aroused not only rational misgivings but an irrational unconscious feeling that my substitute father had betrayed the beloved parent whose place he had to a certain extent taken.

In addition, my marriage into a Republican family had probably served to fortify my hostility to Roosevelt, providing praise and encouragement for my least praiseworthy attacks upon the President's personality. Hindsight forces me to suspect that a by no means admirable desire to show off before my new wife and her family may have played a part.

Once I had gained these insights, I did not feel that the understanding of my own irrationality provided any excuse. I did, however, have a sense of relief at finally comprehending where and why I had gone wrong; and I felt free to make a long-overdue apology to Roosevelt if and when there should be an opportunity to do so.

CHAPTER XIX

A Happy Interlude Cut Short by World Events

HAVING made a fool of myself in a political goldfish bowl, I thought it wise and necessary to let a certain amount of time dim the memory of my behavior. It was also time to think of my personal affairs, the financial security of my family, and my relationship to the bank.

The arrangement under which my two younger daughters spent the winters with their mother in New York had not worked out very satisfactorily for either them or their mother. Recognizing that her work in the theater made it difficult for her to spend evenings at home and that the two girls were being left too much alone, Kay Swift agreed it would be best for all concerned if the children lived the year round with Phyllis and me. Phyllis and I welcomed this decision. We decided to remodel the house at Seventieth Street in such a way as to divide it into three apartments, in one of which we would make our home with the children during the winter while we rented out the other two.

Although my position at the bank provided ample financial security and my associates were anxious to have me remain, I felt that it was time to close this chapter in my career. The New Deal reforms had radically changed the banking business. Investment and commercial banking had wisely been separated. The International Manhattan Company, securities affiliate of the Bank of the Manhattan Company of which I had been president, had been liquidated. The International Acceptance Bank, of which I was also president, was now in good shape. Feeling that my obligations had been discharged, I felt free to strike out along new lines.

Without knowing exactly what I proposed to do, I resigned from my salaried positions with the International Acceptance Bank and as vice chairman of the Manhattan Company, remaining for the time being a member of its board of directors.

Because I had often originated European issues for Kuhn, Loeb & Company and got along well with its partners, the firm offered me a partnership, proposing at the same time to take in my close friend and able associate, Hugh Knowlton. The offer was tempting, because the firm's business was extremely lucrative, but I told my Uncle Felix and other friends at Kuhn, Loeb that, much as I appreciated their invitation, I had a strong feeling against going back into a family concern. I wanted, if I could, to strike out on my own as a free-lance originator of industrial financing in which I would always be glad to co-operate with the firm.

By this time, I had done well enough in rebuilding my father's estate that my mother's and sister's comfort was more than assured. My own income would be small, but, together with certain already assured consultant fees, I thought it would be sufficient to carry my venture and take care of the needs of my wife and children. When I told my mother about my decision, she, too, felt that I would be happiest going it alone and generously offered to provide me with some capital—an offer I now felt free to accept.

Among my old friends whom I had brought into the bank and for whom I felt a responsibility, Blaine succeeded to my position as vice chairman of the board of directors; Knowlton became a partner in Kuhn, Loeb & Company; Morgan and Milholland decided to try their luck with me in my new venture. In addition to these two associates, my new small office high up in the Manhattan tower housed my personal accountant, Louis Siegel, and the two sisters, Julia Hughes and Florence Hemstreet, who had for many years been my secretaries.

My adventure in independent financial activity proved extremely fortunate. John Milholland was a shrewd investor and looked after the management of the family investment corporation my father had founded. John Morgan brought in a number of interesting promotions of which the most profitable turned out to be the Piper Aircraft Company and the Alfol Insulation Company.

Piper Aircraft grew rapidly from very small beginnings into a large and prosperous concern. When I first became interested, William Piper and his two sons were building their first little Cub planes in a vacant garage. At my suggestion, John Morgan and my friend Frank Field went on the company's board of directors and greatly assisted its rapid development.

The Alfol Insulation Company, in which I also acquired an interest, manufactured a new type of aluminum foil and, under the able management of its founder, Jeremiah Giles, grew steadily until it eventually merged at a handsome profit with the Borg Warner Corporation.

The most interesting and eventually by far the most profitable venture during my brief period as a promoter, was my participation in the organization of the Polaroid Corporation. Its future president, Edwin H. Land, later to become a world-renowned scientist, was at this time a young inventor who, under the guidance of his friend and attorney, Julius Silver, was seeking capital with which to exploit two products, both stemming from the invention of a new light-polarizing material.

Land had found a way to imbed and orient iodine crystals in plastic sheeting in such a way as to enable him to block off light or let it through in varying degrees of intensity. One application of this invention was a new type of glare-removing sunglass. The other and more exciting potential application lay in the field of removing the glare of oncoming automobile headlights.

At my first meeting with Land and Silver, I was greatly impressed by the potentiality of Land's invention as well as by the personalities of the two men. Land had an indefinable quality that inspired both interest and confidence. His complete unfamiliarity with financial matters was more than compensated for by the shrewd sophistication of his adviser, who had first met Land when he had been his counselor at summer camp.

When I came into the picture, the banking firm of Schroeder-Rockefeller had already expressed an interest in financing the company Land and Silver wished to form. I offered to see whether I could induce Kuhn, Loeb & Company to lend their prestige to the promotion, although the firm was extremely conservative and rarely underwrote anything but gilt-edge securities. With the enthusiastic help of Hugh Knowlton, I succeeded in interesting the Kuhn, Loeb partners in participating in the underwriting of the preferred stock of the new company. My own willingness to make a considerable investment in what amounted to a speculative bet on the scientific ability of one man and the business judgment of another no doubt helped to bring about the firm's decision.

In one respect, this transaction was unique in the history of Wall Street. Never before had an unknown young inventor been able to obtain through the sale of preferred stock almost a million dollars of capital without giving up the majority control of the common-stock equity in his concern. For my services in bringing about the consummation of this unusual deal, I received a substantial bonus of then worthless common stock, together with an option to increase my holdings in the course of the next few years. I was also invited to become a member of the board of directors.

The company went through some lean years, during which it managed to live on the proceeds of an arrangement with the American Optical Company for the manufacture and sale of Polaroid sunglasses.

Long negotiations with the automotive industry, including many costly demonstrations with cars equipped with polarizing headlights and visors, dragged along without result. The automobile manufacturers were interested, but their interest waned when they realized that no one company could gain an advantage over its competitors. The elimination of headlight glare would become possible only if the system was built into *all* cars. There was also the difficult problem of how to equip the millions of old cars already on the roads. The National Safety Council and a number of insurance underwriters were interested in seeing the system adopted but could do little more than express their favorable opinion. We considered the possibility of getting laws passed requiring automobiles to be equipped with head-light-glare elimination, but this meant that forty-eight state legislatures would have to be induced to enact such legislation—a task even more difficult than getting the relatively small number of automotive manufacturers to act together.

With our major project stalled, Land proceeded literally to invent his company out of its difficulties. After some unsuccessful experiments with glare-removing desk lamps, he applied his genius to a number of defense projects which resulted in substantial government contracts; and, when these were completed, he was ready at the end of World War II with the invention of his revolutionary photographic process which was to put the company permanently on its feet.

At the time, I had no idea that my association with Polaroid would eventually make me a rich man, or that it would become one of my major continuing interests in the years to come.

In the summer of 1937, Phyllis and I took the two younger girls via Montreal and Quebec to Murray Bay. The Manoir Richelieu was an ideal playground for children. Andy and Kay acquired their first boy friends and enjoyed themselves hugely. The Dean Achesons had taken a house at Murray Bay for the summer, and our two families played lawn bowls and tennis and went on picnics together.

The scenery along the hills above the great St. Lawrence River was ideal for painters, and Alice Acheson and I frequently went sketching. She and two other friends, Maude and Patrick Morgan, were accomplished artists from whose criticism I benefited greatly, especially in the use of water colors—a medium I found much more difficult than oils. It was a peaceful and happy holiday, during which I almost forgot my growing concern over the ominous developments in Europe.

A chance encounter with Ohio's Senator Robert A. Taft shook me out of this holiday mood. The senator and his family were regular summer residents of Murray Bay. Although politically in opposing camps, Taft and Acheson were fellow members of the Yale Corporation and on very friendly terms with each other.

It so happened that Senator Taft took the same river steamer that carried us and our station wagon back to Montreal at the end of our holiday. After dinner, the senator invited me to have a talk, which drifted from a discussion of the New Deal into the general subject of foreign affairs. All through the evening and well into a moonlit night, while we sat on the top deck of the steamer, I tried to convince the senator that Mussolini's conquest of Ethiopia, Hitler's rearming of Germany and his march into the Rhineland, and Franco's rebellion in Spain might well be the beginning of a fascist attempt to conquer all of Europe. Taft considered the Franco rebellion a purely local affair of no importance to the United States, although at this time Italian Blackshirt "volunteers" were fighting for Franco at the gates of Madrid and Hitler was testing his latest weapons in Spain, allegedly having sent "only a few technical groups" to that country.

The senator was not troubled by Hitler's rearming of Germany or his seizure of the Rhineland. "After all," he said, "the Versailles Treaty was unjust, and the Rhineland is a part of Germany." He was a little more concerned over Japan's recent expansion into northern China, but the original rape of Manchuria in 1931 had apparently not greatly disturbed him. Nor was he alarmed by the failure of "collective security" under the League of Nations to arrest aggression in Asia or in Europe.

Vainly, I tried to convince him that our Neutrality Acts of 1935 and 1936 had been a mistake, and that the United States was currently conniving in a disgraceful policy of Anglo-French appeasement. On May 1, 1937, President Roosevelt had exercised the discretionary power given to him under a new neutrality resolution to extend all the previous neutrality provisions (which had hitherto applied only to belligerents) to nations engaged in civil war. In so doing, the President had taken a position which clearly favored the rebellion and thus, as I saw it, furthered the designs of Hitler and Mussolini.

When I characterized this action as morally and pragmatically indefensible, the senator, who hated Roosevelt, came to his defense, saying that the Spanish Government was a communist government and was receiving aid from the Soviet Union. I admitted that the Soviet Union had sent some planes and pilots, but I believed that the government against which Franco had launched his rebellion had not contained a single communist or even a single left-wing socialist cabinet member. This was later corroborated by Claude Bowers, our ambassador to Madrid, in his memoirs, published in 1954.[1]

Late that night when I went to bed, I told my wife that talking to the senator about foreign affairs had been like talking into a London fog. Taft was extremely well-informed about the New Deal and all domestic issues, but his mind seemed to be hermetically sealed against the world outside of the borders of the United States. In that world, he appeared to think that we had no vital interests other than commercial trading rights and no responsibility whatever for the preservation of world peace.

Driving homeward the next day through Vermont, I said to Phyllis that I had been fortunate to have had an interlude in which to enjoy my family and to provide—far better than I realized at the time—for our future security. It was time now to turn my attention once more to world affairs.

CHAPTER XX

Intervention versus Isolation

IF SENATOR TAFT seemed unconcerned about the rapidly deteriorating world situation, President Roosevelt seemed no less so. Immediately after his re-election in 1936, he had gone on a tour of Latin America the major purpose of which, apart from implementing his Good Neighbor policy, appeared to be to extend the spirit of the Neutrality Acts to the hemisphere.

[1] *My Mission to Spain*, Simon & Schuster, 1954, pp. 190–94.

The American people, too, were apathetic. If the British and French saw no threat to themselves, why, indeed, should Americans be alarmed over the actions of Hitler and Mussolini?

Convinced that the second world war had already begun in Spain and would spread from there unless arrested, I was tempted to speak out. But I had only recently learned the hard way not to speculate about Roosevelt's often obscure motivations. Nevertheless, I was deeply troubled. If Britain, France and the United States were not going to block Hitler's conquest of Europe, who would? Stalin? In that case, Europe would fall to communism.

It was not until October 1937 that the President showed a sudden realization of the danger. In his famous "quarantine speech" at Chicago, he recognized that an "epidemic of world lawlessness" was spreading and said that "the peace-loving nations must make a concerted effort in opposition to those violations of treaties" which were creating "a state of international anarchy and instability *from which there is no escape through mere isolation or neutrality.*" (Italics added.)

The "quarantine speech" revived my confidence in the President, but it evoked widespread disapproval in the American press, partly because prevailing sentiment was isolationist, and partly because the speech seemed and, indeed it was, wholly inconsistent with the President's own recent conduct of international affairs. Disappointingly, Roosevelt did not pursue the discussion. He seemed to realize that it would be impossible to gain support for a firm interventionist policy so long as France and Britain continued their appeasement.

Early in 1938, Anthony Eden resigned as Foreign Secretary in protest against Prime Minister Neville Chamberlain's continued appeasement. His stand evoked much sympathy in the United States, but the President remained strangely silent. He did, however, send a significant message to Congress proposing a substantial increase in naval construction and retooling of the aircraft and munitions industries.

While a reluctant Congress was debating the need for a two-ocean navy, the next step toward war was already in the making. On March 11, 1938 Hitler proclaimed the annexation of Austria as German troops marched unopposed into Vienna. And no sooner had he annexed Austria than Hitler began his plan for the "liberation" of the Sudetenland.

Neither Premier Daladier of France nor Chamberlain believed that war was likely, much less that it was inevitable. Even after hearing Hitler rant and rave at Bad Godesberg, Chamberlain clung to the conviction that a peaceful settlement could still be reached, and he was not alone in his belief. On September 26, Roosevelt cabled to President Beneš and to Hitler, urging that peaceful negotiations be continued. When Hitler sent a rude and uncompromising reply, the President appealed to him once again and also cabled Mussolini urging him to mediate. Mussolini had already declared that, in the event of war, he would support Hitler; his "mediation" resulted in the abject acceptance of Hitler's terms at the notorious four-power Munich meeting of September 30.

The "Peace of Munich" did more than hand over the Moravian gateway to Hitler, thus opening his way into the Danubian plain. It destroyed at one stroke the whole system of French alliances, alienating Poland, Yugoslavia, and Rumania, as well as the Soviet Union. Within Germany, Hitler's triumph killed the last serious opposition to his policy of aggressive expansion. The hitherto skeptical German generals and the German people would now follow him blindly.

In the United States there was mingled relief, dismay, and disgust. Sumner Welles, Under Secretary of State, officially hailed the Munich Pact, characterizing the President's intervention as "an historical service to humanity." The President himself asked to be "excused from an opinion." And well he might, I thought. He, who a year before had recommended quarantining the aggressors, now found himself in the unhappy position of having helped to bring about a disgraceful surrender to aggression.

Like others who knew Europe, I felt on September 30, 1938 as if the bottom had dropped out of everything, but most Americans were still far from recognizing the dangers that threatened them. Disgust at Anglo-French appeasement buried under a thin blandket of righteous indignation whatever sense of guilt might have been aroused by their own government's connivance.

If Mr. Roosevelt had really meant what he had said in the "quarantine speech"—if he had really wanted to turn the country away from complacent isolationism—his own actions had now caused a resurgence of that sentiment and thus presented the aggressors with valuable time in which to exploit American indecision.

On January 4, 1939 the President told Congress in blunt language that the state of the world demanded that the nation arm itself for self-defense. He then proceeded to enunciate a new foreign policy—the policy of short-of-war resistance to aggression.

. . . the mere fact that we rightly decline to intervene with arms . . . does not mean that we must act as if there were no aggression at all. Words may be futile, but war is not the only means of commanding a decent respect for the opinions of mankind. There are many methods short of war but stronger and more effective than mere words of bringing home to the aggressor governments the sentiments of our own people.

I was not happy with this policy. To proclaim that "we rightly decline to intervene with arms"—a phrase reminiscent of Woodrow Wilson's "too proud to fight"—implied that the United States would not resort to arms if methods short-of-war should fail to halt aggression. The President was no doubt aware of this but probably feared that, if he went further, a refractory and isolationist Congress might not enact even the most vitally necessary measures of defense.

The isolationist opposition was quick to mobilize against even short-of-war measures of intervention. Herbert Hoover told the country the President's policy would take America into war by meddling in affairs that were none of its business. Viewing the world through a strange pair of lenses, Hoover said: "There are more pressures for peace in Europe today than there are for war."

My own feeling was that the only hope of averting a second world war lay in a much stronger policy. Speaking at the Economic Club of New York on March 22, I attacked the whole current concept of neutrality and advocated an immediate declaration by the United States making unequivocally clear to the aggressors that the United States would consider an attack upon the nations of Western Europe as an attack upon itself.

This proposal—in essence the same as the Atlantic Treaty commitment, which, in different circumstances, the United States was to assume ten years later—drew sharp disagreement from Senator Burton K. Wheeler of Montana, and from John Foster Dulles. In disagreeing with my proposal and denying the necessity for any such action, Mr. Dulles said: "There is no reason to believe that any of the totalitarian states, separately or collectively, would attempt to attack the United States . . . Only hysteria entertains the idea that Germany, Italy or Japan contemplate war upon us."

The full text of the debate was published by the Economic Club and later included in a book[1] in which I described the nationwide isolationist-internationalist debate which lasted from 1939 until Pearl Harbor.

That was in March 1939, and international events moved swiftly after that. On September 1, German tanks rolled into Poland. Two days later, Britain and France declared war, and the Dominions followed suit.

In a radio address, President Roosevelt declared that the war that had broken out endangered peace everywhere. Announcing that a neutrality proclamation was being prepared, he asked for an adjournment of partisanship. Unlike Wilson, who in similar circumstances had asked the people to be "neutral in thought and feeling," Roosevelt said:

This nation will remain a neutral nation, but I cannot ask that every American citizen remain neutral in thought as well. Even a neutral has a right to take account of facts. Even a neutral cannot be asked to close his mind or conscience.

In effect, the President was putting the decision up to the American people. He left no doubt as to his own feeling: he wanted the Allies to win, and he wanted to help them win without involving the United States in war. Whether he believed this was possible remained a matter of conjecture. If he should ever decide, as I thought he would sooner or later have to decide, that only American intervention would save Europe from Nazi conquest, he would face a difficult job in persuading the Congress and the people to enter the conflict; he would, I thought, need a lot of help, and I began to see how that help might be given.

On September 16, Soviet troops crossed Poland's eastern frontier and advanced as far as the old Curzon Line frontier

[1] *Our War and Our Peace*, Farrar & Rinehart, 1941, pp. 45–103.

between Russia and Poland, where they met the advancing German armies. Moscow then declared that the Soviet Union would remain neutral in the Anglo-French war against Germany.

The Soviet action against Poland created a furor of resentment in the United States, but if Stalin had been content with recapturing the Polish Ukraine, anti-Russian sentiment in the United States might have subsided. Stalin, however, was more concerned with protecting Russia against a future German attack than with Western opinion. Anxious to create the largest possible buffer area, he demanded strategic concessions from the Baltic states and Finland. When Finland refused to move back its frontier from where it came within twenty kilometers of Leningrad or to grant Russia a naval base at Hangoe, Soviet troops moved across the border. This was too much for the American people. All through the winter of 1939–40, until Finland's heroic resistance was finally overcome, the American press and the American people were far more concerned with the fate of Finland than with the preliminary skirmishes of the "phony war" on the Western front.

After a nationwide debate over repealing the Neutrality Acts, in which Senator Borah and Charles Lindbergh led the opposition, the President concluded that the most he could hope for would be a repeal of the arms embargo. This he obtained after a month of acrimonious discussion. During the debate the five major isolationist contentions, which were to be heard over and over again in a heated argument that was to divide the nation, emerged:

1. *Our help is not needed.*

    (Former President Herbert Hoover and others claimed that the preponderant sea power of Britain and French land defenses assured an Allied victory without our help.)

2. *It's all over. We couldn't help the Allies even if we wanted to, so let us accept a Hitler victory.*

    (This was Charles Lindbergh's contribution to the isolationist cause—an argument that gained weight with the fall of France.)

3. *War means abandoning democracy. If the United States enters the war it will become a totalitarian state.*

(This was another favorite of Herbert Hoover and of the isolationist America First Committee.)

4. *We are secure behind our oceans.*

(This paralleled the Maginot Line mentality fostered by Nazi propaganda in France. Carrying this argument to its utmost absurdity, Lindbergh attacked Canada for "bringing the war to this hemisphere" and urged the United States to take over Canada from Britain.)

5. *This is just another imperialist war of power politics and does not concern us.*

(This was the reasoning of Senator Borah, of many Socialists, like Norman Thomas, and pacifists such as President Robert M. Hutchins of the University of Chicago.)

Along with many of my friends I joined the nationwide Committee to Defend America by Aiding the Allies, organized by the Kansas newspaper publisher William Allen White to combat the isolationist America First propaganda. A full-page newspaper advertisement—"STOP HITLER NOW!"—drawn up by Robert Sherwood, launched the committee's campaign. (It also for the first time brought Sherwood's talent as a propagandist to President Roosevelt's attention.)

Immediately after the fall of France, President Roosevelt ordered the shipment to Britain of large stocks of weapons left over from World War I. These played a vital part in enabling the British people to prepare against an apparently imminent invasion. The President also asked Congress for over $1 billion additional defense appropriations, appointed a Defense Council to co-ordinate production and called for a mechanized army and 50,000 warplanes. In a somewhat daring move, considering that 1940 was an election year, he appointed two outstanding Republican leaders to his cabinet: Henry L. Stimson as Secretary of War, and my friend Frank Knox as Secretary of the Navy.

Whatever had been Roosevelt's shortcomings in the past, this was the time, I thought, when he deserved the support of every American. On June 19, I walked into Marvin McIntyre's familiar office in the White House, asked for a piece of writing paper, and wrote the following note which I asked McIntyre to hand to the President at a convenient time:

Dear Mr. President—
Everybody in these days wants to help if he can. I came down this morning to see my old commanding officer, Admiral Towers, about an idea some of us have developed which we hope may be useful in hemisphere defense. This took me also to the State Department.

Being that near I could not resist the temptation to come across the street to do something I have long wanted to do, and that is to say to you, "I was wrong and I'm sorry." In a way I tried to say this before the election of 1936. I wanted to write you then but felt that by doing so I would place myself in an even more impossible position than by doing what I did do. This has left me with the undischarged duty of making a personal apology.

I make it now wholeheartedly and trust that you will not consider that the statute of limitations has run.

Respectfully yours,
(s) JAMES P. WARBURG

Two days later came the following reply from a man whom many had described as vindictive:

My dear Jim:
Thank you for that letter of June nineteenth, so generous in tone and so magnanimous in spirit. There is no statute of limitations on good will and I want you to know that I accept wholeheartedly everything you say, and appreciate, more than I can tell you, having you say it as you did.

With every good wish,

Yours sincerely,
(s) FRANKLIN D. ROOSEVELT

When the cross-channel invasion failed to materialize, it became clear that the greatest danger to British survival was that of German submarine warfare against British shipping. At this point, a fortunate turn of the wheel in domestic American politics made possible an action that saved the British people from almost certain starvation.

In spite of the no-third-term tradition, President Roosevelt was certain to be renominated by the Democratic Party. The Republican choice apparently lay between New York's Governor, Thomas E. Dewey, whose views on foreign policy were enigmatic, and Senator Robert A. Taft, by this time the outspoken leader of the isolationists. Much to my surprise and delight, the Republican convention at Philadelphia unexpectedly nominated Wendell Willkie, an outspoken supporter of aid to the Allies.

Foreign policy was now to all intents and purposes taken out of the campaign, but both candidates were careful not to throw away the isolationist vote. Both men promised to keep the United States out of war, but both stressed the belief that American interests were deeply involved in British survival and urged all possible short-of-war assistance.

Although I liked and admired Willkie, I came out publicly in support of the President, feeling that his experience and Willkie's total lack of it offset the third-term issue.

During the campaign, a few of us, some Democrats and some Republicans, met at irregular intervals at the Century Club of New York, to discuss possible ways and means of strengthening the aid-to-Britain program. It was largely because of Willkie's friends in this group that he was persuaded to back a plan being quietly hatched in Washington to exchange fifty American World War I destroyers for ninety-nine-year leases on certain British bases in the Western hemisphere. With his adversary's support, the President was able to override the isolationist opposition in Congress and put through a deal that gave Britain desperately needed help in her anti-submarine campaign while at the same time strengthening the position of the United States against the eventuality that it might have to rely upon hemisphere defense.

Likewise with Willkie's support, the President succeeded—by a margin of one vote—in obtaining the enactment of the Selective Service Bill, the first peacetime conscription in American history. Rarely had an opposition candidate so greatly helped an administration to protect the national interest.

On October 17, 1940, I received a message from General Watson, the President's military aide, that the President wished to see me on the following day.

Roosevelt looked older than when I had last seen him, but he was as cheerful as ever. His only reference to the past was a gently teasing remark, made as I entered his office, about the virtues of repentant sinners. I gathered the impression that, with the election out of the way (the outcome of which he took for granted), he would welcome the maximum of interventionist pressure. He was, I thought, worried chiefly about Britain's financial position. In the actual fighting, the British were doing well. They had beaten off the Luftwaffe, had repulsed an Italian attempt to invade Egypt, and had crippled a part of the Italian fleet by a brilliant torpedo-plane attack at Taranto. However, the strain of home defense, fighting in Africa, and keeping the sea lanes open had, I gathered, all but stripped the British Treasury.

In the first week of November, Roosevelt was overwhelmingly re-elected. A month later, I floated a trial balloon by means of a two-column letter to the New York *Times* which said in substance: the British would not be able to continue for long to buy their vital purchases of food and war material in the United States unless they were given financial assistance; and American failure to provide this assistance would amount to a deliberate decision to permit Britain's defeat, as surely as if our government were to re-establish the arms embargo.

As matters stood, the Neutrality Acts of 1935 and 1936 forbade our making loans or grants to Britain. I urged the repeal of this prohibition. The Neutrality Acts had been designed to keep the United States neutral in future wars. We had ceased to be neutral in spirit or in international law when we adopted and began to carry out our policy of short-of-war aid to Britain.

Recalling the unhappy experience with the war loans of World War I, I urged that the same mistake not be made again; that if there was no way to loan Britain money with any reasonable expectation of repayment, we should make outright contributions to Britain's defense and not risk another misunderstanding and estrangement.

Encouraged by the favorable response to this letter in which I had, without knowing it, anticipated the Lend-Lease proposal, I set to work to go one step further in creating sentiment favorable to our actual participation in the war. With the help of Lew Douglas and Dean Acheson, I drafted an open letter to Congress to which we secured the signatures of over fifty university presidents, religious leaders, lawyers, bankers, publishers, and writers. The letter bluntly stated the conviction that, if short-of-war aid should prove insufficient to assure the defeat of the Axis, the United States must be prepared in its own vital interests to take whatever measures might be necessary, including the use of its Navy to keep the sea lanes open.

Our letter was fully reported and widely commented upon in the press. We felt we had cut through the obfuscation of short-of-war aid and raised the real issue that confronted the country.

On January 6, 1941 the President sent a special message to Congress in which he nailed the Four Freedoms to the masthead of the United States. In so doing, he created the first great American propaganda weapon against the Axis.

"We are committed to the proposition," the President said, "that principles of morality and consideration for our own security will never permit us to acquiesce in a peace dictated by aggressors and sponsored by appeasers. We know that enduring peace cannot be bought at the expense of other peoples' freedom."

Roosevelt's words echoed around the world. Unlike Wilson, Roosevelt was not content with a statement of lofty ideals. His speech was followed by a message demanding the largest peacetime military budget in the history of the nation, the setting up of three separate fleets (Atlantic, Pacific, and Asiatic), and the introduction of the Lend-Lease Bill. This unleashed another furious controversy.

The isolationist opposition comprised a strange mixture of disparate elements: sincere pacifists, who condemned all war on moral grounds; Socialists, who considered war the inevitable consequence of capitalist imperialism; and loyal and unsuspecting Americans who unwittingly parroted arguments for isolationism coined in Moscow or Berlin. The isolationist press included such strange bedfellows as, on the one hand, the ultra-nationalist newspapers of William Randolph Hearst, Colonel Robert McCormick's Chicago *Tribune,* and Colonel Patterson's New York *Daily News* and, on the other, the Communist Party's *Daily Worker.*

I participated actively in the nationwide debate.[2]

The Lend-Lease Act became law on March 11, 1941.

Our Century Club group, augmented by a number of like-minded citizens, decided that the time had come to take a more forthright position than that of the Committee to Defend America by Aiding the Allies. Breaking away from the short-of-war

[2] *Our War and Our Peace.*

formula, we founded the Fight for Freedom Committee, with Ulric Bell, an experienced newspaperman, as its paid executive director, and took our stand for outright intervention.

Herbert Agar and I became the committee's principal spokesmen. At one mass rally in Madison Square Garden, I debated Charles Lindbergh in a discussion carried over a nationwide radio network.

The Fight for Freedom Committee was highly successful in raising funds and attracting members from all over the country by means of a series of newspaper advertisements urging the President to take more drastic anti-Axis action, including, if necessary, the use of the armed forces of the United States. Some members of our committee felt the text of one such advertisement which I had drafted was a little too strong in its language and asked Ulric Bell to check it with the White House. Bell reported that the President had read the text and said: "If you're going to give me hell, why not use some really strong language?" Then, with his cigarette holder at the usual jaunty angle, he had added: "You know, pusillanimous isn't such a bad word!"

On June 16, the *Robin Moor,* an American vessel, was sunk by a German submarine. The President branded this act as that of an "international outlaw." Anti-Nazi feeling reached a new peak. Our committee called for the full use of the American Navy to keep the sea lanes open, even if this should involve "a shooting war." It seemed that any day might see the United States enter the conflict. And then the totally unexpected happened. At dawn, on June 22, the Nazis launched a furious, unheralded assault upon the Soviet Union. Overnight, the whole picture changed.

Winston Churchill lost no time in making his country's position clear. "Any man or state who fights against Nazism," he said, "will have our aid."

President Roosevelt, too, announced that Russia would receive short-of-war aid, subject to the prior needs of Britain, and sent Harry Hopkins off to Moscow.[3] But Hitler's attack on the Soviet Union gave the American isolationists a new lease on life.

Herbert Hoover opined that the turn of events furnished "half

[3] Robert Sherwood, in *Roosevelt and Hopkins,* Chapter 14, tells the story of the Hopkins mission to Moscow and the extraordinarily frank disclosures made by Stalin.

a dozen reasons for the United States to stay out of the European conflict." Senator Burton K. Wheeler declared: "I don't think the American people will stand for us to tie up with the communists." John T. Flynn, another of my familiar antagonists, asked: "Are we going to fight to make Europe safe for communism?" A popular sentiment of the time was "Let the Nazis and communists kill each other off."

The most strident of all the voices clamoring for American belligerency now became that of the communist *Daily Worker*. Turning an overnight somersault, the American communists suddenly discovered that what had been "a capitalist-imperialist war" on June 21 had, on June 22, become a holy crusade for democracy.

On August 14, 1941 at their first wartime meeting—the famous shipboard conference off Argentia—Roosevelt and Churchill signed the Atlantic Charter and created the first great propaganda instrument of the anti-Axis coalition, setting forth for the peoples of the world the first clear alternative to Hitler's New Order in Europe.

The Roosevelt-Churchill declaration laid down the principles of a just peace—a peace without territorial annexation by the victors—a peace that would recognize the equal rights of all the world's peoples to determine their own destiny and their own form of government—a peace in which all nations would for all time abandon the use of force as a means of settling international disputes.

In signing this declaration with the British leader, the President asserted the intention of taking a hand in the shaping of the peace, even though the United States might or might not become a belligerent in the war. Recognizing the futility of a unilateral declaration such as President Wilson's promulgation of his Fourteen Points, Roosevelt entered into a joint commitment with Britain which was later to become a commitment of the entire anti-Axis coalition.

I had a special reason for welcoming this declaration, for, by the time it was issued, I was already working for a new agency of the United States Government, whose task it would be to counter the propaganda of the Nazi-Fascist powers, to win the allegiance of the uncommitted nations, to stimulate resistance

on the part of the peoples under Nazi occupation, and to undermine enemy morale. In the first week of August 1941, I had
been appointed a special assistant to Colonel William J. Donovan, the newly appointed Coordinator of Information.

CHAPTER XXI

Information, Propaganda, and Political Warfare

ALTHOUGH the United States was still neutral, it was already apparent during the summer of 1941 that short-of-war aid to the
nations fighting Axis aggression would have to be psychological
as well as material. Hitler's triumphs had not been achieved
solely by military means; his victims had in every case been
softened up by extremely skillful propaganda aimed at spreading fear, dissension, confusion, and the distrust of peoples for
their governments. Since much of Nazi propaganda consisted of
widely disseminated and widely believed lies, the need for
counteraction was obvious.

However, the mere idea of establishing an American propaganda agency would have incurred the wrath of the isolationists
and jeopardized the short-of-war aid program. Hence, a curious
device was employed. The Office of the Coordinator of Information was set up ostensibly only to collect and evaluate intelligence
from all over the world. But, with the President's consent, Colonel Donovan construed his mandate to cover the dissemination
of information abroad, claiming that to obtain information his
agency would have to give something in return. Without the
word "propaganda" ever being mentioned, the United States acquired a propaganda agency.

Colonel Donovan separated his new setup into three major
divisions: The Secret Operations division and the Research and

Analysis establishment were housed in Washington; the Foreign Information Service was located in New York. Bob Sherwood had by this time become an intimate friend of Harry Hopkins and an occasional collaborator with Judge Samuel Rosenman on presidential speeches. At the President's request he was appointed by Donovan to head the Foreign Information Service. I was assigned to work on the formulation of political warfare plans and on the assembling of a foreign-language staff for the Foreign Information Service in New York.

On the planning staff in Washington my associates were Douglas Miller (who had written *You Can't Do Business with Hitler*); Edmond Taylor (author of *The Strategy of Terror*); Wallace Deuel; and Percy Winner. My one or two nights a week in Washington were rendered pleasant and interesting by the fact that Dean Acheson had become Assistant Secretary of State and had extended me a standing invitation to stay at his Georgetown home. In New York, I shared with Joseph Barnes, until then foreign editor of the New York *Herald Tribune,* the responsibility for staffing the Foreign Information Service. Later, we were joined in assembling an extraordinary array of talent by Edd Johnson, an original and extremely talented editor; John Houseman, a well-known theater and film director, and Louis Cowan, creator of "Quiz Kids."

Sherwood and Donovan did not get along well together. Donovan, accustomed to command, was quick, extremely energetic and ambitious. Sherwood, a playwright completely inexperienced in working with, under, or over other people, was slow, unpunctual, and moody. In addition, Sherwood resented any authority other than that of the President and was morbidly jealous of any intrusion upon his White House relationship. The incompatibility of these two men became apparent even before Pearl Harbor precipitated the United States into war.

The Japanese attack and the German declaration of war untied the President's hands, ending the years of debate over American intervention. Most of the former America Firsters now became fire-eating Asia Firsters, demanding revenge upon Japan; but the President wisely decided that priority must be given to the defeat of the Axis in Europe.

As the first American troops gathered in Britain and Northern Ireland, decks were cleared for action in the field of political

warfare. A new executive order abolished the Office of the Coordinator and created two new agencies—the Office of Strategic
Services (OSS) and the Office of War Information (OWI).

Donovan was put in charge of OSS, with responsibility for the
collection and evaluation of secret intelligence and for the conduct of secret operations against the enemy. Elmer Davis, hitherto known only as a talented broadcaster, was appointed Director of OWI, with Milton Eisenhower as Associate Director.

Under Davis were two wholly separate organizations. The
Domestic Branch, with Gardner Cowles as its first Director and
Archibald MacLeish as Associate, was charged with keeping the
American people informed as to the conduct of the war. It was
located in Washington. The Overseas Branch, with Sherwood at
its head, took over the Foreign Information Service and became
the political warfare agency of the United States with offices in
Washington, New York, San Francisco, and London. Barnes became Sherwood's deputy in New York. I was put in charge of
propaganda policy in the European Theater. This interesting
assignment necessitated my commuting between Washington,
New York and London.

The avowed purpose of the OSS–OWI plan was:

1. To combine all the informational activities of the government
in one agency;
2. To separate information activities from secret operations and
to keep the former under civilian control.

Neither of these purposes was fully accomplished, partly because the plan was the result of compromising several major
disputes among the White House, the State Department, the
Joint Chiefs of Staff, and Colonel Donovan; and partly because
the drafters of the plan either did not recognize the distinction
between informational activity and political warfare, or else
shied away for domestic political reasons from drawing such a
distinction.

The Executive Order created a Policy Board on which the
Secretaries of State, War, and Navy as well as the Joint Chiefs
of Staff were to be represented. As Chairman of the Policy
Board, the Director of OWI was made directly responsible to the
President. This was intended to give him a position of cabinet
rank. Unfortunately, Elmer Davis lacked any experience what-

ever in political, bureaucratic, and administrative affairs. He viewed his assignment as primarily a domestic publicity job, failing to understand, when he was first appointed, that he had been entrusted with the management of a political warfare agency of vital importance to the war effort. Instead of inviting top men from the departments to serve on the Policy Board, Davis chose to invite the public relations officers of the armed services and the press officer of the State Department. By this fatal error, he deprived the new political warfare agency of a voice in the shaping of over-all foreign policy.

The first of many unhappy consequences was the adoption of the "unconditional surrender" policy—a slogan that would almost certainly never have been adopted if those in charge of political warfare against Germany had had an opportunity to point out how such a policy would play directly into the hands of Dr. Goebbels. (I later made an unsuccessful effort to induce the President to modify the policy, which throughout the war served only to stiffen German resistance.)

The other major handicap under which we labored from the start was that those who drafted the Executive Order failed to recognize that informational functions directed to the people of the United States and its allies were essentially public; whereas political warfare operations designed to sustain resistance in enemy-occupied countries or to break down enemy morale must by nature be secret.

Strictly informational activities, performed in the full light of day, were properly subject to congressional approval and appropriation, but political warfare activities, if they were to be effective, had to be immune to congressional debate or public discussion; they needed to be financed by secret funds, as were the operations of the Office of Strategic Services. The Office of War Information before long got into serious and unnecessary budget difficulties with the Congress.

Because I am still bound by the British Official Secrets Act, there is not very much I can tell about my experience in the combined Anglo-American operations. It was a chapter in my life that left unforgettable memories of people and incidents and a legacy of new friendships both at home and abroad.

My first wartime trip to England was taken together with Archibald MacLeish, a delightful traveling companion. Neither of us had previously flown across the ocean. Our eighteen-hour flight in a little Sikorski flying boat was uneventful, landing us at dawn on the Irish coast, near the mouth of the Shannon River. Here we learned that the plane that was to take us on to London had been delayed and would not leave Shannon Airport until late afternoon. Looking at a map to see how far it was from Foynes to Shannon, MacLeish discovered that the town of Limerick was only a short distance away and immediately suggested a visit to its library to see what "limericks" it contained. We hired a "jaunting car," and drove to Limerick. To our amazement, the librarian, a jovial, portly gentleman, had never heard of the type of verse known as a limerick. He was, however, greatly pleased to meet the former Librarian of Congress. (It turned out that limericks derive their name not from the town but from a certain Lord Limerick, a onetime resident of London, who is said to have invented the verse form.) Having regaled the librarian with a number of choice bawdy examples, we were asked to compose a limerick then and there and to inscribe it in the librarian's guest book. The following epic was the result of alternate lines by Archie and myself:

> There was a young lady from Foynes
> Who collected all manner of coins.
> The six-penny paces
> She earned by her graces,
> The shillings she won with her loins.

My assignment in London was, first, to work out a separation of OWI from OSS functions in the London office of the now extinct Coordinator of Information, and, second, to lay the foundations for Anglo-American joint planning of political warfare. The second assignment led to my participation in the secret planning of the North African invasion.

I was thrilled to see the familiar London landmarks. At first glance, there seemed to be less damage than I had expected. Here and there were gaping holes filled with rubbish, where houses had stood. The paint was peeling off many buildings. Emergency reservoirs occupied the grassy areas in many squares. I had yet to see those parts of the city which had suffered most. I noted that signs indicating bomb shelters were less prominent than in New York.

Ambassador Gilbert Winant's secretary had been able to obtain two rooms on the top floor of Claridge's—apparently because top-floor rooms were not popular, even though German raids had become sporadic and were no longer undertaken in great force. The Claridge staff welcomed me as an old friend.

MacLeish stayed only a little over a week. During that time, he and I called upon most of the top British officials with whom my work would bring me into contact. First, however, we called upon Ambassador Winant and Major General Dwight D. Eisenhower, the newly arrived American commander to whom we had a note of introduction from his brother Milton. As I think back to this first meeting with the general, two things stand out in my recollection—my first exposure to the captivating Eisenhower grin and a strong aroma of soap and leather.

The general was quick to grasp the importance of political warfare and evinced a particularly keen interest in the potentialities of front-line propaganda directed against the morale of enemy troops. At his request, I conducted a number of seminars with the officers of his staff.

Ambassador Winant, whose stanch support had endeared him to the British, was a man of strangely assorted qualities. He looked a little like Abraham Lincoln but lacked Lincoln's sense of humor and easy accessibility. A man of exceptionally broad vision in world affairs, he was inclined to jealous suspicion of both his superiors and subordinates. He resented Roosevelt's direct communication with Churchill, although he greatly admired both men. He resented even more the fact that, as chief of OWI's London office, I was involved in top-secret planning about which I was not always permitted to inform the ambassador, even though I was technically serving under him. Fortunately, my rather difficult position was well understood by the ambassador's two able assistants, Freeman ("Doc") Mathews and Jacob Beam.

The two British agencies with which we were to work in close co-operation were the Ministry of Information and the Political Warfare Executive. Brendan Bracken, the Minister of Information, had charge of the information services to the British public and to Allied and neutral countries. The Political Warfare Executive came under the Foreign Office and dealt with overt and secret propaganda to enemy and enemy-occupied countries.

The Foreign Secretary, Anthony Eden, reminded me superficially of Dean Acheson, and, like Acheson, considered foreign policy an esoteric matter for experts to handle—a matter with which the ordinary citizen should not too much concern himself. Sir Robert Bruce Lockhart, an imaginative veteran of the British Secret Services and a writer of considerable renown, was the active head of the Political Warfare Executive. General Dallas Brooks of the Royal Marines represented the service chiefs. I liked and admired both.

The chief planner of political warfare operations, who became my closest working associate, was Ritchie Calder, a brilliant writer on political and scientific affairs. Under him was a staff of regional experts, some civilian and some military. Richard H. S. Crossman, a member of Parliament, headed the German section. Clandestine ("black") propaganda was conducted in a secret hideout by a special group managed by Sefton Delmer, a German-born British citizen who had formerly worked for the Beaverbrook press. In his book, *Black Boomerang*, published in 1962 by Viking, Delmer has given an account of his operations, surprisingly detailed in view of the Official Secrets Act.

The Ministry of Information and the Foreign Office worked closely together, but the British had drawn a sharp line between open informational activities and secret political warfare. The fact that no such line had been drawn in our organization considerably complicated my job of co-ordinating Anglo-American efforts. In one capacity, I had to be available to the press; in the other, I was not permitted to disclose my activities to my own staff, much less to the public.

The job of separating the Office of War Information and the Office of Strategic Services personnel, files, and appurtenances might have been a delicate task, in view of the jealous rivalry between the two organizations in Washington, but, fortunately, I found two old friends in charge of OSS in London. William Phillips, Under Secretary of State in the early New Deal days, was Donovan's chief London representative, and David K. Bruce, my onetime friendly rival in Baltimore, was his assistant. No two men could have been less influenced by jurisdictional rivalries at home.

In July 1942, General Marshall, Admiral King, and General Arnold, the American Chiefs of Staff, came to London for the

Anglo-American conference that was to decide whether to invade North Africa, or to attempt a cross-Channel invasion of France. Steve Early and Harry Hopkins accompanied them. A very small number of us were informed in strictest confidence of the decision to invade North Africa in November.

There followed a fascinating period of joint planning for the deception of the enemy, and for the maximum psychological exploitation of the African venture. I learned later that one of our deception plans had actually led the Germans to expect an invasion of Norway.

During these months I developed a system whereby Calder and I drew up each week a Central Political Warfare Directive that, after being approved by the Political Warfare Executive, was cabled to Washington for approval or suggested amendment. The various regional sections in Britain and the United States—e.g., the German, French, or Scandinavian sections—would then each draw up a regional guidance for the implementation of the major themes set out in the Central Directive. This method of operation remained in effect throughout the war.

I was both amused and impressed by the thoroughness with which the British Secret Service checked up on those entrusted with top-secret information. One day, coming out of Norfolk House, I was greeted by a high-ranking British officer whom I had met only once and who somewhat to my surprise invited me to lunch at the Guards Club. During the conversation my host several times referred casually to "Torch"—the code name for the North African invasion. Not knowing whether my British friend was one of the initiated or merely on a fishing expedition, I played dumb, half suspecting this was a trap. And so it was. A former stock broker, whom I happened to know, was in charge of this sort of thing in British counter-intelligence. The next time I saw him, I told him about my experience and asked: "How long do you people go on testing those of us in whom you have decided to place confidence?"

"Oh, my dear chap," was the reply, "it's not just you Americans; we go on doing this sort of thing to our own chaps all the time."

Admiral Stark, under whom I had served in World War I, was one of the scapegoats for the Pearl Harbor disaster and had been exiled to London as Commander of the United States Fleet in European Waters. His "fleet" consisted of one old four-piper destroyer anchored in the Thames. Perhaps out of sympathy, or more likely to rid themselves of a burdensome task, the British had assigned to the American admiral the job of maintaining liaison with Charles de Gaulle, the temperamental leader of the Free French. Somewhat to everyone's surprise, this move turned out to be highly successful. One day when I was invited to lunch with the admiral, I asked him how he managed to get along so well with a man whom everyone else seemed to find extremely difficult.

"That's simple," said Stark. "The British hate nothing more than a scene. De Gaulle gets his way with them by kicking and screaming until the British give in to him. Now, when I go to see Big Charlie, I start yelling and screaming first. That's all there is to it."

The spirit shown by the British people during their ordeal was something at which I never ceased to marvel. They had lived with danger so long that they seemed to have lost all fear of death. One evening I was at a meeting in one of the private dining rooms of the Savoy Hotel with three high-ranking British officers closely associated with political warfare, when a bomb exploded just outside on the Embankment. The windows were shattered, and plaster fell from the ceiling. At the sound of the explosion, I and another American who had recently arrived in England dove under the table. When we crawled out, shaking the plaster out of our hair, there sat the three Britishers, each holding his highball from which not a drop had been spilled. "Hah," remarked one of them, "no damn discipline, you Americans!"

Civilians were as sturdy as the military. One morning, my English secretary came in a little late and looking so pale that I asked her if she was ill. "Oh, no," she said. "I'm frightfully sorry I was late." Half an hour later, she seemed about to faint while taking dictation. When I insisted she tell me what was the matter, she said that she and her mother had been buried for six hours in the ruins of their house after a bomb had demolished it during the night. "That's why I was late," she said, "but I'm really quite all right now." If I had not asked her, I would never have heard of what she referred to as "the incident." Such things were simply taken for granted.

Another "incident" never to be forgotten: The scene: A blacked-out street in Bristol; two buses proceeding slowly, the first full of evacuated children, the second an ordinary bus making its regular run. Suddenly, the sirens scream and almost immediately the busful of children is enveloped in a blinding flash. In the following bus, windows are shattered and people shaken up, some of them badly wounded. In the uncanny silence following the explosion, a child is heard to whimper and out of the dark comes the voice of its mother. "Hush, darling. Don't cry. You'll frighten the other people."

After a certain length of time one gets so one sleeps through sirens, gunfire, and even bombs if they are not too close. Being on the top floor of Claridge's, I asked Bennie, the roof-watcher, to stamp loudly overhead if anything happened that he thought worth seeing. One night I was awakened by Bennie's loud stamping and climbed up on the roof. There, sailing along majestically at a height of not over five thousand feet and coned in the London searchlights, were four German planes with every gun in London blasting away at them and coming nowhere near scoring a hit. It was an amazing display of fireworks. Bennie's comment: "I just wanted yer to see 'ow we wyste the taxpyer's money."

(This was the night on which the Germans first dropped sheets of tinfoil to throw off the radar-directed anti-aircraft fire.)

My favorite Churchill story of this time was told me by a friend. The Prime Minister was working late one night during the blitz, when a messenger came into his study in order to urge him to go to the shelter.

"Shelter? What for?" growled Churchill.

"Well, sir, there's been a rather nasty incident quite near by. Lord Baldwin's house has been completely destroyed."

"Baldwin's house, did you say?" rumbled Churchill. "What base ingratitude!"

(Stanley Baldwin, later elevated to the peerage, had been Prime Minister when the appeasement policy had been inaugurated.)

I saw Churchill only once during the war and then briefly on an occasion that provided no opportunity for recalling the evening spent with him in 1933. I did, however, receive a surprising message from him, saying that he wanted me to know how much he had liked my recently published volume of verse. The book, a slender paperback, entitled *Man's Enemy and Man*,[1] had contained the following two sonnets. I had no idea they would ever come to Churchill's attention:

In Winston Churchill breathes the British race.
Unquestioning faith—the sort of dogged grit
That fights the hardest when the hardest hit—
Yet, with it all, a gentle charm and grace,
A sense of timeliness and place,
A love of beauty and a subtle wit—
These things shine from his eyes and they are writ
Upon the rugged features of his face.
Did ever man assume his world's arrears
With finer calm, without a word of blame
For those whose blunders and decadent fears
Had compromised and almost lost the game?
Will any words ring longer down the years
Than his: "I bring you blood and sweat and tears?"

This was the man who, when hope all but died
When visions vanished and man's faith was blurred
Stood at the shore and shook his fist and stirred
The embers of an ancient people's pride.
This was the man who raised his voice and cried
Defiant courage—spoke the simple word
That kindled faith wherever it was heard—
This was the man who lifted up men's eyes,
Roused up their will to fight and to endure,
Made them believe their victory was sure,
Led them to triumph in the British skies,
Steadied and rallied them and earned their trust
While bombs were blasting British homes to dust.

Two weeks before the date set for the invasion of North Africa, General Eisenhower sent me to Washington in connection with certain preparations that had to be made in the United States. The car which was to take me to the airport was late. The general had given me my instructions, so that there was a mo-

[1] Farrar and Rinehart, 1942.

ment to chat about other matters than the business in hand. I took this opportunity to ask General Eisenhower his views on domestic politics. His reply was one I would frequently recall in later years.

"I have never voted," General Eisenhower said. "My oldest brother is a Republican and works at it. Milton, as you know, is a New Dealer. I like President Roosevelt, but I guess you couldn't call me either a Democrat or a Republican."

As the North African invasion proceeded, two developments worried those of us who were responsible for political warfare.

The first was the "unconditional surrender" declaration made at Casablanca that I have already mentioned. The second was General Eisenhower's deal with the notorious Admiral Darlan to end the unexpected resistance of the French armed forces in North Africa. Necessary though this deal may have been from the strictly military point of view, it could not be reconciled with the political principles for which the anti-Axis coalition claimed to be fighting.

The tendency to subordinate political considerations to military expediency became more and more marked as our forces moved first into Sicily and then up the Italian boot. What most of all concerned us was the absence of clearly stated political aims with respect to the post-surrender treatment of enemy countries, the future of enemy-occupied countries such as France and Poland, or the shape in general of the postwar world. This made effective psychological warfare directed at civilian populations (as opposed to tactical propaganda directed at enemy forces in the field) extremely difficult. Moreover, the Allied default was permitting the communists to identify themselves with revolutionary sentiment throughout Europe, to assume a position of leadership in the resistance movements, and to make Britain and the United States appear to be seeking little more than a restoration of the *status quo ante bellum.*

These difficulties came to a head in a dangerous way when Benito Mussolini resigned and Marshal Badoglio took over command under the Italian King. The strange confusion that occurred in American propaganda and raised a teapot tempest in the press has never, so far as I know, been fully explained.

The news of Mussolini's resignation came over the radio on

Sunday evening, July 25, 1943. Elmer Davis was in Algiers. Robert Sherwood was in Washington. The President was at "Shangri-la." At the State Department there was only a duty officer. I was in New York and took personal charge of our broadcasts that night.

Two days later, the New York *Times* carried a sensational front-page story by Arthur Krock, revealing with horror that the Office of War Information had called the Italian King "a little moron" and Badoglio a "high-ranking Fascist." The story also called shocked attention to an OWI commentary by "John Durfee, an imaginary commentator."

Krock reported that President Roosevelt had denounced the OWI broadcast at his press conference. By inference, according to Krock in another front-page story on July 28, the President repudiated OWI's comment to the effect that the essential nature of the Italian Fascist regime had not been changed by Mussolini's resignation. Worse yet, Krock made the President's rebuke appear to imply that the New York office of OWI was "flouting the government's policy and following a policy consistent with the ideologies of its own staff, which served the interests of the communists and endangered the lives of American soldiers."

Following Krock's lead, front-page stories and editorials blossomed across the country, giving the public the impression that the New York office of OWI had run away with the whole business of foreign propaganda and was acting in contravention of United States policy and in defiance of superior authority.

The New York *World-Telegram* of July 29 carried a photograph, spread three columns wide across its front page, showing OWI's fictitious commentator, "John Durfee," at his typewriter —hat, coat, gloves but no visible flesh supporting them. Thomas Stokes, in his usually sensible column, wondered why, in a nation of a hundred and thirty million people, OWI had to make up a man to speak for America. The accompanying editorial said "the whole thing smells of dishonesty," and demanded that OWI Overseas be turned over to the State Department "which seems to know a little more about American foreign policy than the Office of War Information."

To make matters still more difficult, the President had specifically exempted Sherwood from his rebuke, stating that Sherwood had not authorized the July 25 broadcast and was "raising hell." This was not true, but for reasons known only to himself, Sherwood neither corrected the President's misapprehension as to his own responsibility nor made it clear that the New York office had strictly followed directives. The fact that such was the case was later clearly established by the representatives of the Joint Chiefs of Staff on our Planning Board and by Secretary of State Hull.

Our current Italian regional directive, approved by the Planning Board, had specifically stated that fascist leadership included not only Mussolini and his political and military accomplices but the House of Savoy, which had originally betrayed Italy to fascism. In response to a query from me to General Eisenhower on the eve of the invasion of Italy, we had been told "not to spare the House of Savoy for its support of fascism." On July 25, I, therefore, had issued a guidance to the operations personnel instructing them to treat the resignation of Mussolini without undue jubilation, to emphasize that Badoglio's first words upon assuming command under the fascist King had been a promise to keep Italy fighting for the Nazi-Fascist cause, and to make clear that the war against the fascist Italian regime would continue irrespective of the palace revolution. When Sherwood was located in Washington, this guidance had been telephoned to him and had received his approval.

Meanwhile, the monitoring of London's broadcast showed that the British were departing from the agreed line, exulting over the event, and asserting that, with Mussolini gone, now only one enemy—Hitler—remained.

I sent a code cable to our London office late that night, alerting Wallace Carroll to the discrepancy. In addition, I authorized our operations personnel to broadcast, *in English only,* and beamed to Britain, part of a column by Samuel Grafton in the New York *Post* which came very close to carrying out the tougher line called for by our Anglo-American directive. I did this in the hope that the British Broadcasting Corporation (BBC) would monitor our broadcasts and change its line. It was Grafton's column that had referred to King Victor Emmanuel as "the moronic little king."

Our action on July 25 had been strictly in accord with our directives, but what had happened was this:

Unbeknownst to OWI and even, as it turned out, to the Secretary of State, the President had changed his mind as to the treatment to be accorded to the King of Italy, inclining for the time being to the softer line taken by the British. (A day later, Roosevelt reversed himself and declared in a broadcast: "We will have no truck with fascism. We will permit no vestige of fascism to remain.")

Lack of organization at the top level was responsible for the failure to communicate a change of policy. As Wallace Carroll was later to write, "It was a curious fact that the President who established the Office of War Information never knew what it was doing. In his own right Roosevelt was a great propagandist but he did not understand the systematic use of propaganda in total war."[2]

Failure to understand the nature of political warfare was responsible for permitting newspapers to monitor and publish OWI's foreign transmissions, which carried out the secret political warfare directives, thereby committing a serious breach of security.

The same thing was true of the revelation of our use of fictitious commentators. Fortunately, only one such fictitious character was mentioned by name and thereby destroyed. The fact was both we and the British used fictitious by-line commentators to implement our political directives and the Chiefs of Staff directives for treating events on the various battlefronts.

I was "John Durfee." As such, it was my function to implement the State Department's political directives. Under the assumed by-line of "Wallace Herrick," supposedly a well-known military analyst, I had also for months been writing a weekly military analysis broadcast in twenty-one languages and transmitted by teletype to friendly and neutral countries where it was carried by over two hundred newspapers. Frequently, these "Herrick" commentaries were deliberately slanted to raise false hopes in enemy countries or to minimize enemy successes. The practice had been fully authorized. The Planning Board had regularly reviewed copies of the scripts.

[2] *Persuade or Perish*, Houghton Mifflin 1948.

These were the facts. Had proper precautions been taken, as they were taken in England, there would have been no rebuke by the President, no sensational "disclosures" and no wholly false allegations. But proper precautions had not been taken, and, because Sherwood declined to ask the President to set the matter right, the true story was never told. The country was left believing the false allegations. Public confidence in the Overseas Branch of the Office of War Information was shaken, and its usefulness to the military was gravely impaired.

All this silly nonsense happened at a time when all our energies should have been concentrated upon planning and coordinating with the British the greatest possible psychological warfare support for the forthcoming Normandy invasion. I had been in London again during September and October 1943, working on cross-channel invasion plans with the British. While there, I had spent an evening with Averell Harriman, who was on his way to assume the important position of United States Ambassador to Moscow. He seemed to me the ideal man for the post. He already had behind him a distinguished career as the President's trouble-shooter and had come a long way since the days when I had first induced Moley to bring him to Washington early in 1933. I hoped that he would be able to bring about at least some co-ordination of Soviet and Anglo-American propaganda to Germany.

Sherwood had intended to have me shuttle back and forth between London and Washington during the pre-invasion winter of 1943–44. Now, because of an increasingly acrid jurisdictional squabble between Sherwood and Davis, this plan was abandoned, and our Anglo-American planning operations came to a standstill.

In January 1944, Davis and Sherwood finally took their ridiculous quarrel to the President, each demanding the ouster of the other. Roosevelt, angered by this childish behavior, refused to let either man go and ordered them to settle their differences at once. Davis turned in desperation to Edward Klauber, his former superior at the Columbia Broadcasting Company, and, from him, received the shrewd but unprincipled advice that the way to ruin Sherwood would be somehow to get rid of the three deputies upon whom he depended. When Davis, acting on this advice, proceeded to demand the resignations of Barnes, Johnson, and myself, Sherwood caved in, acquiescing in the resignation of his three deputies and his own exile from Washington.

Had we refused to hand in our resignations, the trumped-up charges brought against us by Davis could easily have been disproved before a court of inquiry. But, once Sherwood had thrown in the sponge, it seemed to us best not to protract the unseemly row and to go quietly. It was no easy task for the three of us to prevent mass resignations from the outraged staff of the Overseas Branch.

In transmitting my requested resignation to Davis, I wrote to him, denouncing his charges as wholly false and adding the assertion that he knew they were false—an allegation Davis had the grace not to deny. Sherwood's peculiar behavior was to us inexplicable. It remains my sole experience of being let down by a friend.

The following exchange of letters with the President wrote finis to the chapter, so far as I was concerned.

February 10, 1944

Dear Mr. President,

It has been a great privilege to serve the country and the Administration in the post which I have been permitted to occupy for the past two and one-half years. I cannot leave this post without thanking you for the confidence you have reposed in me.

Naturally, I am saddened by the fact that the three of us, who had worked with Bob Sherwood from the earliest beginning, have now become casualties in a regrettable and unseemly squabble, and thus are unable to carry our job through to its conclusion. However, when our resignations were demanded, it seemed to us that in the circumstances the only useful thing we could do was to go quickly and quietly.

In a time like the present no one likes to sit on the sidelines, and light casualties frequently do return to battle. I hope I may be one of those who do, and that you will take for granted my willingness to serve wherever and however I can.

Respectfully yours,
(s) JAMES P. WARBURG

THE WHITE HOUSE
WASHINGTON

February 15, 1944

Dear Jimmy:

I want you to know how deeply I appreciate the fine spirit which prompts your letter of February tenth. Many thanks. I, too, regret your withdrawal from the public service.

Bob has told me of the high quality of your work, and I know he too regrets the circumstances which impel you to the decision to leave. I am glad to have your assurance that I can take for granted your willingness to serve wherever and however you can.

Always sincerely,
(s) FRANKLIN D. ROOSEVELT

Despite its shabby ending, the experience of two and a half years in political warfare had been most rewarding. I had never worked with a more talented or devoted group of men and women than those who staffed the Overseas Branch of the Office of War Information. Many of them, well-established writers, editors, and artists, served at considerable personal sacrifice. Many were exposed to physical danger. All were handicapped and often harassed by organizational defects, poor leadership, the absence of clearly defined war aims and the lack of an unambiguous pro-democratic policy.

I felt much the same admiration and affection for many of the Europeans with whom I worked. These included, besides my British colleagues, members of the French resistance and officials of the governments-in-exile. Among the latter, I was particularly fond of Jan Masaryk, the Czechoslovak Foreign Minister. Our friendship had begun when, on one of my wartime Atlantic crossings, I had had the good fortune to be fogged in at Iceland in the utterly delightful company of Masaryk and John Steinbeck. Rarely have I spent two more pleasant days.

Leaving the government service, I felt strongly that the one great defect of President Roosevelt's otherwise superb leadership since Pearl Harbor had been his refusal to discuss the shape of the postwar world and his consequent failure to establish common aims for the anti-Axis coalition at a time when common danger might still have made it possible to agree on a plan for the future.

With the probable date of the Normandy invasion set for June, there were still no firm plans for the post-surrender treatment of Germany at the time when I resigned from OWI. The War Department, the State Department, and the Treasury were in disagreement. Treasury Secretary Morgenthau was urging a more Draconian peace than either Secretaries Stimson or Hull thought desirable. John J. McCloy, the Assistant Secretary of War, was assigned the task of weighing and reconciling the conflicting points of view.

Aware of my familiarity with Germany both before and during the war, McCloy summoned me to his office and asked me to express my views as to what should be the nature and purpose of an Allied occupation.

It was agreed that the victorious powers should pursue four aims: To render Germany incapable of renewed aggression; to free and repatriate war prisoners and forced laborers; to set up machinery for the restoration of looted property, for the payment of reparations and the control of foreign trade; and to impress upon the German people the enormity of their crimes and the reality of their defeat.

These four purposes could, I thought, be accomplished by *a relatively short occupation*, during which the Allies would do their utmost to help the Germans to rid themselves of the Nazi Party machine. Most of the party leaders, the Storm Troopers, and the Gestapo would come under the heading of war criminals.

I recommended that when the Allies had accomplished these purposes, they should terminate full occupation and withdraw, leaving in Germany control commissions to prevent rearmament or the creation of para-military organizations, to supervise the repatriation of foreign slave laborers and the payment of reparations, and to observe and report upon all social, political and economic developments. The period of probation and observation I recommended would end whenever the Allies were satisfied that a German government with which they could deal in confidence and on terms of full equality had come into existence. Only then would a peace treaty be signed and Germany readmitted to the family of nations.

The principle underlying this proposal for a short occupation was my belief that the Germans must effect their own cure—

that they must not once more be prevented, as they had been in 1918–19, from carrying out their own democratic revolution. The alternative, against which I warned, would be a long occupation based upon the assumption that the German people were incapable of curing themselves and the victorious Allies would have to effect the cure. This would mean a protracted guardianship.

I pointed out that Allied assumption of responsibility for the future of Germany would mean that the United States, Britain, France, and the Soviet Union would have to agree as to what sort of a Germany they wished to create and what means were to be employed to bring about the desired result. Such agreement seemed to me wholly improbable.

Admittedly, the course I advocated would almost certainly entail a certain amount of revolutionary disorder. Since no military government could be expected to tolerate disorder, I urged that military government be withdrawn at the earliest possible moment—i.e., when Germany had been rendered wholly incapable of renewed aggression.

My proposal was rejected by the War Department on the ground that "the government of the United States cannot undertake a policy designed to induce chaos." However, McCloy himself wrote: "I think there is no quarrel with the idea of a short occupation and the more desirable punishment of the criminals by their own people."

Unfortunately, McCloy's was not to be the deciding voice, although it was he who later drafted the compromise directive under which General Eisenhower was to operate.

Thus began a period of years in which I was to be a frequent and outspoken dissenter from government policy, particularly with respect to Germany.

CHAPTER XXII

"Foreign Policy Begins at Home"

GOVERNMENT service during the early New Deal and again during World War II left me profoundly impressed with the close interrelation of foreign and domestic policy. I had seen at first-hand how consideration of domestic politics intruded upon the conduct of foreign relations, sometimes forcing action undesirable in the interests of peace and at other times inhibiting or slowing down action vital to the nation's interest.

Immediately upon leaving the Office of War Information, I began work on a book designed to explore this theme and to develop what seemed to me the domestic prerequisites of a constructive foreign policy. Its eventual title when published by Harcourt, Brace & Company in the autumn of 1944 was *Foreign Policy Begins at Home.*

In this study I set forth my misgivings concerning the then current policies—or the absence of policies—on the part of the anti-Axis Allies. I expressed the unhappy suspicion that the pledges of a just peace originally embodied in the Atlantic Charter and later adopted by the entire anti-Axis coalition were in the process of being tacitly abrogated. This was because, at the Teheran Conference in 1943, President Roosevelt and Prime Minister Churchill had apparently agreed to permit the Soviet Union and Poland to annex a certain amount of east German territory. If true (the Yalta conference was yet to come), this would violate the pledges against territorial aggrandizement and against territorial changes not in accordance with the freely expressed will of the peoples concerned.

The prospects for the fulfillment of the Atlantic Charter's economic pledges seemed to me equally dim. "Equal access for all nations to the world's markets and raw materials" would require a degree of co-operative planning that seemed improbable, so long as "planning" remained a dirty word in the world's most powerful nation.

Perhaps I may be forgiven for one short excerpt.

We are living today in what amounts to a new industrial revolution. The day when industry belonged to the "Atlantic Community" has gone forever. The so-called "backward," raw material producing countries are rapidly becoming industrialized; they want machine tools and producing equipment with which to build up their own industries; they want to make not merely their own consumer goods but their own steel and their own machinery. There is danger that a new form of nationalism may arise from the desire for political independence.

This danger can be met if the Western industrialized nations, particularly the United States and Britain, recognize that the development of the backward countries is not only inevitable but desirable, and if they assist it with both exports of producer's goods and capital, *without attempting to tie political strings to their investments.* (Original emphasis.)

As might be expected, my thoughts now turned to the impending elections of 1944. Willkie and Roosevelt were said to have been discussing a new party alignment that would bring together the progressive elements in both of the old political parties, but Willkie had incurred the enmity of his own party's leadership. After his resounding defeat in the Wisconsin primaries, he withdrew as a candidate for the Republican nomination. This seemed to make it reasonably certain that either Taft or Dewey would be nominated. In either case, Taft's isolationist influence upon the Republican Party would be strong.

In spite of the vacuum in President Roosevelt's postwar-policy planning, I felt that a continuance of his progressive domestic policy was essential. And the very absence of clear agreements as to the postwar shape of the world argued strongly against disturbing the personal relationships he had established with Churchill and Stalin.

Where and how, I wondered, could a citizen best contribute to preventing a period of Republican reaction and isolationism from jeopardizing the peace? It seemed to me that the point of maximum leverage in the 1944 elections might well be the newly

organized Political Action Committee of the Congress of Industrial Organizations (CIO–PAC). In spite of warnings from a
number of my friends who erroneously considered this organization to be communist-dominated, I decided to offer my services
to Sidney Hillman, president of the Amalgamated Clothing
Workers Union, who had recently been elected head of the Political Action Committee.

At our first interview, Hillman, somewhat suspicious of "intel-
lectuals," asked me what I thought a banker could do for a
labor organization. Explaining why I considered Roosevelt's re-
election of the utmost importance, I said that I thought I might
be more useful writing campaign material for CIO–PAC than
speaking for F.D.R. in my own name, as I had in 1940. When
Hillman asked whether I would consider ghost-writing speeches
for him, I told him I would be delighted to try my hand at it, but
only on condition that his previous speech writer, John Abt,
would have nothing whatever to do with his speeches during the
campaign. (Abt, an extremely able lawyer, was reputed to be a
follower of the Communist Party line.) Somewhat to my surprise, Hillman nodded his acceptance of the stipulation; he had,
he said, at one time believed it was possible to work with communists in a united front but had, by this time, become disillusioned.

As Hillman's "political warfare adviser"—this was Hillman's
own semi-humorous designation—I was privileged to sit in at
meetings of the top strategy board of the CIO, composed of the
presidents of the major constituent unions. This in itself was a
liberal education for a former banker.

During the campaign, I ground out a series of speeches for
Hillman, gradually becoming more and more familiar with the
mores of the labor movement and with Hillman's own peculiar
idiom. I had to learn that labor audiences reacted best to simple
language and to unqualified declaratory statements in which the
Republican Party was painted in the blackest of colors while the
Democrats and particularly Roosevelt were extolled.

Perhaps the most interesting episode in my work with the
CIO–PAC was the opportunity it afforded me to witness the
backstage maneuvering for the vice-presidential nomination at
the 1944 Democratic convention in Chicago. This was the occasion on which F.D.R. was said to have issued his famous "Clear

it with Sidney" injunction. Whether he ever said this, I do not know.

I do know that most of the CIO leadership wanted Henry Wallace to be renominated. Roosevelt, however, had reached the conclusion that Wallace did not have the qualifications to become a possible successor to the presidency. Failing Wallace, the CIO people would have liked best the man whom Roosevelt himself was said to favor—Supreme Court Justice William O. Douglas. Douglas, however, was anathema to the conservative wing of the Democratic Party, whose favorite candidate was former Senator James F. Byrnes of South Carolina. I witnessed at firsthand how Byrnes's candidacy died at the hands of Hillman and Philip Murray, president of the United Steel Workers, both Wallace supporters. A day later, Hillman returned from breakfast with a man whom he described not very enthusiastically as "the gentleman from Missouri." I gathered that the matter had been settled. The CIO leadership, which had been unwilling to accept Byrnes chiefly because of his segregationist views, was willing to go along with the nomination of Harry Truman. It did not occur to me at the time that I had witnessed the naming of the next President of the United States.

Whether or not it was true, as many people thought after Roosevelt's re-election to a fourth term, that the CIO–PAC had been more effective in bringing out the vote than the regular Democratic Party organization, it was a fact that the Political Action Committee sparked an unprecedented effort on the part of the union membership. More doorbells were rung and more telephone calls made than ever before. In later years, I have wondered why the labor movement never thereafter reached such a point of political effectiveness. Roosevelt's death undoubtedly had much to do with the decline of labor's influence, but there were other reasons as well. The merger of the CIO with the more conservative American Federation of Labor must have had something to do with it. It may also be that union leadership became less militant because it became more collusive in its bargaining with business management. And perhaps the very success of the CIO–PAC in 1944 aroused a stronger resistance to labor-in-politics than had existed before.

I saw the President only once during the campaign of 1944. This was when he made his major speech on international affairs under the auspices of the Foreign Policy Association in New York. He had been campaigning all day in the rain and looked ruddy, though slightly drawn. He showed me a passage in the speech he was going to make in which he referred to the post-surrender treatment of the Germans—a passage he thought would greatly please me since it was designed to draw the fangs of the "unconditional surrender" policy.

Unfortunately, I knew that in the previous month at the Quebec conference, the President had initialed the punitive Morgenthau Plan for making Germany into a goat pasture. More-over, by this time, the landings in Normandy had taken place, Paris had been liberated, and the Allied armies were driving to-ward the Rhine. It was probably too late to prevent last-ditch Nazi resistance. Nevertheless, the passage was noteworthy, if only to show what its impact might have been, had Roosevelt spoken earlier in this vein.

Here are his exact words:

As for Germany, that tragic nation which has sown the wind and is now reaping the whirlwind—we and our Allies are entirely agreed that we shall not bargain with the Nazi conspirators, or leave them a shred of control—open or secret—of the instruments of government.

We shall not leave them a single element of military power—or of potential military power.

But I should be false to the very foundations of my religious and political convictions, if I should ever relinquish the hope—and even the faith—that in all people, without exception, there lives some instinct for truth, some attraction toward justice, and some passion for peace—buried as they may be in the German case under a brutal regime.

We bring no charge against the German race as such, for, as such, we cannot believe that God has eternally condemned any race of humanity. For we know in our own land how many good men and women of German ancestry have proven loyal, freedom-loving, peace-loving citizens.

There is going to be stern punishment for all those in Germany directly responsible for this agony of mankind.

The German people are not going to be enslaved—because the United Nations do not traffic in human slavery. But it will be neces-sary for them to earn their way back into the fellowship of peace-loving and law-abiding nations. And, in their climb up that steep road, we shall certainly see that they are not encumbered by having to carry guns. They will be relieved of that burden—we hope, forever.

What a propaganda weapon this speech would have been in 1942, or even in 1943!

The occasion of his speech in New York was the last time I saw Roosevelt. After his election to a fourth term, I sent him a copy of *Foreign Policy Begins at Home,* and received a note of thanks from him. In February 1945, his military aide and close friend General "Pa" Watson died suddenly. The last letter I received from Roosevelt was written in response to a note of sympathy. A little over a month later, he himself was dead— mourned as no President since Abraham Lincoln had been mourned by a bereaved nation.

An era had ended.

Part Three

Part Three

CHAPTER XXIII

Readjustment and a Venture in the Deep South

DURING the war, I had completely lost touch with the banking world. I had moved my secretaries and my accountant from Wall Street into a small office in my house at Seventieth Street. John Morgan had gone to Idaho to help develop the Sun Valley resort, and John Milholland had married and become a recluse in the Adirondack Mountains. My closest friends on the Union Pacific boards had been Averell Harriman and Bob Lovett; Averell was now in Moscow, and Bob Lovett remained in Washington to perform distinguished services for the Truman Administration.

I decided that the time had come to sever my Wall Street connections and resigned from my various directorships including the boards of the Union Pacific and the Bank of Manhattan, remaining as a director of only the Polaroid Corporation and the Juilliard School of Music.

My oldest daughter, April, had married her Italian singing teacher while I was in England. My daughter Andy had left Barnard College to become engaged. Kay was about to graduate from Sarah Lawrence. It was a strange feeling suddenly to have a home without children.

Phyllis, who loved children, had been unable to have any of her own. For this and other reasons she was not very happy. She had worked with me in the Fight for Freedom Committee and, during the war, had compiled a unique collection of newspaper clippings which she later gave to the Library of International Affairs in Chicago. She had also worked with me in the offices of the CIO–PAC. From my point of view, she was an ideal helpmeet, but the vicarious role of being her husband's assistant and invaluable critic did not satisfy the ambitions of her own strong personality. My being away from home and preoccupied with my work during the war had not helped matters. For the second time in my life, I felt that the happiness of my marriage was slipping away.

In politics as in private life, I felt disconnected and somewhat at a loose end. For more than a decade, I had been in close contact with the top officials in the Roosevelt Administration and with the President himself. With President Truman's sudden accession to power, most of the old familiar faces vanished from the Washington scene. Cordell Hull had retired shortly before Roosevelt's death. Frank Knox had died. Out of Roosevelt's cabinet, only Harold Ickes remained in his old post. Lew Douglas was in London, having been appointed by Roosevelt as ambassador to the Court of St. James's. Marvin McIntyre, Missy Le Hand, Grace Tully, and Steve Early were replaced by a new White House staff. Of all my old friends there remained in Washington only Dean Acheson, who was anxious to return to his law practice; Jim Forrestal, who had succeeded Frank Knox as Secretary of the Navy, and Bob Lovett and Jack McCloy in the War Department.

Marshall Field and I had become fast friends back in the early 1920s, when both of us were working in Wall Street. At that time, Field, fresh from serving overseas in World War I, had formed an investment banking house, Marshall Field, Glore, Ward & Company, which had been irreverently known in "the Street" as "Jesus Christ, Tom, Dick & Harry." Originally, our friendship had been essentially a playtime relationship, based upon mutual congeniality and a common liking for games and sports, but, over the years, we had discovered that we had much in common concerning the more serious sides of life, notably in our views on domestic politics and foreign affairs. Both of us had begun life as conservatives and had grown more progressive as we grew older. We had seen each other through marriage, divorce, and remarriage and maintained a happy relationship. Marshall was, of course, enormously wealthy. He lived like an English duke on his estate at Lloyd's Neck on Long Island, but he had the British aristocrat's sense of *noblesse oblige* and the appealing, fun-loving quality of a child.

Without the slightest inclination to take a personal part in politics, Field had been an ardent supporter of Roosevelt and the New Deal, although he had shared many of my misgivings concerning some of Roosevelt's policies. A loyal Chicagoan at heart, in spite of his English education and life in New York, he had long been distressed that his native city was served chiefly by the violently isolationist and reactionary Chicago *Tribune*. In 1940, he had founded the liberal, Roosevelt-supporting Chicago *Sun* and, in New York, he had backed Ralph Ingersoll's experimental newspaper, *PM*. In these ventures, he had frequently asked for my advice, though I was anything but an expert in this field.

During the war and the 1944 election campaign, Field and I both realized that a large part of the American population lived on a meager diet of information supplied by the little weekly rural newspapers and labor union house organs and that this fact retarded the development of an informed and alert electorate. It occurred to me that something might be done about it.

At my suggestion, Marshall agreed to launch an experimental news service for the weekly rural, labor and farm papers. We formed a partnership, known as Cross Country Reports, in which Field supplied most of the capital while I put up the small remainder and undertook the management.

I rented an office in the Old Grand Central Terminal Building and hired two assistants: Morris Werner, an able writer who in OWI had been known as "God's angry man" because of his capacity for righteous and articulate indignation; and a bright youngster, named Al Reitman, who had worked in the CIO–PAC. We offered four weekly columns of about six hundred words each: one, by David Loth, editor of the *Congressional Quarterly*, covered the Washington scene; another, by me, dealt with international affairs; a third, by Ed Lahey, discussed labor news; and a fourth, by various authors, covered developments in the farm belt.

It did not take us long to discover that the weekly newspapers that were interested in our service lacked the money to pay even the small fee we charged, while those that could afford our four weekly columns preferred to use handouts and boiler-plate features put out gratis by the Western Newspaper Union—a concern interested primarily in selling printer's supplies.

The venture itself was a failure, but it resulted in one at least

temporarily constructive development—the creation of a powerful liberal voice in the deep South. This came about in an un-
planned way. In 1946, Aubrey Williams, whom I had known as
Youth Administrator in the New Deal days, had just been appointed by President Truman as Rural Electrification Administrator. The Senate had refused to confirm the appointment, being
influenced by slanderous attacks upon Williams during his earlier service. Aubrey came to me to see whether Cross Country
Reports might be interested in financing his purchase of the
Southern Farmer, a monthly newspaper published in Montgomery, Alabama. The paper was then owned by a Montgomery
bank official, had a circulation of about one hundred thousand
in seven southern states, and was printed on what was probably
the oldest Hoe printing press in the United States. It ran at a
small profit. Williams thought he could build the paper into an
important liberal journal and believed he could buy it for
$100,000. Field and I, both deeply concerned over Southern
segregation, agreed to finance the purchase.

Within two years, Williams built up the *Southern Farmer's*
circulation to over a million by somewhat unorthodox methods
of promotion by radio. The paper carried Williams' outspoken
editorials on race relations and occasionally articles by me on
foreign affairs. For several years, it bade fair to become an important influence. Unfortunately, Williams overextended himself
when he was forced to build a new plant big enough to print his
very large press runs. He hoped that the plant would pay for
itself through job printing but he had reckoned without the
prejudice his liberal point of view engendered. To make matters
worse, the partner upon whom he relied as plant manager died,
and Williams himself went through a desperate illness. The
Southern Farmer lost circulation and advertising revenue and
eventually was contracted into a non-political farmer's almanac.

While both Field and I regretted this development, we were
glad that, for a few years at least, we had been able to help
Williams' liberal voice to be heard.

After Field's untimely death, in 1956, I donated my interest in
the *Southern Farmer* to the Field Foundation.

CHAPTER XXIV

Aborted Attempt at a German Solution

Except for his colleagues in the United States Senate and the people of his native state of Missouri, few Americans knew anything about Harry S. Truman when he became President in April 1945. Throughout the world, people were asking each other: "What sort of a man is he?"

When the new President took office, he had only two weeks in which to prepare for the conference at San Francisco at which the United Nations Charter was to be written. On May 7, Germany surrendered, and on July 17, Truman met with Winston Churchill and Josef Stalin at Potsdam to settle the future of Germany. On August 6, the first atomic bomb ever to be used in warfare was dropped on Hiroshima. On August 14, Japan surrendered.

At Potsdam, Stalin confronted the two Western leaders with a *fait accompli* so far as Germany's eastern territories were concerned. He had annexed the northern half of East Prussia and had handed over its southern half, plus Upper and Lower Silesia, Pomerania, and parts of Brandenburg and Mecklenburg to Polish administration. Some thirteen million Germans had either fled, been killed or driven out of these territories to find new homes in the West. The Russo-Polish land-grab far exceeded the worst interpretation that could have been put upon the Yalta agreements.

Churchill protested vigorously, but there was nothing he and Truman could do except to insist that the final determination of Germany's eastern frontier be left to the peace settlement. Then the results of the British elections announced during the Potsdam Conference overthrew the Churchill government, replacing it by a Labour cabinet under Prime Minister Clement Attlee. Ernest Bevin succeeded Anthony Eden as Foreign Secretary. Truman was left to confront Stalin with British colleagues scarcely more experienced than he was himself.

I was deeply disturbed by the Potsdam Agreement. By no stretch of the imagination could it be reconciled with the Atlantic Charter pledge against territorial annexations or changes that did not conform to the freely expressed wishes of the peoples concerned. The plan agreed upon for the four-power government of a truncated Germany was full of contradictions and inconsistencies, embodying some of the features of the fantastic Morgenthau Plan for "de-industrializing" Germany while, at the same time, amputating its most productive agricultural territories. Worst of all, the Plan assumed that the four occupying powers would be able to agree upon what sort of a "peace-loving and democratic" Germany they wished to create and how the German people were to be "denazified" and "re-educated."

To complete this unhappy beginning, the United States and Britain, having insisted upon the inclusion of France as a fourth occupying power, failed, for some reason I have never been able to discover, to obtain France's signature to the Potsdam Agreement. This left France with a seat on the Allied Control Council and a veto over its action (since the agreement provided for unanimous decisions), without France's being bound to carry out the terms of the agreement.

Great as were my misgivings over this inauspicious start toward liquidating the war in Europe, I was even more shocked and troubled by President Truman's decision to loose atomic bombs upon Japan. The use of this fearful new weapon of mass murder against a civilian population without any sort of prior warning seemed certain to damage American prestige in Asia as well as to exacerbate the already rising tensions between the Soviet Union and the West. I felt sure that, had President Roosevelt lived, he would have proceeded differently, perhaps inviting Japanese emissaries to witness an atomic explosion on one of the uninhabited Pacific islands, and almost certainly taking the Kremlin into his confidence. As it turned out later, the decision to use the bombs against Japan was based upon faulty intelligence as to the Japanese capability to resist an invasion of the home islands. A report by Admiral Zacharias carrying an ac-

6. *(Above)* Father and son, about 1912.

Fabian Bachrach

7. *(Left)* The naval flying cadet.

18. In the training plane.

19. Bydale.

Freudy Photos, Inc.

20. The steeplechaser (author is on right).

21. Paul Warburg shortly before his death.

22. James Warburg with F.D.R., Prime Minister MacDonald, and the British delegation to Washington in 1933. Author is third from left, back row.

23. James Warburg
at his desk, about 1950.

24. Joan and James Warburg (1948).

25. The amateur painter (Florida, 1963).

26. April, Andy, and Kay Warburg (1927).

27. Philip, Jimmy, Jennifer, and Sally Warburg (1961).

curate evaluation of Japan's desperate position was, for some unexplained reason, disregarded.[1]

On August 31, 1945 President Truman abolished the Office of War Information and transferred its overseas activities to the Department of State. I had just finished a book in which I had analyzed the use of political warfare by both sides in the war and had pointed out the need for an international agreement banning all future political or psychological aggression through propaganda or subversive activity. The book, *Unwritten Treaty*, published in 1946, contained a draft of such an agreement and also a draft of a second agreement providing for universal freedom of information. I took the occasion of Truman's executive order to send him a memorandum summarizing these recommendations and attached the drafts of the proposed agreements.

Nothing came of this approach. I was told that the matter had been referred to the State Department. Evidently, Truman's way of dealing with suggestions from private citizens was going to be very different from that of his predecessor. (Seventeen years and two Presidents later, in May 1962, the United States submitted to the Geneva Disarmament Conference the first American approach to the problem of controlling propaganda and providing universal freedom of information. The text of a proposed U.S.-U.S.S.R. declaration prohibited "all forms of propaganda in whatsoever country conducted which is either designed to or likely to encourage any threat to the peace, breach of peace or act of aggression," and undertook to promote by all available means "the widest possible circulation of news, ideas and opinions conducive to the strengthening of peace and friendship." The mills of the gods are surely not the only mills that grind slowly!)

Within a few months of the signing of the Potsdam Agreement, my worst fears were realized. It was evident that the plan for the four-power government of Germany was not going to work. Indeed, the situation as it was developing in Germany seemed to me more than likely to cause the complete disruption of the victorious coalition.

There was little if any agreement among the four occupying

[1] See Harry L. Stimson and McGeorge Bundy *On Active Service in Peace and War*, Harper, 1948; and Admiral Ellis Mark Zacharias' *Secret Missions, The Story of an Intelligence Officer*, Putnam, 1946.

powers as to what sort of a political structure and what sort of an economy they wished to create in Germany. There was dissension as to what reparations were to be exacted, how they were to be collected and to whom they were to be paid. (The Yalta agreements had been vague and ambiguous on this score.) Worst of all, the French, in their peculiar position of being a party to but not bound by the Potsdam Agreement, were unwilling to allow the experiment in four-power government to get off the ground unless the other three occupying powers would agree to let them annex the German Saar and the Rhineland.

Because of French obstructionism, Germany was not being governed as a political and economic entity. Each of the four zones of occupation had become a hermetically sealed-off satrapy which the respective occupying power was trying to make over in its own image. Neither people nor goods could move freely across the arbitrarily fixed zonal frontiers. In the Western, industrialized areas of the British and American zones, the Germans were living at a near starvation level, supported by what amounted to Anglo-American charity. In the surplus-food-producing French and Soviet zones, the occupiers were carting off food to their own countries. Soviet authorities were appropriating and removing to Russia whatever industrial equipment could be moved.

If this state of affairs were to be permitted to continue it seemed to me certain that Germany would quickly become a festering sore in the heart of Europe.

Partly because of the destruction by bombing raids but even more because of the "level of industry regulations" imposed by the Potsdam plan and the removal of equipment on reparations account, the great coal mines and steel factories of the Ruhr were producing almost nothing at a time when all of Europe was hungry for coal and steel with which to rebuild its war-devastated economy. Meanwhile, Stalin, with a surplus zone of occupation at his disposal, was milking the German cow in the East while Anglo-Americans were forced to feed it hay at the other end.

In other ways, too, the wartime coalition seemed to me to be disintegrating. President Truman's abrupt termination of Lend-Lease had not been accompanied by any evidence that he understood the urgent needs of our wartime allies. A Soviet application for a substantial reconstruction loan had been "lost in the files of the Foreign Economic Administration"; and Britain, after long and wearisome negotiations, had been granted a wholly inadequate loan on terms that seemed to me utterly impossible to fulfill. Truman's hasty abolition of wartime economic controls had set off an inflationary wave of rising prices which added to the difficulties of other countries in buying the food, fuel, fibers, machinery and other goods urgently needed and obtainable only in the United States.

Early in 1946, Winston Churchill, now a private citizen, came to the United States to deliver a speech at Fulton, Missouri, in which he declared that the world was now divided into two hostile camps and that only American possession of the atomic bomb protected the "free world" from communist conquest. This seemed to me not only extravagant but likely to become a dangerous, self-fulfilling prophecy.

Recognizing that the whole structure of peace which Roosevelt had sought to erect rested upon the continuing friendly cooperation of the four chief members of the victorious coalition, I observed these signs of deterioration with increasing dismay. I had never believed that the Yalta agreement had been based upon a realistic hope. It had always seemed to me improbable that Stalin would give up control over the countries his armies had "liberated." On the other hand, I thought that Germany, Austria, and Czechoslovakia could reasonably be expected to remain outside of the Soviet orbit. The crux of the matter now lay in Germany. Nowhere else was four-power co-operation so explicitly on trial. If a workable agreement could be reached with regard to the future of Germany, the mounting East-West tensions might still abate.

I decided to make an effort to bring about a re-examination and revision of our German policy and went to see Dean Acheson. Acheson and the people under him in the State Department were very much aware of the deteriorating situation and willing to listen to any constructive suggestion. Before attempting to make any proposals, I said that I would like to have an opportunity to study the existing situation at firsthand and suggested that it might be possible for me to obtain an assignment to visit Germany as a war correspondent, provided the State and War departments would facilitate my entry into the four zones of occupation. When this idea found favor with Acheson and with Jack McCloy in the War Department, I arranged with Marshall Field to have myself accredited as a special correspondent for the Chicago *Sun* Syndicate.

Thanks to the arrangements made by Acheson and McCloy, all doors in Germany were opened. General Lucius D. Clay, the able United States chief of military government, gave me a thorough briefing on inter-ally relations and ordered his staff to provide whatever available information I might desire. He arranged permission for me to travel where and as I pleased throughout the Western zones of occupation, and placed a jeep at my disposal. Clay's British opposite number, General Sir Brian Robertson, was equally co-operative, as was the French commandant, General Paul Koenig. After some weeks, I was also able to obtain permission from Marshal Sokolovsky to join the first small group of American correspondents allowed to enter the Soviet zone.

Most of Berlin was a heap of rubble. Bomb craters made it look like a telescopic view of the moon. People were living in cellars and in the fragments of houses left partially standing. Few of the old familiar landmarks remained. Conditions in the city were appalling. German currency was worthless. Cigarettes had become the medium of exchange by which the occupiers bought whatever articles the half-starved Berliners had to offer. One American correspondent told me that he bought an Opel sedan in good condition for six cartons of Lucky Strikes. While the American GIs specialized in "liberating" Zeiss binoculars and Leica cameras, the Russian soldiers concentrated upon wrist watches.

Most of the German politicians were reluctant to talk. I had interesting interviews with three who later turned out to be important: Ernst Reuter, the courageous Socialist mayor of West Berlin; Kurt Schumacher, the fiery leader of the Social Democratic Party; and the saturnine Walter Ulbricht, future boss of the East German satellite state and already a rising power in the Communist hierarchy.

One of the prisoners of war who drove jeeps for the Zehlendorf car pool gave me a revealing insight into post-Hitler German mentality. On the way to General Clay's headquarters I asked the driver what he had done before going into the army. He said he had been a chauffeur for a rich Jewish coal merchant who had been forced to flee the country.

"Didn't working for a Jew get you into trouble?" I asked.

"Nah! Not me," he said, and delivered an eloquent denunciation of "that criminal anti-Semitic nonsense."

I listened in fascinated surprise, thinking that here was at least one German who had had the guts to say what he thought of the Nazis. As we pulled up at OMGUS headquarters, the driver turned around and said: "Now, if Hitler had said that the Negroes were *Untermenschen* [sub-humans], that would have made sense."

It gave me a strange feeling to revisit Hamburg and the scenes of my boyhood. I had not been there since 1932. The old heart of the city was relatively undamaged. Some of the working-class suburbs had been demolished. The harbor was in ruins. I visited my parents' and grandparents' former homes. Both had been turned into lodging houses. Max Warburg's home had been destroyed, but the old Warburg banking house still stood on the Ferdinandstrasse. I had a brief visit with Rudolf Brinckmann, the non-Jewish former junior partner whom the Nazis had installed to run the "Aryanized" firm. Brinckmann hoped the Warburgs would soon come back.

The factory towns of the Ruhr were a shambles. Here and there smoke rose from an undamaged tall chimney. Most of the great steel plants were a mass of twisted metal. River traffic on the once busy Rhine was at a standstill.

Everywhere, the people had a gray, haunted look. Most were living on a near starvation diet. There was almost no recognition of guilt. The Germans were sorry for themselves and seemed to feel that they had been in no way responsible for what the Nazi regime had done. But they definitely had had enough of war. "*Das naechste Mal ohne mich*" [Next time without me] was the common way of expressing it.

The relations between the American and British military governments were friendly and co-operative, in marked contrast to the strained relations between the Anglo-Americans and the French. I was agreeably surprised to find that American-Soviet relations at the military level were cordial. Marshal Sokolovsky, the Soviet commander in Germany, told me that he got along splendidly with General Clay; the trouble began only when the diplomats confronted each other across the green baize table. He thought Secretary of State Byrnes "tricky," whereas he felt he could rely on anything that General Clay said.

The relations between Colonel (later General) Frank Howley at the Berlin Kommandatura and his Soviet colleague, General Kotikov, were equally friendly. The Russians respected Howley partly because of his skill as a horseman and partly because, though a small man, he knew judo and could take excellent care of himself in a friendly rough-and-tumble. On one occasion, at one of Kotikov's parties, Howley splashed a Soviet major twice his size off the wall, after warning him that he did not like to be pushed around. Kotikov rocked with laughter and said: "Good, my friend Frank! Next time I get you a bigger Russian!"

On the other hand, I discovered that the Russians turned quickly from playful friendliness to anger and from hostility back to geniality. One night, on the way through the Soviet zone from Halle to Leipzig, my car's headlights picked up a six-wheel lorry loaded with recumbent Russian soldiers. Some were singing. All appeared to be drunk. Just as we were about to pass the lorry, a soldier who had been teetering precariously on the tailboard fell off, lit on his feet, and began yelling and shooting at the lorry to make it stop. Without thinking, I ordered my German prisoner-of-war driver to stop and got out to tell the drunken soldier that we would try to catch up with the lorry and put him back aboard. Unfortunately, this took some time. The lorry was by this time out of sight. After driving at full speed for about fifteen minutes without picking up our quarry, I concluded that the lorry must have turned off the main road. But where?

It occurred to me that driving through the Soviet zone at night in a war correspondent's uniform with a drunken Russian soldier on my lap might not be a very wise thing to do. Accordingly, I told my driver to stop at the nearest village Kommandatura.

Here a burly sergeant eyed us with obvious suspicion. I explained in German what had happened. The sergeant made a number of telephone calls. At the completion of each call, his expression grew more grim, and I was uncomfortably aware that two big Russian soldiers had quietly taken their places on either side of me. Suddenly, the sergeant asked in his broken German: "What was number of lorry?"

Fortunately, the lorry had been in my car's headlights long

enough so that the whole scene, including the number plate, had photographed itself on my mind. I told the sergeant the number was M-1118. This occasioned another telephone call in the midst of which the sergeant's expression changed. He grinned at me, indicating that everything was now in order. He had found out where the lorry belonged. A bottle of vodka was produced and, before I was permitted to go on my way, a toast was drunk to Soviet-American friendship. I have often wondered what would have happened if I had not chanced to remember the lorry's number.

The Soviet commander in Thuringia was Major General Kolnisnichenko, a huge, powerfully built man whose facial expression could also turn in a trice from thundercloud to sunshine and vice versa. I made a deal with the general according to which I would report such comments as I might hear from the Germans about the Soviet occupation without furnishing any names, while the general, in exchange, would allow me the unusual privilege of moving about unescorted and would facilitate my seeing whatever I wanted to see. Some of what I saw revealed unsuspected contradictions within the Soviet administration as well as new insights into the nature of Soviet man.

I spent several days interviewing German farm families recently given possession of land formerly sharecropped for large landowners whose estates had been broken up by the Soviet authorities. These farmers were, on the whole, happy people. Neither they nor I realized that the "land reform" from which they had benefited would turn out to be the first step toward collectivization.

At the fortunately undamaged Goethe Haus in Weimar, I saw dozens of Russian GIs poring over the Goethe manuscripts exhibited under glass. I returned several times to see whether perhaps my first visit had coincided with that of some special group, but each time the place was full of eager Goethe students.

One day, I saw a group of Russian soldiers dismantling what I took to be a sugar factory. The machinery was being removed and carefully loaded on flat cars. A week later, I was surprised to see another group of Russian soldiers unloading the cars and replacing the machinery in the plant. It took some time to discover the explanation. The first group of soldiers had belonged to the Reparations Command which was taking everything that it could lay hands on off to Russia. Then along had come Kolnisnichenko's Military Government Command whose job it was to make the district economically viable.

When I thought I had seen enough in this area, I went to the general to thank him and say good-by. He asked whether there was anything more that I wanted to see. I said I would have liked to visit Buchenwald, the notorious Nazi concentration camp, which I understood was now full of Nazi SS prisoners.

The general frowned and said: "I can't send you out there because it's outside of my command, but how would you like to see another farm?"

This seemed odd, since the general knew that I had just visited a number of farms. However, something in his expression made me reply that I would be glad to.

Kolnisnichenko chuckled and pushed a button. A sergeant appeared and was given instructions in Russian. The general told me to go with the sergeant and come back to see him later. We drove a few miles out from Weimar and stopped in a potato field. The sergeant motioned for me to get out. Then he drove off. Seeing a fringe of trees at the edge of the field, I wandered over, and, sure enough, there was a barbed wire fence with some gray-clad figures behind it. Coming close to the fence, I talked with a number of wholly unregenerate Nazi storm troopers until a Russian guard chased me away. These were the first Germans I had seen who admitted to having been convinced National Socialists. I repeated the experiment at two other points along the fence until I was chased away and then returned to the potato field, where I found the Russian jeep waiting.

Back in Kolnisnichenko's office, the general said: "Well, did you find that an interesting farm?"

"Yes, indeed, General."

"Did you see any farmers?"

"Yes, I talked with quite a few."

"Think they've learned anything?"

"No, General."

"Neither do I." As he said this, the general drew his hand across his throat in an unmistakable gesture.

My final request to General Kolnisnichenko was to be allowed to ride from Weimar to Berlin on a Russian leave train. This, too, was granted. During the four-hour journey in third-class wooden-seated cars, I had an opportunity to observe the behavior of Soviet troops happy to be returning home on leave. They seemed remarkably like American GIs, except that, where American troops would have produced candy bars and beer from their knapsacks, the Russians produced thick black bread, rancid butter, sausages, and vodka. The jokes and the gripes, translated for me by a young Soviet flyer who spoke German, seemed very much like those of our own troops.

I was asked many questions about America. One question concerned the school system in the United States. I explained that the system varied in the different states and that I knew only about New York and my own state of Connecticut. Thereupon a hitherto silent saturnine lieutenant delivered a lecture on the American school system which would have been remarkable even if it had come from an American. When I asked how he happened to know so much about American schools, his matter-of-fact answer was: "I teach United States history and government at Leningrad University."

A little later, a great row seemed to have started among the four soldiers sitting across the aisle. A huge corporal with a lock of black hair hanging over his forehead was pounding his fist on the table and shouting at his companions. I asked the German-speaking airman what the row was about. The latter listened for a moment and said: "That's not a row. The big corporal is simply explaining that Pushkin was not murdered by his mistress but by the Tsar's secret police."

It would be difficult to imagine American troops going home on leave arguing about a comparable subject. Nor could one imagine American GIs taking for granted that a foreigner would instantly be able to identify Walt Whitman or Henry Wadsworth Longfellow.

Back in the American zone, I was shocked to discover the existence of a sort of double Jim Crow arrangement. Vehicles, waiting rooms, toilets, and other facilities were marked *Nicht fuer Deutsche;* others were additionally marked FOR OFFICERS ONLY. An odd way, I thought, to teach democracy by example.

Few Americans learned to speak German. Most of the GIs seemed to have very little interest in why they were in Germany and were preoccupied with wondering when they would be sent home. Although forbidden to fraternize, the American GIs were not unkindly disposed toward the Germans. A frequent comment was: "At least the Krauts are clean."

When I asked General Clay why he did not learn German and emancipate himself from dependence upon interpreters, the general answered that he purposely had not learned German because he wanted "to keep the Krauts at a distance." One could easily imagine Lucius Clay in the role of an ancient Roman proconsul, ruling over a distant province of the empire. He was an extremely able administrator—efficient, tough, but scrupulously just.

The British army of occupation gave the appearance of being quite at home in the job of managing a colony. Little British enclaves had already sprung into being with their own schools and clubs. "The natives" were employed as servants. It was my impression that the Germans understood and respected the haughty British more than they did the friendlier Americans.

By far the worst relationship between victors and vanquished existed in the French zone, where the French, whom the Germans had conquered in a few weeks, now lorded it over them as conquerors. The French occupation troops appeared nervous and somewhat vindictive. The German inhabitants were outspokenly bitter. They knew that whatever the Russians might do to them in the East was not as bad as what their own troops had done in Russia, but to have the defeated French order them around, take away their horses, and appropriate their crops was more than they could bear.

As the result of my three-month stay in Germany, I wrote a series of eight newspaper articles for Marshall Field's syndicate. The last article outlined a specific proposal for a revision of United States policy.

My more detailed report to Acheson and McCloy in Washington was later published in my *Germany—Bridge or Battleground*[2] and need not, therefore, be summarized here beyond saying that it recommended a reopening of the question of Germany's eastern frontier, an upward revision of the restrictions upon German steel production, and the substitution of a "period

[2] Published by Harcourt, Brace in New York and Heinemann in London in 1947; and in German by Franz Mittelbach Verlag, Stuttgart in 1948.

of observation and control" in which other European nations would participate in place of four-power occupation and military government. The latter recommendation was essentially the same as I had made to McCloy during the pre-surrender planning in 1943.

One other feature of this first of many plans for a revision of our German policy which I have submitted over the years, perhaps deserves mention. This was a proposal[3] to settle the Ruhr dispute by creating a European Coal Authority under which not only German but French, Belgian, and Polish coal production would be pooled and allocated to the needs of the various Continental nations. Although it received little official attention at the time, the proposal anticipated the French Schuman Plan of 1950 (actually drawn by Jean Monnet) which was eventually to lay the foundation for the European Economic Community established under the Rome Treaties of 1957. However, whereas my proposal was put forward in the hope that a European Coal Authority would tend to reunify the whole European trading community, the later economic unification of France, Germany, Italy, Holland, Belgium, and Luxembourg in the Common Market became a measure of economic defense against the Soviet bloc, thereby crystallizing the already existing division of Europe into two hostile camps. While the statesmen who created the "Little Europe of the Six," talked in 1950 about a "united Europe," they were thinking in terms of the ancient West European Catholic empire of Charlemagne.

When I reported to Acheson and McCloy in the autumn of 1946, Secretary of State Byrnes was in Paris for a four-power meeting of foreign ministers. Parts of my recommendations were cabled to him as a suggested basis for discussion with the Russians. However, instead of talking to Molotov about a partial revision of the Polish-German frontier, the Secretary went to Stuttgart and, apparently in an effort to curry favor with the Germans, made a speech to a German audience the vagueness of which implied a return to Germany of all the trans-Oder-Neisse territory including Upper Silesia. The result was to increase the strain between East and West, cause the failure of the Paris conference, and render the dangerous deadlock over

3 *Ibid.*, pp. 231–33.

Germany more intractable than ever. Secretary Byrnes then backed away from the German problem altogether.

In the November congressional elections, President Truman lost control of both houses of Congress. This political defeat left him faced with the necessity of obtaining bipartisan support for a foreign policy which was running into trouble not only in Europe but in China, where the United States had become involved in the Nationalist-Communist civil war.

Early in 1946, my mother died at the age of seventy-six. My sister and I laid her to rest beside our father at Sleepy Hollow Cemetery in the plot overlooking her beloved Hudson that she herself had selected and planted. I had been fortunate enough to be able to look after her material comfort, but I was saddened by the fact that, in the last years of her life, I had not seen very much of her, partly because I was away much of the time and partly because she and my wife had not been congenial.

CHAPTER XXV

One-Man Task Force for Peace

IN 1947 THE Truman Administration turned from its attempt to follow the Roosevelt formula for peace through great-power co-operation to the cold-war policy advocated by Winston Churchill in his speech at Fulton, Missouri. However, the turn did not take place until after two important efforts to relax the mounting tensions had been undertaken.

The first of these was the Acheson-Lilienthal proposal, better known as the Baruch Plan to establish a supranational control of atomic energy. I welcomed this proposal, and, viewed from the Western point of view, it was an extremely generous offer on the part of the United States to relinquish its atomic monopoly to the United Nations. From the Soviet point of view, however, it was wholly unacceptable because it would have required the type of inspection that would have laid bare not only carefully guarded Russian secrets but the weakness of the war-shattered Soviet economy. What interested me was that the proposal amounted to the establishment of a limited world government in the field of atomic weaponry—a principle which its authors were far from ready to apply to conventional armaments.

At the beginning of the year, President Truman had decided to supplant Byrnes as Secretary of State. After the fiasco of his Stuttgart speech in September 1946, Byrnes had concerned himself chiefly with negotiating a Trieste settlement and peace treaties with the former Axis satellites. The President needed to find a Secretary of State who could command bipartisan support in the Congress and in the country. No one could more certainly meet this requirement than the wartime Chief of Staff, General George Catlett Marshall.

Advised of the President's wishes, General Marshall returned in January 1947 from his unsuccessful mission to China and began at once to give his chief attention to the German deadlock and to the preparation for the Big Four Foreign Ministers' meeting scheduled for March 10, in Moscow. I was told that he was considering certain aspects of my proposal.

Unhappily, while General Marshall was en route to the Soviet capital, a crisis flared up in the eastern Mediterranean. This whole area had been a British responsibility, but, because of her precarious financial position, Britain now suddenly declared that she was no longer able to cope with the communist conspiracy in Greece and the recent Soviet threats against Turkey. This unanticipated emergency led to the promulgation of a new American policy—the so-called Truman Doctrine—just as General Marshall was about to begin his negotiations in Moscow.

Truman decided to ask Congress to appropriate $400 million for military and economic assistance to the Greek and Turkish governments. However, when he summoned the legislative leaders to secure their support, he was told by Senator Arthur Vandenberg of Michigan, the new Republican chairman of the Senate Foreign Relations Committee, that to obtain passage of this legislation, he would have to make a personal appearance before the Congress and "scare the hell out of it and the country."[1] The resulting message, drafted with this end in view, frightened most of America's friends abroad.

After painting the world-wide communist threat in the most somber colors, the President made the belligerent assertion that the United States would from now on come to the assistance of "any nation threatened by totalitarian conspiracy from without or within." (It was apparent that this pronouncement was aimed solely at communist totalitarianism, not at totalitarianism of the right, such as existed in Spain, Portugal, and parts of Latin America. As a matter of fact, Turkey, one of the two intended beneficiaries of immediate aid, was at that time governed by an anti-democratic military dictatorship.)

The President's hastily contrived and far-reaching pronouncement was, in fact, a declaration of global resistance to communism—a new "containment policy" shortly thereafter to be more fully explained in an article in *Foreign Affairs*, authored by a mysterious "Mr. X.," who later turned out to be George F. Kennan, the State Department's chief of policy planning.

The immediate impact of the President's message was to create anxiety and confusion at home and abroad. When, on a nation-wide radio broadcast, Edward R. Murrow asked me to comment on the Truman message, I said that there was good reason for giving aid to Greece and Turkey, although, in view of the recent successful United Nations intervention in Iran, I would have preferred to see the assistance rendered through the world organization, rather than unilaterally extended by the United States.

On the other hand, I stated bluntly that, in my opinion, there existed no valid reason for the United States to appoint itself as a global anti-communist policeman. No one had asked us to undertake such a commitment; its fulfillment clearly lay beyond the power of the United States alone. Upon what allies were we going to rely to carry out this unilateral global undertaking? Did President Truman consider that only communist dictatorships were the enemies of democracy? Would the United States welcome the support of Franco, Salazar, or Perón in its new anti-communist crusade?

[1] See my *Put Yourself in Marshall's Place*, Simon & Schuster, 1948, pp. 22–23.

Similar questions were being asked in Britain and France. As for Moscow's reaction, the enunciation of the Truman Doctrine put an end to whatever hope there had been of reaching a German settlement. In the face of President Truman's declaration of global ideological war, the Kremlin now looked upon Germany as merely one of many fronts in such a conflict. In these circumstances the Moscow Conference was foredoomed to failure.[2]

There remained one final moment in 1947 when the four-power fiasco might have been redeemed. This came with Secretary Marshall's spectacular announcement at Harvard University, on June 5, of his plan for American aid to all-European recovery. The Secretary's speech at Cambridge had, as a matter of fact, been foreshadowed by a little-noticed address delivered by Dean Acheson on May 8, at Cleveland, Mississippi.[3] (At General Marshall's urgent request, Acheson had agreed to remain for a few months as Under Secretary.)

The brilliantly conceived Marshall Plan was the second major effort to end the cold war. It offered economic assistance to any and all European countries willing to help themselves and each other in bringing about recovery. The keynote of the proposal was struck in one sentence spoken by the Secretary of State: "Our policy," General Marshall said, "is not directed against any country or doctrine but against hunger, poverty, desperation and chaos."

In a number of public speeches, including another nationwide broadcast, I welcomed this return to reason and supported the Marshall program as vigorously as I had attacked the Truman Doctrine.

Had the Soviet Union accepted Mr. Marshall's extraordinary offer—and Congress ratified it—the cold war might have ended then and there, and a German settlement might have been reached. The Kremlin, however, regarded the Marshall Plan as merely a more intelligent form of the Truman Doctrine. At the famous Paris meeting in July 1947, Foreign Minister Molotov walked out after listening to the purposefully uninviting presentation of the proposal by Britain's Foreign Secretary, Ernest

[2] For Secretary Marshall's report on the Moscow Conference, see *Put Yourself in Marshall's Place*, pp. 49–52.
[3] Ibid., pp. 52–54.

Bevin. (Bevin, like many officials in Washington, was not at all anxious to have Russia accept. Many Washington officials feared that if the Soviet Union were included, Congress might refuse to ratify the whole plan.)

Prior to Molotov's walkout, Poland and Czechoslovakia had declared their willingness to co-operate, but now they reversed their position. The Western press, having foolishly crowed over Polish and Czech acceptance as a defeat for the Soviet Union, now interpreted the reversal as proof positive that Poland and Czechoslovakia were nothing more than helpless, subservient Soviet satellites.

So far as Czechoslovakia was concerned, I strongly doubted the validity of this conclusion. The truth could, I knew, be learned from my friend, Jan Masaryk. A telephone call to Marshall Field in Chicago resulted in another assignment, this time not only to make a second firsthand report on Germany but to investigate the situation in Czechoslovakia and to report, if possible, upon the difficult economic situation of Britain.

I was only too glad to obtain this assignment. My wife and I had just regretfully decided to end our marriage—a decision that left me with an abiding sense of gratitude for twelve often tempestuous but, on the whole, happy years and, above all, for the stable home she had provided for my children. I wondered whether perhaps I was too self-sufficient a man to make a satisfactory husband. As I set out for Czechoslovakia, the prospect of once more being a bachelor and coming home to a house without wife or children seemed rather bleak.

Arriving in the alleged communist police state, I found that the formalities at the Prague airport were fewer and more casual than at La Guardia in New York. No questions were asked at the hotel. Strolling down *Vaclavske Namesti*, the main street of the ancient city, I passed numerous newsstands and book shops in which Western newspapers and magazines were offered for sale. The Communist Party newspaper, *Rude Pravo*, displayed in its book stall copies of such conservative newspapers as *Le Figaro* and Lord Beaverbrook's *Daily Express*.

People were friendly but disinclined to converse in German. If, however, having first tried French or English without success, one asked: "Do you speak Swiss?" they were willing to communicate by means of the hated language of the Nazis. No one seemed afraid to express political opinions. The impression of matter-of-fact freedom and independence gained on my first stroll through the city was confirmed by everything I saw or heard during subsequent weeks.

A study of the political scene in Czechoslovakia led me to the conclusion that all was by no means lost. It was true that the Communist Party had gained control of 40 per cent of the seats in parliament in the previous year's altogether free elections. But it was also true that the Czech Communist Party was strongly nationalistic. Neither Jan Masaryk nor our ambassador, Lawrence Steinhardt, thought that Czechoslovakia had abdicated its independence.

For about a week, I traveled through Bohemia and Moravia with Jan Masaryk in his little two-seater. Masaryk's "uniform" was a white shirt open at the neck and with the shirt-tails hanging outside of his trousers. Everywhere we went, people recognized and came to greet him. Frequently, Masaryk would stop and talk to groups of flaxen-haired children. Peasants in the fields would drop their tools and come running to catch a glimpse of him or perhaps even to touch him. One day, when I jokingly commented on Jan's informal attire, he said: "I leave the proper trappings of a Foreign Minister to my communist deputy, Clementis. He goes around in striped trousers and a morning coat. I go like this."

Several weeks of on-the-spot study led to my sending back six newspaper articles and a confidential report to Bob Lovett, who had now replaced Dean Acheson as Under Secretary of State. The gist of my reportage was that, if an Iron Curtain had been drawn around Czechoslovakia, it had been drawn by us— not by the Soviet Union. I said that, by prematurely writing off Czechoslovakia as a Soviet satellite, we might very well force the little country into the Soviet orbit.

Masaryk had given me permission to publish the facts about his government's reversal with regard to the Marshall Plan. Czechoslovakia had not been "ordered" by Moscow to withdraw, as claimed by the American press. The withdrawal had been made necessary by the Western interpretation of Czechoslovakia's original acceptance as a rebuff to the Soviet Union. There had been no coercion.

It was clear to me that, while not subservient to the Soviet

Union, the Czechs felt warmly toward that country—partly because Russia alone had not joined in the betrayal of Munich, and
partly because Soviet troops had been the ones to liberate
Czechoslovakia from the Nazis. (I was often asked why General
Patton's Third Army had sat in front of Pilsen for several days
while the Red Army came up to "liberate" Prague and most of
Czechoslovakia. I am convinced that this, and General Eisenhower's decision to let the Red Army capture Berlin, profoundly
influenced the course of postwar history.)

What impressed me most in the summer of 1947 was that the
Czechs were and felt themselves to be Slavs, while culturally
they were almost wholly oriented toward the West. Given their
choice, they would join neither camp but would try instead to
act as a link between them. ("Not a bridge," Masaryk said,
"because a bridge is walked on by everybody.") The aim of
United States policy should, I thought, be to encourage this attitude of friendliness toward both sides. I suggested to Lovett
that the granting of even a modest revolving credit for the purchase of American cotton would go far toward strengthening
the still precariously dominant anti-communist elements in
Czechoslovakia. The State Department, however, had apparently
made up its mind that Czechoslovakia was lost—either that, or
else it feared that any friendly gesture toward that country
would jeopardize congressional ratification of the whole Marshall Plan.[4]

While I was in Czechoslovakia, I took the opportunity to investigate a subject that interested me greatly. I knew that
Prague was one of the main stations on the "underground railroad" over which large numbers of Jews from Eastern Europe
were making their clandestine way to Palestine in defiance of
the British immigration restrictions. By looking up the representative of the American Joint Distribution Committee, which my
Uncle Felix had founded, I was able to visit several of the
secret hideaways in which groups of Jews, mostly from Poland,
Hungary, and Rumania were concealed, awaiting the next
transport to the Middle East. I did not speak Yiddish, but my
knowledge of German and my half-forgotten Hebrew made it

[4] My published report on Czechoslovakia was later included in *Last Call
for Common Sense*, Harcourt, Brace & Co., 1949.

possible to converse without too much help from my interpreter-guide.

Most of the travelers were in their thirties or early forties. Some had children with them. There were almost no elderly people. The answers to two questions were interesting and almost unanimous:

"If you were able to obtain a visa to the United States and the assurance of employment there, would you go to America instead of to Palestine?"

Answer: "No. Your country won't take us but, even if it would, we want to go to *Eretz*."

"Why?"

"Because we want to go somewhere where to be a Jew is to be a member of the majority. We are tired of being a persecuted minority."

Religious Zionism—the traditional longing of Jewish people to return to Palestine—seemed to play very little part in the motivation of these people. They were almost all Orthodox, but it seemed to be less their religious belief than their wholly understandable secular desire to escape from the intolerable conditions in Eastern Europe that made them willing to undertake the risks and the hardships of attempting an illegal entry into Palestine in defiance of British restrictions.

The night before I left Prague, I had a last dinner with Jan Masaryk in his apartment high up in the ancient Hradčany castle, once the residence of Holy Roman emperors that now housed the Foreign Office. Jan was greatly disturbed by a number of messages received from people whom he considered his friends in the United States. The tenor of these letters and cables was: "How can you continue to hold office in a government that has become Moscow's slave?" (This was almost literally, as I remember it, the text of a cable from a Wall Street banker whom I knew well.)

"What do they want me to do?" Masaryk said. "If I resign, I should again have to go into exile. That I shall never do. How else can I help my people except by holding on? The only other way would be to make a martyr of myself by committing suicide. Is that what my American friends want me to do?"

In addition to being a most lovable human being, Masaryk was one of those rare people who are at the same time passionate patriots and responsible citizens of the world. No man would have made a more ideal Secretary-General of the United Nations.

Having done what I could to interpret the situation in Czechoslovakia, I flew to Berlin for another look at developments in Germany. From here, too, I reported my impressions to the State Department and in a series of newspaper articles. Germany was still an economic desert and a moral morass in the heart of Europe. The four-power snarl remained more hopelessly tangled than ever. The four doctors still disagreed about the patient's malady and the treatment required. The patient was slowly getting weaker—less able and less willing to co-operate in bringing about his own cure. Much of the rubble had been cleared away from the streets of cities. But little, if any, of the rubble had been cleared away from the German mind.

The men on the spot were not to blame for the demoralization of what had been intended to be a four-power government of Germany. General Clay continued to face his impossible task with indomitable courage and determination, but no amount of hard work by military government could arrest the slow wasting away of the physical and moral strength of a population that lacked both the vision of a tolerable future and the incentive to work for anything more than the immediate necessities of life. No amount of courage and determination could fully counteract the wastage of morale among the conquerors themselves, nor the loss of prestige that resulted from their inability to work together.

In 1946, I had found among the Allied officials the hope that before too long Paris, London, Moscow, and Washington would iron out their differences. In 1947, the prevailing mood was one of pessimism. The American and British zones were now joined into "Bizonia." While I was in Berlin, the decision was taken to raise the limits of the "level of industry" restriction—a move I had recommended in 1946. The French protested the decision because they wanted a greater share of Ruhr coal. In addition, they wanted the assurance that raising the permitted level of German steel production to 10,700,000 tons per annum would never allow the German output of steel to exceed that of France. This had created a difficult problem.

French steel capacity in 1947 was about 7,000,000 tons, as against a potential German capacity considerably higher than the new output limit of 10,700,000 tons. The French demand actually meant that German steel production should be held back—not until French production reached present capacity, but until French capacity could be increased by roughly 50 per cent. This would take time and require the building of new French plants, which in turn would require a large quantity of steel. It would mean that the whole of European recovery would be delayed by lack of steel in order to give France the lead over Germany that she desired. This, General Clay explained, was why we and the British could not meet French desires.

The answer, I thought, would be to create the European Coal Authority I had suggested the previous year.

Just before the Anglo-American decision to raise the limits on Ruhr steel production was publicly announced, I was able—with Clay's permission—to obtain a firsthand reaction from a group of Soviet officials at their headquarters in Karlshorst. What they said was: "You are closing the door on the unification of Germany." I pointed out that we and the British had been waiting two years, contributing some $500 million a year to sustain our zones while their zone was yielding them a profit. The Russians came back with the usual recital of their desperate need for reparations, of Soviet sacrifices and losses in the war, and their chagrin at our failure to take these factors into account. One agricultural expert asserted that Britain and the United States would not have to pour money into Germany, if they managed the economy of their zones properly.

"You don't have to build up industry to make your zones self-supporting," he said. "All you have to do is to make your Germans grow and deliver more food. If you make your Germans cut down some of the forests and plow up some of the pasture land, your zones could produce enough food to provide a low-calorie diet for their population."

It was clear to me that the Russians were not yet ready to integrate their zone with Western Germany because it had not yet been milked dry. The French were reluctant to merge their zone with "Bizonia" for the same reason; they, too, had a surplus-producing zone.

Before going to London to study the financial and political situation in England, I decided to spend two weeks learning something about Asia, by attending the Far East Conference at Stratford-on-Avon held under the auspices of the Royal Institute of International Affairs. There were a number of representatives from Asian countries, but the conference was predominantly a conference *about* Asia held by representatives of the West. By far the largest delegations were from Britain and the United States. For one who badly needed education, the well-prepared documents about each of the Asian states and the round-table discussion by experts such as Owen Lattimore, John Fairbank, Arnold Toynbee, and Lionel Curtis, were most instructive.

The Nationalist government of China was represented, but not the communist North. One of the Kuomintang delegates, a General Chen-li, asked me to have dinner with him one evening. Much to my surprise, the general spent most of the evening inquiring about living conditions in the United States. The next morning, I told Owen Lattimore about this curious conversation. Owen's eyes sparkled with excitement.

"Don't you see what that means?" he said. "It means that the rats are getting ready to leave the Kuomintang ship. You apparently don't know that your friend, the general, is one of the top men in Chiang Kai-shek's secret police organization." Lattimore knew his China. This was two years before the Central Government collapsed and Chiang Kai-shek fled to Formosa!

My next and last assignment on this trip was the most difficult. I spent several weeks discussing Britain's economic position with wartime friends in and out of government and with some of my older acquaintances in the London financial community. Not being at all sure that I had been able to analyze Britain's precarious condition fairly and accurately in the short time at my disposal, I telephoned Professor Harold Laski, the one-man Brain Trust of the Labour government, to ask whether I might send the drafts of my three short articles to him for criticism.

"Send them, no," Laski said. "Come for supper and read them to Frida and me."

The series was entitled: *What's the Matter with Britain?* Its primary purpose was to explain to an American audience the importance to the United States of a strong and healthy United

Kingdom and Britain's urgent need for help in readjusting her economy to peace. I had stressed the fundamental health of the British economy and declared that the nationalization of the ailing coal industry had probably made matters neither better nor worse. The main point of the series was to counter the growing feeling in the United States that Britain was on the road to communism or at least to ruin because a Socialist government was in power.

That evening, as I finished reading my pieces to the Laskis, Harold jumped up, walked over to a corner of his library, and, apparently without looking, took down a book. Then, again apparently without having to look for the place he wanted, he read out about four sentences—sentences that someone had at some time addressed to the British people in a time of crisis. The last sentence read:

"In prosperous times you are dull and uninspiring, but in adversity you are grand—with a pulse like a cannon."

Laski put the book down and said: "Of course you know who wrote that?"

I confessed that I did not know. Asked to make a guess, I said: "If I weren't reasonably sure that Emerson never visited England, I would suspect he was the author . . ."

"Ignoramus!" happily shouted Laski. "Of course he was in England during the Corn Law crisis of 1848. What I read was from a speech he delivered at Manchester. You ought to be highly flattered that your pieces reminded me of it."

(Laski's library was unique. When he died a few years later, Supreme Court Justice Felix Frankfurter suggested that I approach Laski's American friends to raise a fund to purchase the library for the London School of Economics—a job I undertook with enthusiasm.)

Upon returning to the United States, I decided to become a one-man task force for peace and embarked upon a strenuous period of writing and speaking about the need for a revised American foreign policy, especially with respect to Europe. In the midst of this work my secretary resigned. My daughter Kay suggested that I interview a friend of hers who, she thought, would be an ideal research assistant and secretary because she had worked for a well-known radio commentator. I lost no time in following up this suggestion. Kay's friend, Joan Melber, became the most competent and also the most attractive secretary I had ever had. Little did Kay or I realize at the time that no daughter had ever done her father a better turn.

Joan's first task was to help me in the preparation of a course of six lectures covering General Marshall's first eventful year as Secretary of State, which I had been invited to give at the New School for Social Research in New York. (These lectures were later published by Simon & Schuster in book form as *Put Yourself in Marshall's Place* and also in French by Edition Self, Paris, as *Pourquoi de Plan Marshall?*)

At her own suggestion, Joan sat in the audience and made notes of whatever comments she heard during the discussion periods—an extremely useful practice which she continued throughout the following year.

In the last lecture, I discussed future policy with respect to Europe and warned as emphatically as I could against adopting the suggestion, recently put forward by former President Hoover, that we should combine the three Western zones of Germany into a new, separate West German state and sign a separate peace treaty with it. I expressed the opinion, which unfortunately was to prove correct, that to follow this course would entail two most undesirable consequences: the almost certain creation by the Soviet Union of an East German, communist-dominated satellite state; and the strong likelihood of a Soviet attempt to oust the Western powers from Berlin.[5]

Before the end of 1947, the focus of world events shifted to the Levant, where, under almost incredible British mismanagement, the Arab-Jewish question was coming to a head. On November 30, the British Government, under considerable pressure from Washington, surrendered its mandate over Palestine. Under American leadership, with the Soviet Union concurring, the United Nations voted to partition Palestine into separate Arab and Jewish states.

While I appreciated the need for constructive action and the warmhearted sympathy that had prompted President Truman's sponsorship of the creation of a Jewish state, I had certain misgivings about the probable effect of this decision. I would have

[5] *Put Yourself in Marshall's Place*, p. 37.

preferred the creation of a bi-national Arab-Jewish state, affording equal rights to Jews and Arabs—a solution originally advocated by my teacher, Judah Magnes, and by other farseeing leaders of the *Ichud* group. Dr. Magnes had become president of the Hebrew University in Palestine. He opposed the arden- Zionists under the leadership of Chaim Weizmann and asserted that the creation of a separate Jewish state would lead to conflict, whereas a bi-national state might restore the centuries-old friendly symbiosis between Jews and Arabs in the Near East.

Apart from this, I felt that Truman's sponsorship of a separate Jewish nation would involve him in a conflict with his own desire to win the Arabs as allies in his containment policy. I had little hope that the President would resolve this dilemma by abandoning the idea of building a barrier against communism in the Middle East. It seemed far more probable that the sponsorship of Israel would involve the United States in the pursuit of two mutually exclusive aims.

The outlook at the end of 1947 was not promising. It seemed more than likely that the constructive philosophy of the Marshall Plan would be superseded by a global anti-communist crusade.

CHAPTER XXVI

Last Call for Common Sense

THE HOPE that the East-West tensions might subside was shattered on February 25, 1948, when the Communist Party seized power by a *coup d'état* in Czechoslovakia. Within a few days, the Czech press was muzzled, the non-communist parties were purged, and Czechoslovakia disappeared behind the Iron Curtain.

The West was shocked and angry. Sadly, I noted how similar

were the newspaper headlines to those which, six months earlier, had written off Czechoslovakia when its freedom and independence might still have been preserved. Deeply concerned for Jan Masaryk, I cabled him: "Horsey, keep your tail up!"

I learned later that Masaryk had been cheered by the message, but, by that time, a saddened world already knew of his tragic end. He had plunged to his death from the window of the very room in which he and I had had our last conversation. In my ears rang his words: "What do they want me to do? Commit suicide?"

If Stalin had deliberately wanted to arouse the West and to create a solid anti-communist front, he could have chosen no more effective manner of accomplishing this purpose than that of extending the orbit of his power westward. Within less than a month, Britain, France, the Netherlands, Belgium, and Luxembourg signed the Brussels Pact committing themselves to mutual defense. On the same day—March 17, 1948—President Truman addressed a special message to the Congress, reaffirming the doctrine of global containment he had enunciated a year earlier and indicating that the United States would support the nations that had signed the Brussels Pact.

With this much I agreed, but I was profoundly shocked by the over-simplified and one-sided analysis of the state of world affairs which the President then presented to the Congress and to the American people, and I took the occasion to say so on April 5 before the American Academy of Political and Social Science in Philadelphia.[1]

Two gentlemen, neither of whom I knew, came up to speak to me at the conclusion of the session. One introduced himself as Carleton Savage, executive secretary of the State Department Planning Board; the other was General Don Zimmerman, head of the Advance Military Study Group recently organized by General Eisenhower in his capacity as Chief of Staff. Each invited me to come to Washington for further discussion.

When, shortly thereafter, I met with the State Department Planning Board and the Military Study Group, I found that neither the civilian nor the military planners wholly accepted President Truman's over-simplified analysis. Both subjected me to vigorous cross-examination. Both were inclined to agree that

---

[1] The text of this address appears in my *Last Call for Common Sense,* Harcourt, Brace, 1949, pp. 17–37.

the Soviet threat was not primarily military and that the United States should lay greater emphasis upon rendering the non-communist world immune to subversion. On the other hand, both groups felt that the West European countries should, as soon as consistent with their economic recovery, place themselves in a stronger military posture. On the whole, the military planners were more outspokenly favorable to an affirmative policy, in place of purely negative anti-communism, than their civilian counterparts.

The Academy address marked the beginning of a long period during which I became an outspoken dissenter from the heated climate of opinion generated by Winston Churchill's Fulton speech and President Truman's messages of March 1947 and March 1948.

During the spring and summer of 1948, I took my dissent to the American public, delivering speeches and broadcasts in various parts of the country. Most of these talks were informal affairs, designed to stimulate discussion. Occasionally, when it seemed appropriate, I released a prepared text to the press. The wide newspaper coverage accorded to my efforts produced a voluminous correspondence with citizens from all over the United States and Canada. In response to requests for reprints, some of the prepared lectures were distributed in pamphlet form under the trade name of the Current Affairs Press to a rapidly growing mailing list.

Reprints of my occasional letters to the New York *Times* caused a number of out-of-town newspapers to invite me to contribute to their columns, so that what amounted to an informal syndicate for such communications developed. In areas not reached by the *Times*, my letters began to appear in a number of leading journals, such as the Chicago *Sun*, the St. Louis *Post-Dispatch*, the Louisville *Courier-Journal*, the Des Moines *Register*, the Minneapolis *Star-Tribune*, the Denver *Post*, the San Francisco *Chronicle* and the *Christian Science Monitor*. At times I contributed articles to *Harper's*, *The Nation*, *The Progressive* and the New York *Times* Magazine.

All this one-man task force activity created a heavy work load for Joan Melber, whose devotion, efficiency, and charm aroused more than the gratitude of her employer. In August 1948, she consented to become my wife. My scruples about marrying a girl half my age were brushed aside by Joan and her sympathetic widowed mother. And so, I, a somewhat battered veteran, entered upon what was to become both the happiest and the most creative part of an already long and variegated life.

In view of her keen interest in world affairs, I took Joan on a work-play wedding trip to Europe. We attended the first international conference of the World Movement for World Federation at Luxembourg where Joan met many of my Federalist friends.

Stringfellow Barr and I were asked to draw the resolutions the conference finally adopted. It was not easy to work out a consensus among the many varieties of Federalists. We were all agreed that a world shrunk by science and technology must, in order to survive, be governed by a supranational organization; but opinions differed widely as to how this goal might be reached. Some favored making a start through regional federations. Others wanted at once to draw up a constitution for a world government. Still others held the view that a beginning should be made by uniting only the non-communist nations under a single government. There were those who wanted to develop the United Nations into a parliament of man, and others who thought that a wholly new world organization should be created. Barr humorously remarked that federalizing the Federalists was more difficult than bringing the world's nations under a single government.

Since Joan had never before been to Europe, we motored through Belgium and Holland, flew to Scandinavia, and from Gothenburg took a small ship to England. We skipped Germany because of its unhappy state and because none of my relatives was left in Hamburg, but we visited my Uncle Fritz, the sole male survivor of my father's generation, in Stockholm. In Copenhagen, we called on the Henriques family whom I had not seen since before the war; Carl Otto proudly showed me that the office had acquired a flush toilet.

In England, Joan was enthusiastically welcomed by many of my old friends, some of them wartime colleagues, others dating back to my banking days. It was a novel experience for me to see London as a tourist and most enjoyable to show my wife all the familiar old landmarks. We went to the museums in which my father had taught me to distinguish the characteristics of the great masters, and I thought how much he would have enjoyed Joan's quick and eager appreciation.

At Oxford, Joan met the famous Isaiah Berlin and was completely baffled by his rapid-fire Oxonian, spoken through clenched teeth. She was fascinated by the various styles of architecture in the different colleges and, much to my delight, preferred Worcester and New College to the more famous Magdalen.

Before sailing home we motored to Winchester, Stonehenge, and Salisbury. As good luck would have it, we came upon Stonehenge in a thick early morning fog. Joan, looking at the great pillars mysteriously wreathed in mist, said to me: "I feel as if I had just seen the beginning of the world."

Back in the United States, Joan barely had time to settle down at Bydale before we took off on a speaking trip to preach the gospel of world government in the Middle West. I had been one of the original members of the United World Federalists and, at the organization's second annual convention in Minneapolis, was elected to its executive committee. On this governing body, I embarked upon an unsuccessful effort to persuade my colleagues that an organization whose goal was to establish world government must concern itself with more than the question of how to transform the United Nations into a representative federal government of the world; that it must also take stands on the current issues of foreign policy that would either make possible the ultimate achievement of world peace through world law or forever block the road to its attainment.

The most urgent of the current issues seemed to me the deadlock over Germany. A Soviet blockade of the land routes to Berlin had been instituted when the three Western powers had combined their zones, carried out a long-overdue currency reform and introduced the new Deutsche Mark in the Western sectors of the city. The blockade was being met by an airlift, brilliantly improvised by General Clay, and by an Allied counterblockade of the Soviet zone. The situation was ugly and would grow even uglier if, as I feared, the Western powers were to proceed with the Hoover plan for making their three zones into a separate West German state.

The majority of the United World Federalist executive committee, however, feared that taking positions on specific issues, such as Germany, would split the Federalist constituency. Dean Paul Shipman Andrews of Syracuse University's Law School made the classical statement of this position. "My daddy once told me," he said, "always to stick to one thing and then, like a postage stamp, you will arrive at your destination." I replied, "And, like a postage stamp, you will arrive canceled."

Eventually, I decided to remain a member of the United World Federalists but to devote my time to an individual effort to arouse my fellow citizens to the immediate dangers posed by the ever more threatening cold war.

Foreign policy played little part in the Presidential election campaign of 1948, except in so far as it was injected into public discussion by former Vice President Henry Wallace, running as the candidate of a newly organized Progressive Party. Early in the year, when Wallace had first decided to run as a third-party candidate, he had invited me to lunch and asked, "In view of your dissent from Truman's cold war policy, with which you know that I heartily agree, why aren't you in my corner?"

I liked Wallace for his idealism but considered him an impractical politician except in his own field of agriculture and so I replied, "Because you have not as yet developed an affirmative program in place of the policy you rightly criticize, because I am afraid that your independent candidacy may elect Dewey, and because, quite honestly, I don't much care for some of the people who are already in your corner." (Wallace, a former Republican turned Democrat under Roosevelt, was certainly no crypto-communist or communist sympathizer, but some of his closest advisers were the very left-wingers I had learned to distrust when working with Sidney Hillman. I doubted whether Wallace possessed the political sophistication that had enabled Hillman to keep these gentry at arm's length.)

When Joan and I returned from Europe shortly before the November elections, most people seemed to take it for granted that Dewey would be an easy victor over Truman. I took no part in the campaign. Much as I disliked President Truman's foreign policy, I saw no reason to suppose that Dewey's would be any better, particularly since John Foster Dulles was slated to become Secretary of State in the event of a Republican victory. In domestic affairs, Truman would, I thought, pursue a more liberal course, and, chiefly for this reason, I decided, without

much enthusiasm, to vote for his re-election. The President's unexpected triumph at the polls was a distinctly personal victory
due to his indefatigable campaigning and his rugged exploitation
of the "do-nothing, Republican-controlled eighty-worst Congress."

Although past experience made it doubtful that a personal
plea from me would have any effect upon President Truman's
foreign policy, I wrote him, urging that he devote the major part
of the nation's available resources to world-wide rehabilitation
and social and economic development, rather than attempt to
build a physical wall around the vast periphery of the communist
orbit. Pleading once more for a new approach to the German
problem, I warned against freezing the partition by creating
and making a separate peace with a West German state.

More than six weeks elapsed before I received a perfunctory
acknowledgment from the public affairs officer of the Department of State. Having failed to interest the President, I ascertained from Clark Clifford, one of his assistants, that there would
be no objection to the publication of my message in a forthcoming book. The letter with its accompanying memorandum
was published in *Last Call for Common Sense* (pages 261 to
271). No review ever pleased me more than Carl Sandburg's
generous comment on this book, which he wrote to my publishers:

If it should be that World War III comes, James P. Warburg is
already shriven of all guilt. Warburg comes as a reporter and historian of the present scene. "Last Call for Common Sense" is perhaps the greatest pamphlet of our time—amazingly clean of malice,
anger and hate not required for this hour. He reminds one of Lincoln's "House Divided" speech and its opening line: "If we could
first know where we are and whither we are tending, we could better judge what to do and how to do it."

CHAPTER XXVII

Unhappy Break with an Old Friend

PRESIDENT TRUMAN's inaugural address was noteworthy chiefly for one brief paragraph in which he announced the inception of "a bold new program" of technical assistance to the world's "underdeveloped areas." Because this announcement was the fourth point made by the President, the program became known as the Point Four Program.

The new program came as a welcome surprise and raised the hope that the philosophy of the Marshall Plan would now be applied to Asia, Africa, and Latin America. It soon developed, however, that Truman was not thinking of extending economic aid analogous to that given to Western Europe; he was thinking of technical advice—in his words, "a sharing of American know-how." As it turned out, the program was neither very bold nor very new; the United Nations were already giving technical advice and assistance to a number of countries; the Administration had not, as a matter of fact, developed any specific plan of action; it had simply coined a slogan. The mere announcement, however, raised such hopes and was so enthusiastically welcomed abroad that it became urgently necessary to translate the President's words into action.

It was fortunate that Truman's victory at the polls had carried with it a restored Democratic control of both houses of Congress because General Marshall's illness had deprived the Administration of the services of the one man who, more than any other, had commanded the support of both parties. While saddened by General Marshall's forced retirement, I felt that a reversion to traditional foreign-policy making was to be welcomed. It seemed to me desirable that the party in power assume full responsibility.

The appointment of my old friend Dean Acheson as Marshall's successor seemed a happy omen. As Assistant Secretary and then as Under Secretary, Acheson had been largely responsible for the brilliant concept of the Marshall Plan. He had got along well with the President and with Congress. His year in private practice had left him uninvolved in those recent developments in European policy which seemed to me loaded with dynamite.

Immediately after Acheson's appointment was announced and about a week before he was to take office, I went to see him at his Washington law office. He told me that he had been almost completely out of touch with European developments during recent months and would welcome whatever information I could give him. I concentrated upon three subjects: Ruhr coal; the German problem; and the reported negotiations for American participation in a North Atlantic Defense Pact.

In place of the recently drafted Ruhr Coal Agreement under which German coal was to be allocated among the participants in the European Recovery Program, I urged consideration of my 1946 proposal to create a European Coal Authority under which all European coal would be pooled and allocated to any nations willing to participate as producers, consumers, or in both capacities. This, I argued, would tend to draw the entire European community together and would not discriminate against any one country.

I renewed my warning against the creation of a separate West German state, arguing that the economic unification of the three Western zones was sufficient to bring them into the European Recovery Plan, and that their political unification as a state would undoubtedly cause the Russians to convert their zone into a satellite state and freeze the partition.

Next, I brought up the projected defense alliance with Western Europe. On June 11, 1948, Congress had passed the Vandenberg resolution authorizing United States participation in mutual defense treaties with other countries in accordance with Article 52 of the United Nations Charter. On the basis of this precedent-breaking resolution, the Truman administration had been negotiating with the Brussels Treaty powers for the possible participation of the United States and Canada in a North Atlantic Treaty. The details of these negotiations were still a closely guarded secret. I told Acheson that I favored the general idea of an Atlantic alliance, provided that our commitment would not tie the United States to any predetermined strategy of defense or theater of action in the event of war. I warned against including Germany or any part of Germany in such a defense alliance, since this would, in my judgment, provoke rather than prevent conflict.

Acheson listened with interest and asked me to set down the ideas I had expressed in the form of memoranda, so that he could give them careful consideration.[1] As I left, I felt encouraged to hope that American policy in Europe would be given a thorough re-examination—a hope soon to be sorely disappointed.

In April, the North Atlantic Treaty was sent to the Senate for ratification. On May 10, 1949, I was asked to testify before the Senate Foreign Relations Committee for or against the proposed treaty. This occasion involved me in a direct conflict with Acheson—a conflict that eventually marred a cherished friendship.

The day before I testified, Acheson had assured the Senate Committee that the proposed treaty would not involve sending additional American troops to Germany; that Western Europe would not be diverted from recovery to rearmament since it was planned only to modernize the existing twelve West European divisions; and that the United States would in no circumstances agree to the remilitarization of Germany. I found myself compelled to take issue with each of these statements.

It was clear, I said to the senators, that the West Europeans and especially the French would not be satisfied with a treaty that merely guaranteed that the United States would come to their aid in the event that they were attacked; they had no wish once more to be liberated from enemy occupation. Henri Queuille, the French Premier, had explicitly said with regard to the pending negotiations, "Next time you liberate us, you will be liberating a corpse."

I was not opposed to the treaty as such. In fact, I pointed out that in 1939 I had suggested precisely such a declaration of solidarity with Western Europe as the only way to prevent Hitler from attacking the Low Countries, Britain, and France. But it

[1] *Last Call for Common Sense*, pp. 183–239.

was one thing to say that the United States would consider an attack upon Western Europe as an attack upon itself, retaining freedom of action to fight an aggressor by whatever means and in whatever theater it might deem best; and quite another to stretch the treaty into a promise to prevent Western Europe from being invaded—in other words, to defend Western Europe at its easternmost frontier in central Germany. The French attitude was, I thought, entirely understandable, but the commitment the French wanted us to undertake could not possibly be fulfilled if, as Acheson had testified, the treaty implied nothing more than the modernization of twelve antiquated West European divisions. Such a commitment, I said, would involve not only a much more far-reaching rearmament of Western Europe but also the permanent stationing of a large American garrison in Germany and eventually the rearming of the West Germans themselves. I said that either the French were being misled as to the meaning of the American commitment or the Senate and the American people were being misled as to what was implied by the commitment they were being asked to take.

Both Senator Tom Connally of Texas, the Democratic committee chairman, and Senator Arthur Vandenberg of Michigan, its senior Republican member, asserted that the treaty commitment would not be stretched to imply a guarantee against invasion—that, in Senator Vandenberg's words, "There will be no Maginot line."[2]

The Foreign Relations Committee and later the full Senate ratified the treaty with this understanding, but it was only a few months before it became apparent that the Truman Administration was, as I had suspected, undertaking to defend Western Europe at its Iron Curtain frontier in central Germany. This made it inevitable that Acheson's promises would fall by the wayside—that a substantial American garrison would have to be stationed permanently in Germany; and that sooner or later there would be a demand that the West Germans contribute to their own defense.

Throughout 1949, until the point of no return was passed, I did my utmost to persuade Acheson not to create a separate

[2] For a full account of this hearing, see the New York *Times* of May 11, 1949; also pp. 77–105 of my *Germany—Key to Peace*, Harvard University Press, 1953.

West German state and to restrict the treaty to the terms upon which it had been ratified. Failing in this direct approach, I tried unsuccessfully through numerous speeches and pamphlets to arouse public opinion.

Neither Acheson nor the President ever openly admitted or explained their strange reversal of policy, nor would they concede that the fulfillment of their extended commitment would involve the remilitarization of West Germany.

The Soviet blockade of West Berlin was lifted in May 1949, but Truman and Acheson proceeded with their plan to create a separate West German state. In July, I made another attempt to show the Senate Foreign Relations Committee that the basis upon which it had ratified the North Atlantic Treaty was being ignored by the Administration.[3] As might be expected, this did not endear me to Acheson, who was proceeding under a full head of steam to bring into being a West German state.

On August 14, 1949 the Federal Republic of Germany was created, and Konrad Adenauer was elected as its Chancellor. On October 1, the Russians announced the creation of an East German, so-called Democratic Republic of Germany. The partition was now frozen.

In the course of several speaking trips to the Middle West, the Rocky Mountain states, and the Pacific coast, I discussed with university and citizen groups the probable implications of the North Atlantic Treaty and the partition of Germany. I also tried to work up support for the Point Four program, which seemed to me the only promising development of recent months. At a conference in Philadelphia organized by Stringfellow Barr and Norman Thomas to consider the carrying out of this hopeful program, I undertook to produce a pamphlet to be sponsored by the Public Affairs Institute of Washington, D.C. This booklet aroused wide interest and was reprinted several times. It was followed by Stringfellow Barr's even more popular *Let's Join the Human Race*, published by the Chicago University Press.

Eventually, these efforts to strengthen a policy that had so far failed to live up to its promise as a "bold, new program," bore fruit in the creation of a permanent, well-staffed lobby in Washington, organized by the United World Federalists, the American Association for the United Nations, the C.I.O., and

[3] *Germany—Key to Peace*, pp. 112–15.

the Cooperative League of the United States. It was largely due
to the efforts of this lobby that enabling legislation was enacted.
A similar lobby, organized by the United World Federalists and
others interested in disarmament and world government, succeeded in obtaining the introduction of Senate and House resolutions favoring the strengthening of the United Nations.

Events in the world arena moved rapidly in the next year.
In September 1949, the Russians exploded their first atomic device. In November, Chiang Kai-shek gave up the struggle on
the mainland of China and fled with the remnants of his battered forces to the island of Formosa. Ugly talk among right-
wing Republicans asserted that "China had been lost to communism," because the State Department had been infiltrated by
communists or communist-sympathizers.

In May 1950, French Foreign Minister Robert Schuman startled his British and American colleagues with his proposal to
launch a European Coal and Steel Community. And in June the
Soviet-equipped North Korean Army suddenly erupted across
the thirty-eighth parallel and invaded the Republic of South
Korea.

Republican spokesmen at once accused Secretary Acheson of
having "invited" the communist attack by having stated in a
recent speech that Korea lay outside of the defense perimeter
of the United States. Much as I disagreed with Acheson over
European policy, this accusation seemed unjust. The original mistake had been to commit American troops to the defense of an
arbitrary boundary between the American- and Soviet-occupied
parts of a distant Asian peninsula and then to agree upon a mutual withdrawal without training and adequately equipping
South Korea's defense forces to the point where they could hold
their own against the Soviet-trained and equipped North Korean
Army. If blame were to be assessed, it seemed to me more
logical to place it upon the American military authorities than
upon the admittedly ill-timed and ill-chosen remarks of the Secretary of State. (General Eisenhower was at this time Chief of
Staff.) Whoever had been to blame, once the invasion took
place, the Truman Administration acted, as it had in the case of
the Berlin blockade, with courage and vigor.

The shock produced in Europe by the North Korean aggression was similar to that occasioned by the *coup d'état* in Czechoslovakia. The Korean adventure seemed to prove that, given what looked like a favorable opportunity, the Russians would not hesitate to further their expansionist aims by the use of military force. Would similar tactics be applied to Europe? Would satellite armies invade West Germany?

I did not think so. But in September 1950 the Truman Administration openly demanded the rearmament of West Germany and its inclusion in the NATO alliance. The result was what I had expected. A long and bitter struggle broke out in Western Europe and in Germany—a struggle that was to last for four years before the first steps toward rearming Germany could be taken.[4]

During these troubled times, a happy event occurred in my personal life. On the second anniversary of our marriage, Joan presented me with a big, healthy boy. Not until the arrival of James Paul, Jr., had I realized how much I had wanted to have a son.

Shortly after the baby's arrival, we decided to live year round in the country. We converted our house on Seventieth Street into a small apartment house in which we retained the top floor as a *pied-à-terre*, and rented the remaining eight two-room apartments. At about the same time, we converted what had been the stable at Bydale into a library in which, for the first time in my life, I had room for all my books and could work in peace and quiet.

My domestic life had never been happier, but our poor country was moving into one of the most disgraceful periods in its history—the era of McCarthyism.

In the mid-term election campaign of 1950, the Republicans seized upon "the loss of China" as an issue, attributing Mao's triumph to the Truman Administration's alleged "softness toward communism." President Truman had himself laid the foundations for such an attack first by being careless of a certain amount of communist espionage and infiltration (which he described as a "red herring"), and by then adopting, in the "loyalty order" of 1947, security regulations that sanctioned the doctrine of guilt

[4] *Germany—Key to Peace*, pp. 129–51.

by association and the practice of discharging suspected security risks from government service without confronting them with their accusers or with the charges brought against them.

With the sanction of the Truman Administration, the Attorney General prepared a list of organizations which he labeled as "subversive" or "communist front." Membership in any organization on this list—whether past or present—became "evidence" of an individual's doubtful loyalty. Some of these organizations were no doubt communist fronts; others, originally innocent, had become communist-infiltrated; still others were wholly innocent. These distinctions mattered but little. If the Attorney General—or, for that matter, anyone else—said that such and such an organization was "subversive," then anyone who had belonged to it, no matter when or for how long, became an object of suspicion. It needed only the conviction for perjury of Alger Hiss to establish the widespread belief that the State Department had been infiltrated by communists and that a hidden communist fifth column was shaping American foreign policy. In this climate of suspicion and fear, informers flourished; unsubstantiated denunciation took the place of evidence; and unscrupulous opportunists, like Wisconsin's junior senator, Joseph McCarthy, reaped a political harvest.

Two of my closest friends, Owen Lattimore and Joseph Barnes, were among the victims of irrational and baseless persecution. By publicly coming to their defense, I myself became an object of suspicion.

The effect of this reign of terror upon the nation's foreign policy was disastrous. The Truman Administration began to compete with its critics by endeavoring to prove that it was more anti-communist than they. It accepted the thesis of the extremists that any and all negotiation with communist governments would constitute "appeasement," and so worked itself into a position of complete inflexibility. By falling in with the McCarthyite witch-hunt, the Administration destroyed the morale of the State Department and the Foreign Service, eventually depriving the department of some of its ablest Far Eastern experts.

Equally disastrous was the effect of the witch-hunt upon our schools, colleges, the media of communication and the American people as a whole. Many faculties were purged of teachers suspected of the slightest leftist leanings. Laws were introduced in some state legislatures forbidding the teaching of "controversial subjects." Otherwise sensible citizens became suspicious of neighbors and afraid to discuss politics or international affairs. The pursuit of suspects extended into Hollywood studios, newspaper offices, and radio stations. Nonconformist writers were banned from most magazines. A miasma of fear, hate, and suspicion threatened to strangle all freedom and distorted the nation's image throughout the world. (I am sure that, had I not once been a banker, I myself would have been hailed before a congressional investigating committee, especially because of a book written in 1950—*How to Co-exist without Playing the Kremlin's Game*—which contained [pages 46–89] a chapter entitled "An Inquiry into the Causes of Our Fear.")

The last three years of the Truman Administration were years of lost opportunity to settle the future of Europe, of frustration in Korea and abortive endeavor in the Middle East. In Chapters 5 through 10 of my *Germany—Key to Peace* (pages 77–244), published by the Harvard University Press in 1953, I have given an account of the European developments which culminated, in 1952, in Acheson's apparent triumph through the signature of the treaties that were to restore full sovereignty to West Germany and a rearmed West Germany's inclusion in the NATO alliance, only to encounter a European revolt against their ratification. In Chapters 26 through 29 of *The United States in a Changing World* (pages 385–461), published by Putnam in 1954, I have reviewed the whole Truman-Acheson period, including MacArthur's march to the Yalu, the defeat of his forces by the Chinese, his sensational recall, and the resulting stalemate at the thirty-eighth parallel, as well as the failure of the containment policy in the Middle East.

In retrospect, I am inclined to think that the most far-reaching developments of this period occurred in Asia. Britain's graceful withdrawal from India, Burma, and Ceylon, together with the defeat of the American-supported Kuomintang government of China, set in motion a revolt against Western domination which involved the Netherlands in Indonesia, France in Indo-China, Britain in the Arab Middle East, and ultimately all of the European colonial powers in Africa. The Truman Administration's attitude toward these developments was ambiguous. It futilely backed the Nationalist Government of China and the

French in their effort to re-establish colonial rule in Indo-China. On the other hand, it freed the Philippines and supported the Indonesian demand for independence. Traditional American anti-colonialism was at loggerheads with a policy that, in its obsession with containing communism, seemed likely to become a global defense of an already indefensible status quo.

Harry S. Truman, by no means a weak President, had come to power as the prisoner of Roosevelt's optimistic postwar policy, which only Roosevelt himself might have brought to fruition. He finished his almost eight years in office as the prisoner of an intellectual and emotional paralysis for which his own miseducation of the American people had been largely responsible. He left to his successor a nation torn by internal dissension, suspicion, and fear, uncertain as to the nature of the challenge it faced and no longer in possession of paramount power. The Berlin Airlift provided a demonstration of courage, ingenuity and determination, though it did not and could not redeem the blunders that had brought about the Berlin crisis. The Marshall Plan, though frustrated in its original bold and generous conception, had saved Western Europe from economic chaos and, very likely, from communist subversion; this remained a major achievement. The Point Four program was at least an intellectual departure from the sterile negativism of military containment. Finally, whatever the judgment of history might be on the origin and conduct of the Korean War, the decision to intervene was bravely taken and probably saved the United Nations from oblivion. However myopic and inflexible Truman's basic foreign policy, the crucial decisions to implement it were courageously made and gallantly executed.

As the 1952 elections approached, one major question preoccupied my mind: Would the forthcoming campaign bring about a long overdue debate concerning the basic aims of our foreign policy, or would the next President merely accept and carry on the well-intentioned but inadequate policy of his predecessor?

CHAPTER XXVIII

A New Star Flashes across the Political Firmament

WEARINESS with the stalemated Korean War and disgust over a series of minor scandals in the Truman Administration gave the Republican Party an opportunity in 1952 to exploit the slogan "It's time for a change." Its leading candidates for the Presidency were Senator Robert Alonzo Taft (now known as "Mr. Republican") and General Dwight D. Eisenhower, with Governor Earl Warren of California a dark-horse possibility.

With President Truman's support, an effort had been made to induce General Eisenhower to accept the Democratic nomination, but the general had declined, having by this time come to the conclusion that his sympathies lay more with the conservative Republican Party than with the Democrats. On the other hand, he did not wish to see Taft elected because of the senator's isolationist views; it was this consideration that led him somewhat reluctantly to seek the Republican nomination.

Among the Democratic candidates were Senator Estes Kefauver of Tennessee, Senator Richard Russell of Georgia, and my friend Averell Harriman, now governor of New York. The two men most strongly favored by the liberal Democrats—Supreme Court Justice William O. Douglas and Illinois Governor Adlai E. Stevenson—had declined to become candidates. (In a personal conversation with Justice Douglas, I learned that the Justice would not accept the nomination even if drafted, because he felt strongly that to do so would set a bad precedent; the Court, he felt, should never become a steppingstone to the Presidency.)

Kefauver, the most industrious campaigner in primary elections, had a liberal record in Congress but did not seem to me to
possess the attributes of a great President. His views on foreign
policy were unknown. I felt that Harriman had many qualities
that would make him a good President, but, unfortunately, he
had wholeheartedly supported Acheson's European policy and
was, in any case, too loyal to Truman to appeal to the people as
an exponent of change from the preceding Administration. The
only liberal Democrat who might conceivably break away from
the Truman-Acheson foreign policy, I thought, was Governor
Adlai Stevenson of Illinois, provided he could be persuaded to
seek the nomination.

I had known Stevenson since the thirties, when both he and I
had worked against inflation in the early days of the New Deal.
Later, I had occasionally seen him while he was a member of
the first American delegation to the United Nations. He was a
close friend of Marshall and Ruth Field. On January 28, 1952, I
wrote to him:

Naturally, we have followed recent events with the greatest possible interest. (This referred to the reports that President Truman
intended to back Stevenson for the nomination.) I can't quite bring
myself to believe that a certain gent, who shall be nameless, would
have enough sense to wish to sublet his present dwelling to you but,
if he should—and if you were to evince any interest in that transaction
—I want you to know that one coat is ready to be taken off and one
pair of sleeves ready to be rolled up—Ike or no Ike.

My guess is that you won't be wanted if Taft looks like the Republican nominee but that, if it looks like Ike, you will, because then it
will take more than whistle-stops à la 1948. Realistically, I wouldn't
appraise too highly the chances of beating Ike, but that doesn't seem
to me the only thing to consider. If the Democratic Party could clean
itself up, become the party of progress and sanity—as it would with
you as its standard-bearer—and lose decently, I'm not sure that this
wouldn't be the best thing that could happen right now. You would
then build a record of constructive "loyal opposition" and, I think,
walk in in 1956.

That, I know, is not a particularly alluring prospect. It requires
great personal sacrifice. On the other hand, playing it that way just
might be the way to pull an unexpected miracle and actually win
this year. (And who the hell asked for *my* advice?)

Governor Stevenson replied on February 2, 1952:

I am most grateful for your letter. I think you make a most realistic appraisal of the situation. I wish I had ambitions because I think we are agreed that Taft must not be President. I have found this job, however, about all I can handle and then some . . .

On March 17 I wrote to him again.

In traveling about the country as an itinerant preacher pleading for a more creative foreign policy, I am almost invariably asked: "Which candidate, if any, do you think would if elected bring about the sort of reorientation that you are talking about?"

My answer is that the only man who I *know* would do this is un-available—namely, Supreme Court Justice William O. Douglas. I then go on to say that I *think* you would but don't know for sure and that it would be easier for you to do so if you were nominated on your own, rather than as Truman's designee.

The purpose of this letter is certainly not to embarrass you by asking for any answers. I merely thought it might be useful to state a quandary in which many of us find ourselves . . . It comes down to this:

Those of us who would want to pitch in and help where we could would feel far greater enthusiasm if you sought and won the nomination on your own, instead of accepting it as Truman's heir. Maybe you cannot do that, or can but don't want to. I am not presuming to offer any advice. I am simply stating the belief that there are two things to be seriously considered at the present time:

The first is that, if you want to change our foreign policy, it will be difficult to do so, if you have to campaign for election on the basis of defending it. (The relevance of this factor depends upon the extent to which you would want to change it.)

The second factor is that, to be elected, any Democrat will have to overcome the very powerful popular demand for a change—the feeling that, if a two-party system is to survive, it is about time that the Democrats were turned out. (This quite apart from the resentment against corruption and so forth, in this particular Administration.) To overcome this sentiment a Democratic candidate must, in my humble opinion, clearly stand for change, and not for a continuation of the present regime.

Assuming that you have any desire to become President, and assuming that you would not want to continue the present foreign policy, if you were elected, these two factors in combination make the case for an independent candidacy which I wanted to put before you. Don't bother to acknowledge this letter and please forgive my impertinance in writing it.

Early in April, Stevenson had been in Washington and was reported to have declined President Truman's suggestion that he seek the Democratic nomination. He had declared his intention of running for re-election as governor of Illinois.

On April 10, I wrote the governor:

Things seem to be moving your way. Best of all, you are now clear of the impediment which I feared when I last wrote you.

Assuming that you are nominated and that Ike is your opponent, there could be one beautifully clear issue between you—namely our policy with respect to Germany. Ike won't be able to attack it because he helped to make it. You won't have to defend it because you did not make it. Thus you will be in a position to turn the tables with regard to what I consider the most vulnerable aspect of your party's record.

Because of the crucial importance of this issue, I am taking the liberty of sending you this advance copy of a pamphlet to be issued on April 19th. I hope it will persuade you—if you need persuasion— that Dean has been basically wrong about European defense.

I'm not asking you to commit yourself on this. Indeed, I think you would be most unwise to commit yourself so far in advance even to what I would consider the wise position. Too much is bound to happen in the next few weeks and months. I'm asking only that you give this some very serious thought, if you will—because, in my humble opinion, this is the decisive factor in war or peace.

The pamphlet referred to was an advance copy of *Our Last Chance in Germany—Stop, Look and Negotiate*, which summarized my recent testimony before the Senate Foreign Relations Committee.

Adlai Stevenson wrote me on April 12:

Thanks for your letter and the Senate testimony, which I certainly *will* read. I owe you an apology for not acknowledging long before this your very interesting and helpful letter of March 17. I have had no doubt from the start about my position on the presidential business in view of my official candidacy for Governor, but the pressures have been appalling, as you will appreciate, I am sure.

I replied to the Governor's letter on April 18, regretting but respecting his decision.

His next letter of April 25 quite definitely reaffirmed his determination not to seek the nomination.

On May 19 I wrote him again.

I was asked some time ago to submit some ideas to Senator Kefauver on what he should say in a foreign policy speech. On condition that my making such suggestions would in no way commit me to the Kefauver camp, I sent along a number of short background papers and three position papers—on rearmament, negotiation and the development of a positive plan for peace.

When these exploratory papers seemed to fall on not altogether arid soil, I agreed to draft the sort of foreign policy speech which I considered should be made and which I believed to be politically wise as well.

Thinking that you might be interested in this attempt, I am enclosing a copy. In the unlikely event that Kefauver should actually make something recognizable as a derivative of this speech, I would of course rely upon your discretion in keeping its origin locked in your bosom.

Meanwhile, should you feel like commenting in confidence on this draft, I should be most interested . . .

Stevenson replied on May 30:

I have read and re-read your splendid speech for Senator Kefauver and will doubtless borrow from your ideas freely and without byline or prosecution, I hope . . . Perhaps I sense the horrors of the next few years more clearly than he and some of the other gentlemen who seem so eager to assume burdens and decisions that dwarf the imagination . . . Please keep feeding my empty head.

Senator Kefauver did not make the speech I had drafted for him, and so, believing that the ideas in it should be thoroughly aired before the Democratic convention even if they could not be presented as the views of a presidential aspirant, I decided to deliver it myself as "The Unspoken Speech" before the Columbia University Summer Session. The address, which received nationwide press coverage, denied that war was inevitable, affirmed the belief that victory in war would destroy the very values Americans desired to protect, and criticized the existing over-emphasis upon seeking peace by preparing for war. It held that rearmament, while necessary, should not be provocative and must not be permitted to undermine economic strength; and it laid out an affirmative program consisting of a multilateral approach to world economic development wholly divorced from the cold war, and a simultaneous approach to the abolition of war through universal national disarmament enforced by a supranational authority endowed with the exclusive right to maintain armed forces.

The day after Eisenhower was nominated, I wrote Stevenson:

It is more than clear after yesterday's events at Chicago that there is a real foreign policy issue in the campaign, provided that the Democratic nominee is not bound by a silver cord to the Truman Administration and its foreign policy.

The choice of Eisenhower and the foreign policy plank adopted by the Republican convention repudiate the Taft-MacArthur doctrine of writing off Europe; endorsing instead NATO and the inclusion of Germany in NATO . . . Dulles has sold the party his notion of some sort of an ideological offensive behind the Iron Curtain. (This is an issue in itself, but not the one to which I want to call your attention at this moment.)

The point to which I want to draw your attention is this:

In a strange outburst to the Nebraska delegation, two days before his nomination, Eisenhower let the cat out of the bag as to his own view of NATO and Europe. He, who has been talking about France and to the French as if France were the keystone of the arch of European defense, suddenly burst out with a statement accusing France of "moral disintegration." He was quoted as having said:

"One place where France has gone astray is that they have fifty percent of their people agnostic or atheists. It takes no brains to be an atheist—you find no atheists in foxholes."

(Translation by JPW: "France is no good. NATO must be built upon Germany." The statement contains other implications as well, but this is the important element in it.)

Now—the Truman Administration has reluctantly agreed, under pressure from Europe, to hold some sort of talks with Russia on German unification. Adenauer has failed to get ratification of the EDC Treaty before such talks can be held . . .

French ratification will, I should think, wait on German action. If Germany does not ratify, the French will heave a sigh of relief; they will be out of the shot-gun marriage without having incurred the wrath of Washington. If Germany does ratify in September, you can be quite sure that there will be the hottest kind of fight in the French Assembly during the last and decisive month of our election campaign.

The potential issue is this: Ike will inevitably take the pro-German anti-French line . . . No Democratic candidate can take up that challenge who has endorsed promoting the shot-gun marriage.

This does not mean that the Democrat would have to oppose a "United Europe." He could—and should—endorse the Schuman Plan as a sound step in that direction. What he must attack is the putting of the military cart before the political and economic horses. Ike himself saw this in February 1951, when he recommended postponing German contributions to NATO. Given Ike's own promises to bring our own boys back "as soon as Europe is in a position to defend itself" and to reduce the military budget and taxes, this means just one thing: making Germany the dominant power on the Continent.

Verb. Sap. Here endeth the exercise.

Superfluous couplet:

I know who I'd like
To run against Ike.

The governor replied on July 16:

Your letters always fascinate me and the last two are no exception. I wish I could see things differently but I feel utterly dedicated, obligated and preoccupied with my present job. Moreover, there seem to be plenty of aspirants for the Presidential nomination.

I shall study long and carefully your comments about Germany, about which I know all too little.

My next letter was written while the Democratic convention was in session at Chicago:

For three days I've wanted to send you a telegram reading:

Now that you're stuck with it,
Brother, good luck with it.

Superstition has prevented my sending it, but I'll risk the hoodoo of sending it so it won't reach you until after you are made the nominee late tonight or early tomorrow morning. You have my very real personal sympathy, but, as a citizen of the United States and of the world, I am very happy. You can and will win. You can and will be a great President . . .

If I can ever lighten, even by a little, the burden you will be carrying during the campaign and, later, in the White House, I should consider it a great privilege. The one thing I think I might be able to do for you from time to time is to present a clear analysis of a problem that lies within the limited area of my competence, along with an analysis of alternative solutions. You won't get anything from me that you couldn't produce better yourself, but you won't have the time to produce it once you get on the treadmill. The mess as to Germany is a good current example, and will be lying right on top of the agenda on your desk in the Oval Study . . .

The Democratic nominee wrote to me on August 4:

Your couplet is splendid and reflects my state of mind exactly. I shall do my best, and I wish I were as confident of the future, not just the elections returns, as you are. I had never fancied myself in this appalling predicament.

As to what you can do, I should, of course, welcome any drafts of speech material which you could pass along. Also I am hopeful, speaking politically, that some activity will develop along the lines of Stevenson-Sparkman Committees or Stevenson for President Clubs or something of that kind to work among the independents. I think an old friend of mine, James B. Alley, a lawyer down town, may be interested in promoting something of the kind. It is difficult for me to get my mind on it in view of the infinite problems here, but I am sure that sort of spontaneous nonprofessional work was invaluable to me in Illinois and will be in this campaign where I have to overcome, basically, the "time for a change" idea.

Stevenson's campaign from beginning to end set a new high in American politics. Throughout the campaign, I supplied material and partial drafts of speeches as requested, marveling at the way in which Stevenson would take up a roughly suggested idea and clothe it in his own sparkling style. Much as I had admired him, I had had only an inkling of the man's true greatness of heart and mind until it was unfolded during the grueling weeks of campaigning from one end of the country to the other.

With respect to foreign policy, Stevenson took a forthright position in favor of never closing the door upon negotiation and of making a greater effort to promote world-wide economic development. He did not, to my regret, take specific positions on issues such as Germany, feeling, perhaps wisely, that to do so might tie his hands in the event of his election.

As for General Eisenhower, whom I had liked and admired during the war, I was shocked by his endorsement of senators Jenner and McCarthy, by his compromises with Taft, and by his unfair exploitation of "Truman's Korean war." I expressed these feelings in a bit of doggerel published anonymously by the Volunteers for Stevenson:

JUNE ILLUSION

I like Ike. I like his grin.
I like the jutting of his chin.
Here is a man, sincere and just,
A man in whom to put our trust,
Whose character will not be bent
By wanting to be President.
Here is a man to bear the load
Beneath which weaker men would crack
Who clearly sees the long, hard road
And will not seek to turn us back.
Here is the man to clean up graft.
And—best of all—he is not Taft.

OCTOBER AWAKENING

Alas, my friends, I do not like
This new and strangely altered Ike.
I have not liked him since the hour
When he became Ike Taftenhower.

And so, my friends, though I, for one,
Thought that a change was overdue,
I think I'll vote for Stevenson
And recommend the same to you.

Without success, I persistently endeavored to persuade my friend, Arthur Sulzberger, publisher of the New York *Times,* to switch his support to Stevenson, pointing out that Stevenson had taken a clear stand for the principles advocated by the *Times,* while Eisenhower, through his compromises with Taft, had all but repudiated them.

Apart from Stevenson's own magnificent efforts, his campaign was poorly run. On the night of Eisenhower's election, I wired Stevenson:

No man has ever achieved a greater victory in defeat or given those who supported him more reason to be proud of their candidate. Nothing could be more important than giving this country what it has lacked for twenty years, namely, a loyal opposition which offers not obstruction but responsible constructive criticism. That is what I'd like to talk to you about when you have had a good rest, apart from wanting to shake your hand and to congratulate you in more ways than one.

Adlai Stevenson replied on November 11:

So many thanks for your good telegram. I quite agree with you about the proper posture of the party in the future, and I hope I can lend a little weight to that end. I am going to be away for a few days, but except for the Thanksgiving week-end I shall be here continuously and, of course, would be glad to see you at any time.

I shan't attempt to thank you for all you did on our behalf and for your many contributions to our intellectual fare.

My trip to Libertyville to see Stevenson was postponed by the unexpected tardiness of Joan's second child in arriving. (I told Joan that I was sure the baby was a girl since only a woman could fuss that long before making her appearance.) Instead of going to visit Stevenson, I wrote him a lengthy letter expressing my admiration of the campaign he had conducted and my pleasure at learning from his telegram that he intended to be active as the leader of a constructive opposition party. I suggested that, as soon as possible after finishing his term as governor, he should take a leisurely trip around the world, stopping in Europe, Africa, the Near East, India, Indonesia, and Japan, pointing out that not one American political leader was informed about Africa, which seemed to me likely soon to follow Asia in shaking off colonial rule. I suggested that the trip would be invaluable in preparing a constructive alternative to the sterile foreign policy likely to be continued by the Eisenhower Administration.

On November 20 Joan gave birth to a little girl. Stevenson had a day or so before announced that he was going to "lie in the bullrushes for a while." On behalf of my new daughter, I wrote to him:

Dere Guvnor:
I hear you're going to lie in the bullrushes. I hope you have a good rest but please take along a pillow because the bullrushes and weeds might tickle your ear.

> *Much love*
> Jennifer Joan Warburg

A few days later, Jennifer received a letter she will always treasure:

Executive Mansion
Springfield, Illinois

December 15, 1952

Dear Jennifer:
 Thank you so much for your superb letter. I have never had a better letter from one so young. Indeed, I have never had one from one so young.
 And thanks for reminding me about the pillow when I lie in the weeds. But if you were a weed, I would very much like you to tickle my ear; and I should like to have you tickle my ear anyway.

Your very old friend,
(s) Adlai Stevenson

What a warmhearted, lovable human being! Looking back ten years later, I still regret that he was not elected in 1952, even though I was disappointed by his second campaign against Eisenhower in 1956. In retrospect, I am sure that no man could have been elected against Eisenhower in 1952 or probably in 1956. If Stevenson did nothing else, he lifted American politics for a short time to a new level of decency, humanity, and mature intellectuality. People who were unable to appreciate this great service to the nation scornfully called Stevenson an egghead and resented his gentle humor. But apart from his later distinguished service at the United Nations the fact remains as a monument to Stevenson that he made both intellectuality and humor in politics respectable. Had he not done so, I doubt whether John Fitzgerald Kennedy would have become President in 1961.

CHAPTER XXIX

A Benevolent General Reigns but Does Not Rule

IN SPITE of the fact that I had been an articulate Stevenson supporter, my contacts with the White House and its entourage during the eight years of Dwight D. Eisenhower's presidency were far more friendly and pleasant than they had been during President Truman's incumbency; and this in spite of the fact that I remained an outspoken critic of the Administration's foreign and domestic policies.

In retrospect, I feel that President Eisenhower's judgment was better than he himself knew and that his misfortunes arose chiefly because he trusted the judgment of others more often than he exercised his own. Strangely enough, he seemed to me as President to lack the very qualities that had made him a great military commander: self-confidence, decisiveness in resolving conflict of opinion, and the ability to pick the right men for the right tasks.

In fiscal policy, his oracle was George Humphrey, a Treasury Secretary alongside of whom Calvin Coolidge's Andrew Mellon would have appeared as a progressive. In foreign affairs, he relied implicitly upon John Foster Dulles, "the greatest Secretary of State of this century." I knew Dulles well and personally rather liked him, though not as much as I liked his brother Allen; but, as Secretary of State, I considered Dulles a disaster. Even more than Dean Acheson, he saw the world in self-righteous terms of blacks and whites, without Acheson's pragmatic sense of the limits of American power.

It is my considered belief that in foreign affairs at least Dwight D. Eisenhower might have gone down in history as a great President had he at the outset taken matters into his own hands. Whenever the chips were down, he showed both wisdom and determination. Twice, he personally prevented war by restraining the hotheads in his official family. Certainly, no one can doubt that he earnestly tried, even though in the end he tragically failed, to find the road to peace.

The lists of my books and pamphlets appended to this and the next chapters and the order in which these publications appeared give a sufficient picture of the subjects about which my growing concern was expressed during the Eisenhower years to the White House, to the Congress and to the public. I shall fill in here only a few items of personal experience.

Before the new Administration took office, I made an attempt to persuade General Eisenhower and some of his advisers to take a new look at our European policy, especially as it concerned Germany. The effort was wholly unsuccessful. This was the response which I received:

June 15, 1953

Dear Mr. Warburg:

May I thank you for your letters concerning our German policy, and for sending me a copy of your pamphlet, "France, Germany and NATO." My recent absence and the preparatory work for Bermuda have caused some delay in my correspondence.

I find myself in strong sympathy with your view that the United States must positively support efforts to achieve German unity; and that we should envisage the unity of Germany as a step toward a new peaceful and secure all-European community.

However, under current circumstances, I feel that EDC is a step, and probably an essential step, on the road to German unity.

I have taken the liberty of forwarding your letter and pamphlet to the Secretary of State who will, I am sure, find them both interesting and helpful.

With me, he will be most grateful for your kind and encouraging personal observations.

Sincerely,
(s) DWIGHT D. EISENHOWER

President Eisenhower's letter made it plain that the new Administration would be no less adamant that its predecessor in insisting upon the ratification of the treaties which would bring a rearmed West Germany into NATO.

Indeed, Secretary Dulles, who had criticized Acheson's policies, soon threatened an "agonizing reappraisal" of the American attitude toward Europe unless Acheson's Bonn and Paris (EDC) treaties were promptly ratified.

Neither the rapidly deteriorating situation within the Western alliance nor the death of Stalin in March 1953, persuaded Dulles to consider a new approach, even though, after Stalin's death, there were distinct signs of a change in Soviet policy.

In August 1954 I decided to see for myself what was happening in Europe. I arrived in France on August 30—the day on which the French parliament spectacularly rejected the EDC treaty, thereby causing an unprecedented crisis in the Western alliance.

Through my friend, Claude Bourdet, a non-communist leftist, whose weekly *France Observateur* had opposed ratification of the treaty, I met several members of the Mendès-France cabinet. From them I gained some insight into the strange and confused state of French opinion. Hubert Beuve-Méry, the brilliant editor of the influential *Le Monde,* and Jacques Servan-Schreiber, editor of the weekly *L'Express,* further provided background to their country's ambivalent feelings. Both had opposed the treaty.

On the one hand, France feared Russia; on the other, she feared a rearmed Germany. I concluded that what most Frenchmen wanted was a calf with five legs—a German Army bigger than that of Russia and smaller than that of France! (The Soviet Army consisted of 175 combat-ready divisions; France had at most six.) My old friend David Bruce, now the American ambassador to NATO, had done his utmost to resolve this dilemma, without success.

From Paris, I went to Bonn, where the *Bundestag* was in session, for the moment preoccupied with the defection of a high secret-service official. At several sessions of the *Bundestag,* I had an opportunity to observe the autocratic contempt with which the Chancellor treated the parliament. I made no attempt to see Dr. Adenauer, because I had known and learned to distrust him in my banking days, when, as mayor of Cologne, he had tried to float an American bond issue. I did see the Chancellor's amiable press chief, Felix von Eckhardt, and his State Secretary, Hans Globke—a highly controversial character—to whom the Chancellor delegated most of his authority in internal affairs. (The relationship between Adenauer and Globke was rather like that between President Eisenhower and Sherman Adams.)

I was not surprised to find that "democracy" under Adenauer was little more than a farce. This was perhaps as much the fault of the German people and the opposition parties as it was the fault of the Chancellor. The German people still wanted to follow a leader rather than to govern themselves. The Social Democratic opposition was woefully weak, more inclined to complain than to offer constructive criticism. When I asked its leader, Erich Ollenhauer, why he did not occasionally bang his fist on the rostrum, he replied: "That would only hurt my own fist." Professor Carlo Schmidt, the second man in the Social Democratic hierarchy, was a charming, highly civilized philosopher who commanded affection and respect, but lacked force. The only forceful character in the opposition party with whom I came into contact was Herbert Wehner, an ex-communist of somewhat inscrutable orientation.

Dr. James Conant, the former president of Harvard University, whom I knew slightly, was at this time our ambassador to Bonn, having replaced Jack McCloy in 1952, when the post of High Commissioner was abolished. I had learned that Dr. Conant rarely saw anyone not in sympathy with the Chancellor's regime and tried not very successfully to convince him that it might be wise to treat the German opposition leaders as loyal Germans and not as if they were enemies of the republic and, therefore, of the United States.

The net impression gained by several weeks in the Federal Republic was not encouraging. Even more than in the United States, dissent was too often equated with pro-communism. Democracy had not yet put down any sturdy roots. The German people were quite satisfied to leave things to their "betters"; they were preoccupied with prosperity and the "economic miracle." Two Germans meeting on the street would often not say, "Good morning," but rather, "How is your new house?"

Ludwig Rosenberg, one of the top labor leaders in Düsseldorf, gave me an interesting insight. When I asked him why the underpaid German workmen never struck for higher wages, he said, "Because the strike benefits, while larger than in your country, are not large enough to enable a striking worker to keep up his installment payments on his motorcycle or his electric refrigerator. Your American installment payments have broken the strength of the German labor movement."

Another, perhaps even more revealing insight into the West German mind was provided by German youth. While at Bonn, I spent several Sundays talking to groups of young Germans who debarked from Rhine steamers at one or another of the many little restaurants along the west bank. When I asked these young men and women what sort of jobs they hoped to get when they had finished their education, the most common answer was, "Any job with good pay and a pension."

The attempt to "denazify" and re-educate the Germans had resulted in their adopting the worst rather than the best traits of the America they were trying to ape. They had achieved an economic but not a political miracle. They had become affluent without becoming mature. The shameful Nazi past was covered over by a thin layer of pretense that such a past had never existed. (It was not until 1958 that German history textbooks contained any reference to the Nazi period.) Few Germans were ready to admit either individual or collective responsibility for the past or to assume any responsibility for the future.

While all the political leaders were vociferously demanding reunification, very few of the people seemed to care, except those with relatives in the East, and their concern was mainly personal. While the political leaders talked about reunification, they developed no initiative toward its attainment; they said that the initiative must come from Washington or London; yet, whenever either Washington or London had shown the slightest signs of taking the initiative their own Chancellor had strenuously objected.

From Germany, I flew to England and found London agog with political discussion. Some of my friends in Whitehall and the City were openly pleased by the French rejection of EDC. The Labour Party had strongly opposed German rearmament and so had many right-wing Tories who followed the anti-German line of Lord Beaverbrook's *Daily Express*. However, most of the people I knew were seriously alarmed over the future of the Western alliance and fearful of what might now be the outcome of Dulles' "agonizing reappraisal."

During a turbulent month of discussion at London, it was not Dulles but Eden who came up with a solution to the crucial

NATO dilemma. In a rapid tour of the West European capitals, Britain's Foreign Secretary proposed the ingenious scheme of reviving the old Western Union formed by the Brussels Pact powers in 1948, and to admit the Federal Republic of Germany to NATO through the back door of membership in this semi-moribund organization.

In the end, it was Eden's display of unusual toughness that persuaded a harassed Mendès-France to agree to this solution, and, strangely enough, the French parliament ratified his action. The *Chambre* had rejected a treaty which would have permitted West Germany to rearm only to the extent of furnishing contingents to a European Army; it now accepted an arrangement which gave the Germans the right to rebuild a twelve-division Army of their own commanded by German generals, plus a limited Air Force and Navy.

The fact that German rearmament had now become a certainty four years after Secretary Acheson had first demanded it induced the Kremlin once more to seek a negotiated settlement. Dulles remained deaf to Moscow's call for a high-level conference. For the time being, he had other fish to fry in Asia and the Middle East.

Returning from Europe in October, I reported my impressions of the critical state of world affairs to Adlai Stevenson. The governor had himself traveled extensively in 1953. He had been to Africa, Asia, and Europe and had everywhere been received with great enthusiasm. My more recent report on the deterioration of the situation in Europe and my misgivings about Dulles' activities in Asia and the Middle East deeply disturbed him. Noting with pleasure the amazing extent to which Stevenson had familiarized himself with the problems of the various countries, I suggested that this would be a good time for him to get ready for the 1956 election by beginning to crystallize his views with respect to American foreign policy. Stevenson was by no means certain that he wanted to be the Democratic candidate again, but I suggested that, candidate or not, he would undoubtedly wish to take part in the campaign.

The idea of preparing a number of tentative position papers appealed to Stevenson, if only because they might be useful as speech material during the next two years, when he would in any case be the titular head of the Democratic Party. He asked me to go ahead and draft some working papers and then to see what the half dozen others whom he named might think of them.

A month later, my activities were suddenly and sharply curtailed by an attack of angina pectoris which required a short period of hospitalization, followed by a strict diet and a regimen of reduced activity. I found this extremely irksome, especially since it not only involved a reduction of travel and political activity but put an end to all but the mildest form of outdoor activity with my wife and children. Joan loved tennis and was an excellent doubles partner. Little Jimmy was just reaching the age at which a father enjoys teaching his son to throw and catch a ball. A second son had recently been born to us.

I was told I was lucky to have had a timely warning signal as well as the excellent medical care that had quickly brought the trouble under control, but, for a time, I felt as if old age had suddenly come upon me, even though a most understanding wife did her best to assure me that such was not the case.

As it turned out, the readjustment was relatively easy. It meant little more than taking it easy for a year and learning to do things more slowly. The only permanent casualty was tennis —a game that I, having once in my teens been beaten by an octogenarian, had confidently expected to be able to play for at least another ten years.

MAJOR PUBLICATIONS 1953–54

Does not include broadcasts and frequent letters to the editor, nor titles of many lectures in the United States and Canada.

FRANCE, GERMANY AND NATO. A memorandum to President-elect Eisenhower; Current Affairs Press, New York and (in German) Goettinger Arbeitskreis, Goettingen.

WHICH WAY TO LIBERATION? Annals of the American Academy of Political and Social Science, Philadelphia and Current Affairs Press, New York.

INTERNAL SECURITY WITHOUT SACRIFICE OF FREEDOM. Current Affairs Press, New York.

GERMANY—KEY TO PEACE.° Harvard University Press, Cambridge.

PROBLEMS OF UNITED STATES POLICY. Lectures at the Army War College and the Air War College; Current Affairs Press, New York.

THE GREATEST THREAT TO OUR LIBERTY. Current Affairs Press, New York.

THE UNITED STATES IN A CHANGING WORLD.° A diplomatic history; Putnam, New York.

CO-EXISTENCE OR NO EXISTENCE. Current Affairs Press, New York.

° denotes full-length books.

CHAPTER XXX

The Collapse of Dulles Diplomacy

THE NEWS during the first months of 1955 was not such as to aid the recovery of a cardiac patient. In December 1954, the NATO Council had decided to equip its ground forces with tactical nuclear weapons in order to make up for failure to meet the force goals set in 1952. This made it almost certain that any war in Europe would escalate into a major nuclear conflict. In February 1955, Moscow declared its intention to create a military alliance between the Soviet Union and its East European satellites as a counter-balance to NATO, and Dulles announced his new strategic doctrine of "massive retaliation" which frightened our friends and allies far more than it frightened Moscow or Peking.

On May 15, however, Moscow surprisingly agreed to an Austrian peace treaty providing for the withdrawal of all foreign troops and the military neutralization of a liberated Austrian republic. Thinking that this might indicate the pattern the Kremlin wished to apply to Germany, I wrote to President Eisenhower, asking whether he did not think the time had come to take the initiative toward a German peace settlement based upon a reunified Germany's military neutralization. I suggested that the decision to reduce the NATO force goals from eighty to thirty divisions equipped with nuclear arms had greatly reduced the need for a West German military contribution. President Eisenhower replied:

Thank you for your comments on recent developments in the European situation. I have read them with interest and am bringing them to the attention of the Secretary of State. I expect that he will wish to write you in some detail. Your concern with these important questions is very much appreciated.

I did not hear from Dulles. However, in July, the chiefs of state of the United States, Britain, France, and the Soviet Union and their foreign ministers met at Geneva to discuss the German problem and the question of European security. Although no agreement was reached, the conference did seem to mark the first clear recognition by both sides that war had become unacceptable as an instrument of policy. In particular, President Eisenhower's unmistakable devotion to the cause of peace made a worldwide impression, offsetting the belligerent inflexibility of his Secretary of State.

Still partially incapacitated, I spent the summer of 1955 drafting about a dozen position papers on over-all foreign policy on Europe, the Middle East, Asia, Africa, and Latin America for Stevenson, obtaining ideas and useful criticism chiefly· from George F. Kennan at Princeton and my friend John Kenneth Galbraith at Harvard.

While at Princeton, I called on Professor Albert Einstein, who had for several years been encouraging my efforts. One remark of Einstein's has stuck in my mind ever since: "Everything has changed," he said sadly, "except man's mode of thinking [*Alles hat sich verändert, nur nicht wie der Mensch denkt*]."

In September the world was shocked by President Eisenhower's sudden heart attack. Not only the American people, but people throughout the world had pinned their hopes for peace upon the President and were now thrown into a state of acute apprehension. President Eisenhower's recovery and gallant resumption of office aroused universal sympathy and renewed hope; they also greatly reduced the chances of a Democratic victory in the 1956 elections. It seemed to me evident that only a well-reasoned attack upon Secretary Dulles' foreign policy, with which Eisenhower's spirit at least had often seemed in disagreement, could overturn the Republican administration. Yet this sort of tactic apparently did not appeal to Stevenson. His advisers were telling him that there was "no mileage in foreign policy." I disagreed emphatically, but there was nothing I could do.

With Stevenson's readily given consent, I decided to make a paperback book out of the position papers I had prepared for him, without disclosing their original purpose. It was my hope that such a book might at least produce a public debate. With an eye to the widest possible distribution, I had this book printed on newsprint in a format resembling that of a weekly news magazine. This enabled my Current Affairs Press to sell it at ten cents a copy. Its title was *Turning Point toward Peace?*

Of all my books published in the postwar period this one reached the widest audience. Senator Wayne Morse of Oregon inserted the entire book in the Congressional Record. The first printing of 10,000 copies was exhausted within a month. Second and third printings of 100,000 copies each were underwritten by a foundation and a bipartisan group of individuals to provide free copies to libraries and to a nationwide selected group of opinion leaders. The most generous contributor to this distribution was, interestingly enough, Ernest T. Weir, president of the National Steel Company and a stanch Republican generally considered to be one of the inner circle in the Eisenhower Administration.

My contact with Weir, whom I had not known before, had an entertaining sequel. Several months later, early in 1956, he asked me to come to his office in New York. Without any preamble, he bluntly asked: "Whom do you think we should get to replace Foster Dulles?"

Startled, I replied, "You know, Mr. Weir, I am a Democrat. My way of getting rid of Mr. Dulles would be to elect Adlai Stevenson President this autumn."

"Don't be silly," said Weir. "You know perfectly well that Ike is sure to be re-elected. You may be a Democrat, but you're also a good American. Whom do you suggest?"

On the off-chance that Weir might actually be spearheading a drive to replace Dulles, I quickly ran over in my mind the names of a number of Republican friends. Bob Lovett's health would probably not permit him to take on another onerous task. The suggestion of Jack McCloy evoked no response from Weir. At the tentative mention of Paul Hoffman, who had rendered distinguished service in administering the European Recovery Program, Weir merely grunted, "Too liberal." Finally, I came up with the suggestion of Christian Herter.

"What do you know about him?" Weir asked.

I said that I had known Herter for many years; that his quiet courtesy, his intimate knowledge of Europe, and his perfect command of French would be great assets in dealing with the tangled European affairs; and that his long experience in the House and as governor of Massachusetts should make him a capable administrator and excellent negotiator on the Hill.

"Sounds good," said Weir. "Find out if he'd take it!"

With some reluctance I agreed to write Chris Herter and to send Weir whatever reply I might receive. In fulfilling this strange mission, I gave Herter a full account of the peculiar circumstances; he replied in a very friendly manner, saying that he wished to finish out his term as governor and then devote himself to his family. I passed this information on to Weir. No one was more surprised than I when, not very long afterward, Herter accepted an appointment as Under Secretary of State.

Throughout the early months of 1956, an almost incredible bipartisan silence with regard to foreign affairs continued. I tried, through an article in the New York *Times Magazine*, to get a discussion started. I endeavored once more to persuade Governor Stevenson to take up the cudgels. Finally, I made an attempt to arouse the Senate Foreign Relations Committee, whose chairman, Walter George of Georgia, had expressed considerable interest in the proposals for policy revision

I had put forward in the previous year. In writing to Senator George, I sent a copy of my letter to each member of the committee with a personal note asking for an expression of opinion.

Significantly, not a single senator defended the existing foreign policy. Several went out of their way to welcome the suggestion that a serious study be undertaken by the Foreign Relations Committee. Senator George did appoint a study group but charged it only with an examination of foreign economic policy —not with the study of foreign policy as a whole.

However, the NATO Council was aware of the deterioration of solidarity within the Western alliance and appointed a committee of "three wise men," with Canada's Foreign Secretary, Lester Pearson, as chairman, to study the problem. As I had long known and admired "Mike" Pearson, I suggested to him that the political organization of the Atlantic community should be undertaken outside of the NATO framework and on a wider basis; that a new, non-military organization be created to coordinate economic aid to the development of the emerging nations and to formulate a common political policy; and that the door to this new association of non-communist nations be left open to European neutrals, such as Switzerland, Sweden, and Austria, as well as to such non-European nations as Australia, New Zealand, Japan, and the democracies of Latin America.

This proposal, which I elaborated in the June 1956 issue of *The Reporter*, resembled the "Grand Design" to be developed five years later by the Kennedy Administration. In 1956, it fell upon barren ground.

American attention was once more focused upon an approaching presidential election. This time, Adlai Stevenson actively sought the nomination and obtained it in spite of a savage attack by former President Truman whose brutal characterization of Stevenson as a candidate who could not win hurt the Democratic Party's already slim chances of victory.

The Democratic foreign-policy plank, adopted at the convention, was a hodgepodge of pronouncements and promises designed to appeal to various groups of voters, rather than a statement of foreign policy. Much to my regret, Stevenson accepted it without reservation. In his acceptance speech, he spoke eloquently of the need for restoring American prestige and leadership but gave no indication of the measures by which this end was to be attained. If he had in mind any substitutes for the policies which he criticized, it was already late in the day to bring them forward. The final stages of a presidential campaign would not readily lend themselves to the kind of calm, careful elucidation required to bring about a basic reorientation of public opinion.

Regretfully, I came to the conclusion that the campaign would be fought chiefly over issues almost wholly irrelevant to the basic problems confronting the world. I decided to supply Stevenson with whatever material he might request but not to make further efforts to induce him to present clearly stated alternatives to the Eisenhower-Dulles policies. This, however, was no reason not to continue the attempt to promote public understanding and interest.

In August 1956, I set to work on a sequel to *Turning Point toward Peace* entitled *Danger and Opportunity*. Its first chapter, headed: "Sleep-walking into Disaster," attacked the complacent belief that the American economy was superbly strong and healthy and asserted that over-expanded consumer credit, together with over-conservative fiscal policies, would very soon produce a recession which would stand in the way of the nation's meeting the rapidly growing Soviet challenge in the economic field. It urged a less orthodox fiscal policy designed to meet long overdue public needs—such as education, housing, and medical care—while at the same time stimulating private investment.

In foreign affairs, the pamphlet sharply criticized the existing foreign-aid program as being 90 per cent directed to creating military strength and only 10 per cent toward aiding economic development, proposing much greater emphasis upon economic aid, a multilateral rather than a bilateral approach, and the total divorce of economic aid programs from the cold war. In the cold war itself, the booklet urged greater flexibility and a greater willingness to negotiate, advocating disengagement wherever possible, especially in Germany. It recommended bringing China into the disarmament talks and into the United Nations. In view of this outspoken criticism, I was touched to receive the following generous letter from President Eisenhower:

October 13, 1956

Dear Mr. Warburg:

It was thoughtful of you to send me your pamphlet, "Danger and Opportunity."

While, as you are aware, I don't always agree with you, I am quite cognizant of the very considerable public service you render by your efforts to further intelligent consideration of the basic issues that confront us all. I hope that you continue to do this and that your own concern may prompt others to do likewise.

There has never been a time in our history when widespread discussion of public policy was more necessary than it is today. The issues are sometimes complex and difficult to penetrate, but this should not prevent useful discussion from taking place.

Many thanks again for thinking of me.

With best wishes,

Sincerely,
(s) DWIGHT D. EISENHOWER

After a lackluster campaign in which Stevenson showed only rare flashes of the qualities which he had demonstrated four years earlier, President Eisenhower was overwhelmingly re-elected. Even had Stevenson taken a stronger stand on foreign policy, the crisis over Hungary and Suez, which occurred during the closing weeks of the campaign would have argued strongly against swapping horses in midstream. Stevenson's last-minute call for a cessation of nuclear tests and the abandonment of conscription fell into the vacuum created by his failure to set forth foreign policy alternatives. Not having laid the foundation for taking advantage of Dulles' blundering in the Middle East, Stevenson was in no position to capitalize on the crisis that erupted there during the last days of the campaign.

In December 1956, a disarmament conference was held at Gould House (Ardsley, New York) under the joint auspices of the Committee for World Development and World Disarmament and the Postwar World Council. Some forty government officials, technical experts, and private citizens participated in the three-day discussions, among them Senators John Sparkman (D) of Alabama and Ralph Flanders (R) of Vermont, both members of the Senate Foreign Relations Committee. We gave particular attention to a recent very interesting Soviet note proposing a regional European approach to disarmament to which no reply had as yet been made by Washington. At my suggestion, the conference adopted a memorandum to President Eisenhower suggesting that, in answer to the Soviet note of November 17, proposing a European security agreement to replace the NATO and Warsaw Pact alliances, the United States government might say that it looked with favor upon the proposal for eventual complete withdrawal of Soviet, British, and American forces from all of Europe west of the Soviet frontier, and that it might offer to take certain steps toward this, if matched by comparable Soviet steps. For example, the first step might be the withdrawal of the NATO forces to the west bank of the Rhine and the withdrawal of Soviet forces to the east banks of the Oder-Neisse rivers, with suitable arrangements for air and ground inspection. These arrangements, we suggested, might include Soviet ground-control posts, including a radar screen, on the east bank of the Rhine, and Western ground-control posts, including a radar screen, on the west banks of the Oder-Neisse. Suitable arrangements would, of course, be made for the preservation of the status quo in Berlin.

Senators Sparkman and Flanders took this statement to the White House and discussed it with President Eisenhower. Afterward, Senator Sparkman told me that the President had seemed to regard the proposal with friendly interest but had considered it "not feasible because Foster and Adenauer wouldn't like it at all."

I was discouraged but in no mood to give up. When the newly elected Congress assembled in January 1957, each senator and each member of the House found on his desk my *Memorandum to the 85th Congress*—an analysis of the dramatically changed world situation together with a plea for a far-reaching readjustment of United States foreign policy. It stressed the cleavages that were beginning to appear in the Sino-Soviet alliance.

With public attention focused upon the Middle East, I also published a number of articles about this area. One spelled out how the Middle East might be converted into a laboratory in which to test out the possibilities of a regional approach to disarmament and economic development. Another proposed the establishment of a United Nations Middle East Development Authority toward the support of which both the oil-rich Arab states and the international oil companies would contribute a share of their respective royalties and profits.

A third pamphlet applied a similar principle to other under-developed areas suggesting that if the bulk of all aid to economic development could be channeled through the United Nations, instead of being extended by unco-ordinated bi-national arrangements, it might become possible to lift the promotion of world-wide social and economic progress out of the sterile context of the cold war. This proposal was endorsed by the American Association for the United Nations in the tenth annual report of its Commission to Study the Organization of Peace.[1]

In October 1957, a near panic was occasioned by the launching of the first Soviet Sputnik and the subsequent testing of the Soviet's first intercontinental missile.

Here at home, doubt was cast upon the adequacy of the whole American defense effort and upon the quality of American education and scientific research. Abroad, America's friends began to question both the ability and the willingness of the United States to hold a protective nuclear umbrella over them, now that American cities had suddenly become vulnerable to Soviet attack. I used these doubts and fears to redouble my plea for disarmament.

In August 1957, I brought out a book entitled *Agenda for Action—Toward Peace through Disengagement,* in which I once more put forward specific proposals for relaxing tensions in Europe and the Middle East. The section devoted to the Middle East included an analysis of the historical factors that had combined to create Arab-Jewish hostility and the anti-Western Arab sentiment that had culminated in the Suez affair.

Shortly after this book appeared, a new impetus toward European disengagement came from an unexpected source. Poland's Foreign Minister, Adam Rapacki, introduced the novel and constructive idea of including Poland and Czechoslovakia as well as the two German states in a denuclearized zone in Central Europe. The Rapacki Plan was endorsed by Moscow but was rejected out of hand by Washington as "communist propaganda."

When Rapacki came to New York in September to attend the United Nations General Assembly, he invited me to lunch, ap-

[1] *Strengthening the United Nations,* Harper, 1957, pp. 8 and 9, 47 and 48, 200–6, 234, and 235.

parently having followed my long advocacy of seeking a détente in Europe. Welcoming the notion of including Poland and Czechoslovakia along with the two German states in a denuclearized zone, I suggested that the plan be expanded to provide for the eventual withdrawal of all foreign troops from the denuclearized zone. Rapacki said this was entirely in accord with his thinking; he had merely thought it more judicious to put forward his plan step by step. He agreed that, if any enthusiasm for his proposal could be generated in the West, Poland would come forward with a more complete proposal for a demilitarized zone. (Rapacki did so amend his proposal a year later.)

The whole idea of disengagement then received unexpected and powerful support from none other than George F. Kennan, the original author of the containment policy. In a brilliant series of Reith Lectures over the British Broadcasting Corporation's transmitters, Kennan aroused world-wide interest in an approach to peace that had up to this point never been fully understood by most Europeans or Americans.

In June 1958, I received a welcome invitation to appear once more before the Senate Foreign Relations Committee. Rhode Island's venerable Senator Theodore Green, who had recently succeeded Senator George as chairman, requested me to come to Washington and to present "an independent critique of our European policy."

After reviewing once more the succession of blunders that had led to the existing impasse over Germany and the general disarray of the Western alliance, I suggested to the committee that a modification of the Rapacki Plan be taken as a point of departure in developing a new Western negotiating position. The committee listened attentively and appeared to be interested, but Senator J. William Fulbright (D) of Arkansas, perhaps its best-informed member, soon to become its chairman, expressed grave doubt as to whether the Senate could properly initiate a major policy revision. My testimony ended with a fervent expression of the belief that the time for complacent, wait-and-see Micawberism had passed, and that the time for action had come.

The action came a few months later, but not from Washington. It came in the shape of a rude ultimatum from Nikita Khrushchev demanding that within six months the Western powers withdraw their garrisons from West Berlin and agree to convert the Western sectors into a "free city" under United Nations protection. I was surprised only that this second Soviet effort to drive us out of Berlin had not come sooner.

In the year 1958 the chickens came home to roost. It brought in quick succession the total collapse of Dulles' Middle East policy; the overthrow of the Fourth French Republic and the re-emergence of De Gaulle; another explosive crisis in the Far East over the Chinese offshore islands[2]; and, here at home, a long overdue economic recession. Meddlesome brinkmanship abroad and a false conception of fiscal conservatism in domestic affairs were bearing their bitter fruit.

Few Americans realized during the anxious winter of 1958–59 that their Secretary of State was heroically fighting a losing battle against a cruelly painful recurrence of abdominal cancer. (He had suffered a previous attack in 1956.) In the early months of 1959, the disease had progressed to the point at which Dulles was living on a bare subsistence diet of liquids and soft foods. Shortly after his return from the last of his many trips abroad, he was hospitalized, but for a few weeks nevertheless directed United States policy from his sickbed.

Fortunately, Britain's Prime Minister Macmillan fully understood the need for action and, entirely upon his own initiative, undertook a journey to Moscow to explore the possibility of opening negotiations without doing so under the threat of an ultimatum.

The Macmillan-Khrushchev communiqué, issued in Moscow on March 3, 1959, indicated that the exploratory talks had ranged beyond the question of Berlin and had set that question in a broader context of the relation of Germany to the whole problem of European security. The two statesmen agreed that

[2] In May 1958, the long smoldering crisis in the Taiwan Strait erupted in a Chinese Communist attack upon the Nationalist-held offshore island of Quemoy, bringing the United States once more within a hairbreadth of involvement in a major conflict. On this occasion, I resorted to placing a full-page paid advertisement in the New York *Times* in order to arouse public protest. The result was a flood of letters and telegrams to Washington from all over the country. Vice President Nixon denounced the State Department for revealing the magnitude of the protest, but President Eisenhower intervened to prevent the threatened involvement of American forces.

the subject should be further pursued at an early meeting of the Big Four Foreign Ministers.

Macmillan's reconnaissance at once aroused the angry suspicion of Chancellor Adenauer and the jealous resentment of President de Gaulle, as well as the anxiety of the fatally stricken American Secretary of State. Reading between the lines of the Washington dispatches, I suspected, however, that the President looked with favor upon the British initiative and that, although willing to leave foreign policy in the hands of his most trusted adviser, he had probably never shared his Secretary of State's inflexible intransigence. Eisenhower had always been willing to "go the last half mile" toward negotiation, whereas Dulles, like his predecessor, considered negotiation with the Soviet leadership a waste of time.

When John Foster Dulles died, on May 24, 1959, President Eisenhower ordered the nation's flags to be flown at half-mast and arranged for Dulles to be buried at Arlington Cemetery. Much as I had disagreed with the Secretary's conduct of foreign affairs, I admired his courage, his indefatigable devotion, and his loyalty to the President whom he served. Perhaps history will judge his diplomacy less harshly than I.

MAJOR PUBLICATIONS 1955–58

1955

*TURNING POINT TOWARD PEACE?** Current Affairs Press, New York and Congressional Record, Washington, D.C.

1956

WANTED—A VITAL DEBATE ON FOREIGN POLICY. New York *Times Magazine.*

THE MIDDLE EAST CRISIS. Current Affairs Press, New York.

DANGER AND OPPORTUNITY. Current Affairs Press, New York.

* denotes full-length books.

1957

MEMORANDUM TO THE 85TH CONGRESS. Current Affairs Press, New York.

THE MIDDLE EAST AS A LABORATORY FOR DISARMAMENT AND DEVELOPMENT. The Reporter and Current Affairs Press, New York.

THE CITIZEN'S RESPONSIBILITY FOR WORLD LEADERSHIP. Annals of the American Academy of Political and Social Science, Philadelphia and Current Affairs Press, New York.

OUR SECOND CHANCE IN EUROPE. Current Affairs Press, New York.

A UNITED NATIONS DEVELOPMENT AUTHORITY. Current Affairs Press, New York.

BREATHING NEW LIFE INTO NATO. The Reporter, New York.

TIME TO PUT UP OR SHUT UP. Current Affairs Press, New York.

AGENDA FOR ACTION°—TOWARD PEACE THROUGH DISENGAGEMENT. Monde, New York.

THE ROLE OF THE CHURCH IN A CHANGING WORLD. Current Affairs Press, New York.

LESSONS WE MUST LEARN OR PERISH. Current Affairs Press, New York.

1958

BARE ESSENTIALS OF A NEW APPROACH TO PEACE. Current Affairs Press, New York.

UNITED STATES POSTWAR POLICY IN ASIA. Annals of the American Academy of Political and Social Science, Philadelphia, and Current Affairs Press, New York.

PROGNOSIS FOR THE UNITED NATIONS. Current Affairs Press, New York.

TOWARD A REVISED FOREIGN AID PROGRAM. Current Affairs Press, New York.

AGENDA FOR A SUMMIT MEETING. Current Affairs Press, New York.

UNITED STATES POLICY IN EUROPE. Congressional Record, Washington, D.C., and Current Affairs Press, New York.

FOREIGN POLICY AND JUDEO-CHRISTIAN MORALITY. Current Affairs Press, New York.

CHAPTER XXXI

Slow Ascent and Rapid Fall from the Summit

No LONGER restrained by Dulles' counsel, Eisenhower lost no time in taking the initiative toward reducing the tensions of the cold war. Through Herter, now Secretary of State, he sounded out the possibility of inviting Premier Khrushchev to visit the United States for a face-to-face discussion. When the Soviet leader jumped at the opportunity, Eisenhower issued a formal invitation which resulted in the famous Khrushchev tour of the United States and the Eisenhower-Khrushchev talks at Camp David. The visit seemed to have convinced the Soviet leader that neither the President nor the American people wanted war; it also convinced most Americans that Khrushchev wanted to transfer the East-West struggle into the politico-economic arena in which he confidently expected ultimate Soviet victory. When the visit ended with Eisenhower's acceptance of an invitation to visit Moscow in 1960, most of the world breathed a sigh of relief, but suspicion was aroused in Bonn, Paris, and Peking.

Adenauer and De Gaulle, fearing an Anglo-American-Soviet deal with respect to the future of Europe, each insisted upon coming to the United States before any summit meeting should take place. Khrushchev's stopover in Peking failed to convert Mao Tse-tung to the idea of peaceful coexistence and led to Mao's announcement that the People's Republic of China would not be bound by the "complete and general disarmament agreement" Khrushchev had proposed to the United Nations. (While the Bonn-Paris reservations came as no surprise to me, the Peking reaction confirmed a belief I had long held and publicly expressed; namely, that the Sino-Soviet monolith would sooner or later turn out to be a myth.)

Throughout 1959, I continued to speak and write in support of peaceful solutions, working closely with a growing number of organizations engaged in similar work. Many of them used and widely distributed my books and pamphlets, especially one book, *The West in Crisis,* published by Doubleday both in hard covers and as a paperback. More than in any previous year, I found this work rewarding, but there is much truth in the old saying that a shoemaker should stick to his last.

In November 1959, I ventured somewhat naïvely into the emotion-charged and highly controversial field of political activity on behalf of Israel on the part of American Jews. In so doing, I stirred up a hornet's nest. My study of the Middle East and my interest in peace in that troubled area, rather than concern with American Jewish affairs, led me into a time-consuming controversy.

Like most American Jews, I had for years contributed to local Jewish charities and to the agencies that provided relief to oppressed Jewish minorities in other parts of the world. After the creation of Israel, I repeatedly urged the United Jewish Appeal to segregate funds raised for charitable purposes from those raised for the support of the Israeli Government or of political parties in Israel. When the UJA management refused to do this, I discontinued my contribution.

In a speech to the Congregation Mishkan Israel at New Haven, I brought this matter into the open, urging that contributors to UJA insist upon a segregation of charitable from political funds. There was no reason, I said, why someone who wished to contribute to charitable enterprises should be forced to contribute to political parties in Israel or to the support of the state. Each individual member of the American Jewish community had a right to make up his mind whether and to what extent he might wish to make any political contributions. He should not be coerced or browbeaten into supporting parties or policies on the ground that all Jews everywhere had a duty to support the Israeli state. Each individual should be free to decide whether support given to a foreign state would be in the interest of the United States and in the interest of the cause of world peace. Personally, I felt that some Israeli policies, such as the state's catering to a bigoted theocracy, should not be supported. Nor was I willing to have any part of my contribution diverted to the support of the ultra-nationalist Herut Party, or to the maintenance of a chauvinistic Zionist lobby in Washington.

This attack upon the Zionist-dominated UJA management aroused a furious controversy and was misinterpreted in some Jewish quarters as an attack upon Israel. Actually, I had merely raised certain questions about Israeli policy that, I contended, should be thoughtfully considered by each individual friend of Israel—questions that, as matters stood, were being arbitrarily settled for all contributors to the UJA by a management engaged in political action under the guise of charity.

The charge of using some of the funds for political purposes was at first indignantly denied and then tacitly admitted by a partial reorganization of the UJA. What had really got under the management's skin had been my raising the question of whether it was proper for contributors to UJA to deduct as tax-exempt charitable contributions funds partially used for political purposes.

After this not very pleasant encounter with highly emotional Jewish parochialism, I undertook a broader discussion of the behavior and treatment of minority groups in a paperback booklet entitled *Reveille for Rebels,* published by Doubleday in 1960. This work was written specifically for high school and college students and raised some of the major problems they would soon encounter as citizens. It dealt with a variety of subjects I had found to be of interest among the students at the various schools and colleges at which I had been invited to lecture.

In December 1959, a group of liberal Democratic congressmen under the leadership of Robert Kastenmeier of Wisconsin and James Roosevelt of California decided to invite a number of scholars to contribute essays to a symposium which they called the Liberal Project. Their purpose was to develop liberal alternatives to the various domestic and foreign policies currently being pursued. I was invited to contribute the basic paper on foreign policy.

In the course of carrying out this interesting assignment, I made several trips to Washington to discuss with the group of congressmen and their legislative assistants the various sections of the paper I was preparing. The draft presented to the group in January 1960 was accepted with relatively few modifications, even though it recommended a number of drastic revisions of policy and policy-making procedures.

The twelve congressmen involved in the Liberal Project had planned to release the foreign-policy paper to the press early in 1960, but the release was delayed until late May by an unsuccessful effort to obtain the endorsement of a larger number of Democratic congressmen. By this time, a disastrous turn had taken place in world affairs. (A dramatic, delayed-fuse reaction to the Liberal Project occurred two years later, when a collection of twelve of the essays was published.[1])

I have elsewhere fully described the events that, in the spring of 1959, led up to the tragic failure of the May summit conference at Paris, the collapse of Eisenhower's well-intentioned efforts, and the humiliating request of Japan's Prime Minister that the President's visit to Tokyo be postponed.[2]

To all intents and purposes, the Eisenhower Administration was now rendered impotent in dealing with the major problems of foreign policy. American prestige had sunk to its nadir after the shooting down of the spy plane over Sverdlovsk and the incredibly inept and disingenuous manner in which the affair had been handled. It was evident that any further development of United States relations with the Soviet bloc or, for that matter, with friendly nations, would have to await the election of a new President.

World events, however, did not pause during the ensuing months of American paralysis. Castro took over Cuba; a crisis developed in the Congo; De Gaulle withdrew part of the French fleet from NATO command and openly demanded a revision of the whole structure of the alliance; Western Europe was literally at sixes and sevens as the rift widened between the six Common Market nations and the seven Free Trade Area countries led by Britain. Finally, while the American people were again involved in an election campaign, the Eisenhower Administration had to deal as best it might with the turbulent sessions of Fifteenth

[1] *The Liberal Papers,* Doubleday, 1962.
[2] *Disarmament—Challenge of the 1960s,* Doubleday, 1961, pp. 77–107.

General Assembly of the United Nations, at which Khrushchev and Castro vied with each other in denouncing the embarrassed host country.

The slow, patient ascent to the summit ended with an avalanche of mutual recrimination that carried both American and Soviet leadership back into the somber canyons of the cold war.

MAJOR PUBLICATIONS 1959–60

1959

AGAIN THE BERLIN CRISIS. Current Affairs Press, New York.

OBSERVATIONS ON "FISCAL CONSERVATISM." Current Affairs Press, New York.

THE CENTRAL EUROPEAN CRISIS. Annals of the American Academy of Political and Social Science, Philadelphia, and Current Affairs Press, New York.

THE WEST IN CRISIS.° Doubleday, New York.

THE GERMAN CRISIS IN PERSPECTIVE. Current Affairs Press, New York.

CALL TO LEADERSHIP ACTION. Current Affairs Press, New York.

AFTER GENEVA, WHAT? Current Affairs Press, New York.

TO SPREAD OR BAN NUCLEAR WEAPONS. Current Affairs Press, New York.

MILESTONE IN HISTORY? (Khrushchev's visit). Current Affairs Press, New York.

HAVE WE A VESTED INTEREST IN THE COLD WAR? Current Affairs Press, New York.

KEY TO TENSIONS IN EUROPE. Current Affairs Press, New York.

ISRAEL AND THE AMERICAN JEWISH COMMUNITY. Current Affairs Press, New York.

REPERCUSSIONS AND RESULTS OF A CONTROVERSIAL ADDRESS. Current Affairs Press, New York.

° denotes full-length books.

1960

A RE-EXAMINATION OF UNITED STATES FOREIGN POLICY.
Congressional Record, Washington, D.C., and Doubleday, New York.

HOW USEFUL IS NATO? Annals of the American Academy of
Political and Social Science, Philadelphia, and Current Affairs Press,
New York.

REFORM IN THE UNITED JEWISH APPEAL? Current Affairs
Press, New York.

*AFTER THE PARIS FIASCO—WHERE DO WE GO FROM
HERE?* Current Affairs Press, New York.

OUR GREATEST DANGER—WAR BY ACCIDENT. Current Affairs
Press, New York.

REVEILLE FOR REBELS.° Doubleday, Paperback, New York.

CHAPTER XXXII

Brave New Beginning Cut Short by Tragedy

NOT SINCE James Buchanan had any American President left to
his successor a legacy of unsolved problems comparable to that
which would be inherited by President Eisenhower's successor.
As I contemplated this legacy, I could not help wondering why
anyone in his right mind would be anxious to inherit such a
burden, while at the same time I hoped that the Democratic
Party would come up with a candidate able and willing to assume it.

With Vice President Richard Nixon clearly slated for the Republican nomination, it seemed to me that Stevenson, if nominated, would stand an excellent chance of being elected, but
I doubted whether the Democratic convention would put up a

standard-bearer who had twice suffered defeat, unless a number of convincing victories in primary elections had first demonstrated that Stevenson's popularity was unimpaired. The governor had, however, already declined to enter any primary contests and, to the regret of his supporters, had made it clear that he did not wish to run for a third time.

Four United States senators were actively seeking the Democratic nomination. John F. Kennedy of Massachusetts and Hubert H. Humphrey of Minnesota fought each other in the Wisconsin and West Virginia primaries, with Kennedy defeating his rival in both states. The Texan Senate Majority Leader, Lyndon B. Johnson was busily gathering delegates in the South and West. Truman was backing his fellow Missourian, Senator Stewart Symington. As the convention date approached, it seemed that the ultimate contest would be between Johnson and Kennedy, unless Stevenson were to make a strong last-minute move; I did not believe that he would.

Of the four senatorial candidates, I knew Humphrey well and liked him, but he seemed out of the running. Johnson I knew slightly and admired his political skill, but I thought—quite unjustly as it turned out—that he was too much of a Southern conservative. I did not know Kennedy, and, while respecting his record in the Congress and liking his writings, I was at first inclined to consider him too much of a young man in a hurry. However, as I watched his campaign, I was much impressed by the forthright manner in which he handled the tricky issue of his Roman Catholic religion, by the contagious charm of his personality, the vigorous clarity of his speeches and the smooth efficiency of his organization. The fact that Ken Galbraith and Arthur Schlesinger, Jr., both former ardent Stevenson supporters, were now in Kennedy's camp provided further food for thought. Any man who could enlist the support of these two highly intelligent friends of mine obviously possessed more than an attractive personality. What the country needed, and needed badly, was new and vigorous leadership by a man who really wanted to undertake the fearful burden. Perhaps, I thought, John Kennedy is just the right man for the times.

The last-minute drive launched for Stevenson at the San Francisco convention without the governor's approval seemed to me unfortunate. I would have liked to have seen Stevenson throw his support to Kennedy once he had decided not to seek the nomination himself. In that event, I had hoped that he would become Kennedy's Secretary of State.

After Kennedy's nomination, I wrote to him:

My congratulations on a well-earned victory and my best wishes for a further triumph in November toward which I should feel privileged to help in any way I can. As an old friend and last-ditch supporter of Adlai Stevenson, I can honestly say that I believe the country will be better served by you as President with Stevenson as a foreign policy adviser than it would have been in any other way. That is the highest tribute of which I am capable.

Senator Kennedy replied:

Thank you very much for your letter of July 18. I greatly appreciate your generous commendation. It is especially heart-warming from one who by friendship and conscience supported Governor Stevenson. I shall need and value all his friends' interest and help. I have asked Professor Cox,[1] of whom Ken Galbraith can tell you, to bring together ideas and advice upon policy questions. I know that he will welcome yours. I shall also make sure that he brings any important ideas to my attention.

In August I exchanged a number of letters with Professor Cox. To obtain some general guidelines, I sent him the foreign-policy essay I had written for the Liberal Project, inquiring to what extent, if any, the views therein expressed might be in accord with those of Senator Kennedy. But Cox was not in a position to give this kind of guidance. Later that month, I was so impressed by an article written for *Life* magazine by Senator Kennedy that I sent him a telegram of congratulation. Busy as he was, Kennedy took the time to reply:

I want personally to acknowledge your congratulatory telegram regarding my article in Life. Your kindness is indeed appreciated.

I have long admired your views and comprehension of our nation's foreign affairs and consider them to be of paramount importance in our policy decisions. Therefore, may I impose upon you further by asking if you would be so kind as to send any ideas you possess for me on foreign policy themes to my assistant, Theodore C. Sorensen, throughout the entire campaign.

My reason for asking you to direct them in this manner is that I

[1] Professor Archibald Cox of Harvard University.

personally have told him of my interest in your comments and he will keep me apprised of your communications during my campaign travels.

Thank you again for your very thoughtful message.

Since both Kennedy and Sorensen were almost continuously on the wing in a fast-moving campaign, I was able to pass on only two suggestions: a warning against taking too strong a position on Cuba (which I later wished I had made more emphatic); and a plea not to be tempted or tricked into saying anything that would later stand in the way of successfully negotiating a détente with the Soviet Union. My only other contribution was an open letter endorsing Kennedy and opposing Nixon which appeared in the New York *Times* and other newspapers. Once more, Kennedy took the trouble to express his thanks in a personal note.

Thus began a relationship in which I was privileged, until the day of President Kennedy's tragic assassination, to submit a fairly steady flow of ideas and suggestions, happy in the knowledge that my long years of often lonely dissent from government policy had come to an end. Some of the ideas suggested were put forward publicly and are listed at the end of this chapter. The list might have been longer had my work not been interrupted by illness.

Early in 1961, I was named as a consultant to my old friend, John McCloy, to whom the President had entrusted the formation of a new Arms Control and Disarmament Agency as well as the conduct of disarmament negotiations with the Soviet Union. During the late summer, I was privileged to submit suggestions for the President's address to the Sixteenth General Assembly of the United Nations on the subject of disarmament and the establishment of peace under world law. By the time this address was delivered, I was in the hospital, having been suddenly forced to undergo radical surgery for carcinoma of the tongue—an ordeal greatly lightened by the incredible solicitude of a devoted family and a host of friends. The first flowers I received came from the President, and the first two letters my wife read to me came from the White House. President Kennedy wrote:

I could not be sorrier to hear about your hospitalization. You have my warm best wishes during this ordeal. I know of few Americans who have served the country so well in stimulating the discussion of foreign affairs, and I look forward to hearing your views for a long time to come.

I very much appreciated your recent letter. The Berlin problem has been a complicated one, but I am hopeful that we can bring the affair to a peaceful resolution.

I trust that we will soon hear good news from you. With every good wish,

Sincerely,
(s) John F. Kennedy

Ted Sorensen also wrote sending his wishes for a rapid recovery, and adding that my recent suggestions had been "most useful and you may have detected their impact in the President's speech on Berlin and his probably forthcoming speech to the United Nations."

Who could fail to recover with such encouragement?

Early in 1962, I was able to resume studying and writing, but my activities were curtailed by a speech impairment which took time to overcome. In April, I wrote the President suggesting the idea of seeking a partial test-ban treaty, leaving aside the question of inspection of underground explosions for the time being and seeking an immediate ban on test explosions in the air, in space, or under water that could be monitored without international inspection.[1] The President reacted favorably to this suggestion, although he thought the time not quite ripe. (A little over a year later, in August 1963, precisely such a partial test-ban treaty was signed at Moscow.)

The first time I ventured to try out my re-educated speaking apparatus was in November 1962, when I was awarded the Gandhi Peace Prize. Ironically enough, this occasion coincided with the height of the crisis over the discovery of Soviet missile installations in Cuba—a crisis which had brought the whole world to the brink of nuclear war. I was happy to have the opportunity publicly to express my great admiration of President Kennedy's courage, restraint, and diplomatic skill in meeting this challenge and to defend his action both against pacifist critics and against belligerent war hawks who would have had him invade Cuba.

---

[1] The idea was put forward for public discussion in a letter to the New York *Times* dated April 12, 1962.

There was for me personally an added and deeply touching element on the occasion of the Gandhi award. In the midst of his crucially important activity as United States Ambassador to the United Nations, Governor Stevenson had taken the time and trouble to send the award committee a tribute I valued more highly than any peace prize.

Stevenson's message read:

I am happy to join with you in paying tribute to James P. Warburg, citizen extraordinary. His fresh approach to troubling problems, no less than his ability to articulate his ideas, put us all in his debt. Jim Warburg is in the great tradition of the 18th century pamphleteers who did so much to form American opinion and his voice is one we do well to value. I would be grateful if you would convey to him my esteem and my affection, as well as my regret that I cannot be with you to express them personally on this occasion.

The Cuban crisis and President Kennedy's careful but resolute approach to an understanding with the Soviet Union, culminating in his magnificent foreign policy speech to the American University on June 10, 1963, opened a new era in American foreign policy. Shortly thereafter, I had occasion to witness at firsthand the enthusiasm aroused in Europe by the President's visit. For the first time since 1945, I felt that we had at last set our feet on the road to enduring peace. No public figure had in my lifetime matured faster than had John Fitzgerald Kennedy in the three years during which he had occupied the White House. Not only in foreign affairs but in dealing with the domestic scene, particularly in the field of race relations, Kennedy was clearly on the way toward making himself a place in history alongside of the greatest American Presidents . . .

And then, on November 22, 1963, came the unspeakable and outrageous tragedy of his assassination.

As I conclude this last chapter, I am still too shocked and too full of grief to speculate about the future. I know only that a gallant, energetic, highly intelligent, and lovable young leader of rare grace and charm has been taken from us just as he was growing into true greatness. Somehow, I believe that the work which Kennedy began so well will be completed—that we stand at the threshold of a new era into which he opened the door, and that John Fitzgerald Kennedy will go down in history as the man who, like Moses, led his people to the frontiers of the promised land, though he himself was not permitted to enter it.

The day after Kennedy's assassination, I wrote to Lyndon B. Johnson, the man upon whose shoulders the great burden of responsibility had fallen:

In the midst of the outraged grief which we all feel over yesterday's tragedy, my thoughts have been with you who have lost a beloved friend and inherited his burdens and responsibilities. I should like to express my deep sympathy and my confidence in your ability to carry on the work of a man who, in my judgment, had already shown himself to be one of the few truly great American Presidents.

You are entitled to the support of all of us and, if there should be any way in which I might be of the slightest service, I should of course deem it a privilege. With best wishes for the success which I feel sure you will achieve and a feeling of gratitude that our nation's leadership is in your capable hands,

Respectfully,
James P. Warburg

CHAPTER XXXIII

Retrospect and a Look into the Future

THERE remains only the pleasant task of rendering a brief account of the private happiness I have enjoyed over the past fifteen years—by far the happiest years of the sixty-seven I have lived.

In spite of being forced to cut down my physical activities, I feel younger now than I did fifteen years ago when I married Joan Melber. In large measure, this is due to Joan herself, and, in part, to her bringing into my life a host of new friends who are her contemporaries, rather than mine. Most of all, I feel young because I have four young children—two boys and two girls. There is no better antidote to growing old.

On summer weekends, Bydale swarms with friends who come with their children for swimming, games, and cookouts under the old maple trees. I thoroughly enjoy these occasions, whether our guests are of Joan's generation or mine.

Joan's seventy-five-year-old mother is a more or less permanent member of our household and I am glad that the children can know at least one of their grandparents. Often, I wish that my parents might have known Joan and our children.

The musical talent of our oldest son, James, Jr., would have been a particular delight to them. While Jimmy is all boy, Jennifer, almost eleven, is all girl. Until Sally, our youngest, was born in 1959, Jennifer, sandwiched in between two boys, kept asking when she could have a little sister. When we brought Sally home from the hospital, she was beside herself with joy. Dolls were no longer of the slightest interest; she now had a live doll to mother. Jennifer has compassion and a great capacity for love. She will make some man a wonderful wife. Philip, at age nine, reminds both my sister and me of our father. He is the quietest and most thoughtful of our children. My sister calls him "the philosopher." Sally, not yet five, shows signs of developing the same sort of charm as the formidable great-great-grandmother, Sara, for whom she was named. She is an inveterate chatterbox, full of high spirits, looks a little like Jimmy, and seems to have a similar musical talent.

Through the constant pleasure I derive from my second brood of children I have ruefully realized what I missed by being so much away from home during the time that the three daughters of my first marriage were growing up. Much of this loss is now compensated by the happy relationship that has developed between my daughters and Joan—a relationship more like that between sisters than between a stepmother and her husband's children. This, in turn, has brought me closer to my daughters and their children than I had been in many years. I am inclined to think now that a man is not really fit to be a father until he is in his early thirties. In my case, I feel that I became a father both too soon and too late. I know where I failed as a father in my first marriage. In my second, my one great regret is that in all likelihood I shall not live long enough to see my second brood of children reach maturity.

Since we have lived the year around at Bydale, Joan has become involved in many community activities. Her term as head of the Round Hill Nursery School led to our having summer play groups at our home three times a week for the past nine years, but her major local interest is the Greenwich Center for Child and Family Service which she was recently elected president. I am proud of her work as a conscientious and effective citizen of our community.

My own outside interests apart from public affairs are the Juilliard School of Music and the Polaroid Corporation. Last year, after my protracted hospitalization and convalescence, I resigned as chairman of the Juilliard board on which I had served for almost thirty years, but I hope to keep in close touch with the school through my friend, William Schuman, who has recently become the president of Lincoln Center for the Performing Arts, of which the Juilliard School will soon become a part. The Schumans are our close friends and have recently become neighbors in Greenwich as well. I continue to serve as a director of Polaroid, fascinated year after year by the inventive genius of Ed Land.

During the last two years, I have picked up my long neglected painting, especially since we built ourselves a winter vacation home in Florida. Joan and I greatly enjoyed designing, building, and furnishing this refuge from the cold northern winters. The children love it, and I have derived particular pleasure from converting the sandy wilderness along the shore of our peaceful lagoon into a natural garden of palms, fruit trees, and flowering shrubs. Taking care of plants, like taking care of growing children, tends to keep one's thoughts on the future rather than on the past.

In the grim days of the Great Depression, my father and I once agreed that he was by nature a sad optimist while I was a cheerful pessimist. I think this was true then, but if I am now a cheerful optimist it is largely because my father once told me a story that has since become my life's guideline:

A little frog fell into a glass of milk and swam about frantically trying in vain to get a foothold on the slippery sides of the glass. More and more exhausted, he was about to give up and let himself drown but decided to give one last big kick. As he did so, the milk turned into butter and the little frog stood on dry land.

I have thought of this tale whenever I have felt discouraged and inclined to lose either my cheerfulness or my optimism. These moments have not been many. Mine has been an active, variegated life, fully savored and lustily lived—a life enriched by friendship and far more love than I think I have deserved.

Inevitably, this autobiography has been to a large extent interwoven with the history of the first sixty years of the twentieth century. I recognize that, as history, the story I have told is sketchy and incomplete, while as a personal memoir it is perhaps too heavily loaded with impersonal matters. As for the history I have failed to include in these pages, I refer to my published writings in which I have given a fairly full contemporary account of developments as they occurred. With regard to the personal memoir, I can say only that I have tried to write the sort of account that I wish my father had written for me to read—a story about his life, about the things in which he was interested, and about the times in which he lived.

Unlike my father, who died with his world tumbling about his ears, I have had the good fortune to live through an era of increasingly menacing crises and disasters until the very recent moment when I could sense that, at long last, a turn had come in the fortunes of mankind. If I were to die tomorrow, I would feel that the world was nearer to becoming what I hoped it would be when I was a young man than it has been at any time during my lifetime. So also, after many mistakes, vicissitudes, and disappointments in my private life, I have at length found peace, tranquillity, and happiness. That is why I have gratefully called this book:

THE LONG ROAD HOME

MAJOR PUBLICATIONS 1960–63

1960

TASKS OF THE UNITED STATES UNDER NEW LEADERSHIP. Current Affairs Press, New York.

THE COMING DEBATE OVER DEFENSE. North American Newspaper Alliance (NANA).

1961

DISARMAMENT–CHALLENGE OF THE NINETEEN SIXTIES.
Doubleday, New York.

THE GOLD CRISIS. New York *Times Magazine.*

DISENGAGEMENT AND THE ECONOMICS OF DISARMA-MENT. Current Affairs Press, New York.

WHAT CORNERSTONE FOR OUR FOREIGN POLICY? Current Affairs Press, New York.

FOREIGN AID, GOLD AND THE BALANCE OF PAYMENTS.
Current Affairs Press, New York.

THE UNITED STATES, CHINA AND THE UNITED NATIONS.
Current Affairs Press, New York.

A CHALLENGE TO BUSINESS MANAGEMENT. Current Affairs Press, New York.

THE FIRST THREE MONTHS OF THE KENNEDY ADMIN-ISTRATION. Current Affairs Press.

BERLIN–BACKGROUND AND FUTURE–MEMORANDUM TO THE PRESIDENT AND CONGRESS. Current Affairs Press, New York.

1962

PROPOSAL FOR A PARTIAL TEST BAN TREATY. The New York *Times.*

CUBA–TIME FOR RESTRAINT AND FORTITUDE. Current Affairs Press, New York.

WHAT TO DO ABOUT BERLIN. The *Progressive.*

1963

THE BONN–PARIS AXIS. New York *Times.*

PROPOSAL FOR AN EAST–WEST DÉTENTE. The New York *Times.*

FAREWELL TO THE POSTWAR PERIOD. Current Affairs Press, New York.

THE TEST BAN TREATY. Testimony before the Senate Foreign Relations Committee, Current Affairs Press, New York.

IN DEFENSE OF FOREIGN AID. The New York *Times.*

TODAY'S CHALLENGES TO DIPLOMACY. Bulletin of the Atomic Scientists, and Current Affairs Press.

DEFENSE AGAINST GAULLIST ISOLATIONISM. Annals of the American Academy of Political and Social Science, Philadelphia and Current Affairs Press, New York.

POSTSCRIPT

A Letter to My Young Children and Grandchildren

HAVING written this autobiography largely for you, I am not at all sure that you will find it useful. You are going to live in a world very different from that in which I have lived and in which you have been raised.

The Great Awakening of the hitherto passive, underprivileged majority of mankind has only begun. Your world will be ruled less and less by the relatively affluent white-skinned minority of the human race.

Our country will not be a model for other peoples to follow unless "the American way of life" adapts itself to rapidly changing circumstance. Our present ideas and institutions will require modification if anything like "democracy" and "free enterprise" are to survive even in the United States.

I cannot predict the future, except to say that it will differ radically from the present. I hope it will be better; it may be worse. In any case, it will not be the same. I cannot give you advice, as to how to become useful and responsible citizens except in these very simple terms:

Keep abreast of developments. Be informed. Read, Read, READ! and Travel! Learn to understand the differing needs, traditions and value systems of other peoples.

Form your opinions on the basis of knowledge acquired. Listen to the opinions of others but weigh them against what you know or think you know. Don't be afraid to stand alone for your convictions, but also don't take pride in standing alone. Your convictions will not be of much use if you cannot win the support of others.

Be fearless in recognizing where you have been wrong and equally fearless in fighting for what you think is right.

Be participants—not spectators. Learn to test yourselves in competition and how to win or lose gracefully, but remember that your aim in life is not to compete but to co-operate.

For the rest, live your lives fully without feelings of guilt. Work hard. Play hard. Love, marry, have children, make your mistakes, recognize them if you can, and *learn from your children*, as I have learned from you.

That is about all I can tell you. You are wonderful people, and I am content to leave the future in your hands.

F